D0454898

Boots on
the Ground

Boots on
the Ground

The Fight to Liberate Afghanistan from
Al-Qaeda and the Taliban, 2001–2002

Dick Camp

ZENITH PRESS

First published in 2011 by MBI Publishing Company and Zenith Press, an imprint of MBI Publishing Company, 400 First Avenue North, Suite 300, Minneapolis, MN 55401 USA

Zenith Press titles are also available at discounts in bulk quantity for industrial or sales-promotional use. For details write to Special Sales Manager at MBI Publishing Company, 400 First Avenue North, Suite 300, Minneapolis, MN 55401 USA.

To find out more about our books, visit us online at www.zenithpress.com.

Cover design: Andrew J. Brozyna
Interior design: Helena Shimizu
Design Manager: Brenda C. Canales

Library of Congress Cataloging-in-Publication Data

Camp, Richard D.
 Boots on the ground : the fight to liberate Afghanistan from al-Qaeda and the Taliban, 2001-2002 / Dick Camp.
     p. cm.
 ISBN 978-0-7603-4111-7 (hb w/ jkt.)
 1. Afghan War, 2001---Commando operations--United States.
 2. United States. Army. Special Forces--History--21st century.
 3. Afghan War, 2001---Campaigns. I. Title.
 DS371.412.C355 2011
 958.104'742--dc23
                        2011029203

Printed in China

10 9 8 7 6 5 4 3 2 1

*With great admiration for the service and sacrifice of the Marines,
Special Forces, and the National Clandestine Service during Operation
Enduring Freedom.*

*Till the last landing made
And we stand unafraid
On a shore no mortal has seen.*

*Till the last bugle call
Sounds taps for us all
It's* Semper Fidelis, *Marine*

*Special thanks to Richard Kane for shepherding the book through the
publishing wickets, Scott Pearson for working his editing magic, and Lt. Col.
"Wild" Bill Cody USMC (Ret) for producing the wonderful maps.*

Contents

Part III: Boots on the Ground, Southern Afghanistan

Prologue

THE GUESTS SLOWLY FILED INTO the lavish dining room of the recently refurbished Afghan presidential palace. Eleven-year-old Najiba recalled, "It was like something from a movie: the staircases, the golden lift, the chandeliers, and the glitter—the beauty of it." As the guests took their seats, Afghan President Hafizullah Amin invited them to partake of his favorite soup, a creamy vegetable specially prepared by his Soviet cook. One guest thought that it was particularly tasty. The cook, KGB secret agent Lt. Col. Mitalin Talybov, was particularly pleased. He noted that the soup bowls came back to the kitchen empty, a sign that his mission was successful. As the guests left the luncheon table, several remarked they were feeling very sleepy. Within minutes the sleepiness had progressed to immobilizing agony. Amin's wife called for assistance. Two Soviet military doctors quickly responded. As the doctors entered the palace lobby, they were confronted with dozens of people lying on the floor and on the stairs, some unconscious and others in considerable pain. Amin was found in a deep coma, near death. The doctors diagnosed the problem at once—widespread poisoning—and immediately began life-saving procedures. After several hours of treatment, they were successful in saving the president.

No sooner did the half-drugged Amin regain consciousness than shots and explosions racked the palace. He ordered his aide to notify his Soviet military advisors that the palace was under attack. "The Soviets will help us," he exclaimed.

"Nonsense," the aide shouted sarcastically. "The Soviets are doing the shooting!" At that moment, not only were Soviet Spetsnaz (special forces) attacking the palace with orders to kill Amin and install a pro-Soviet stooge, but upwards of 80,000 Soviet army soldiers were invading Afghanistan to bring the country more closely into its sphere of influence. This massive

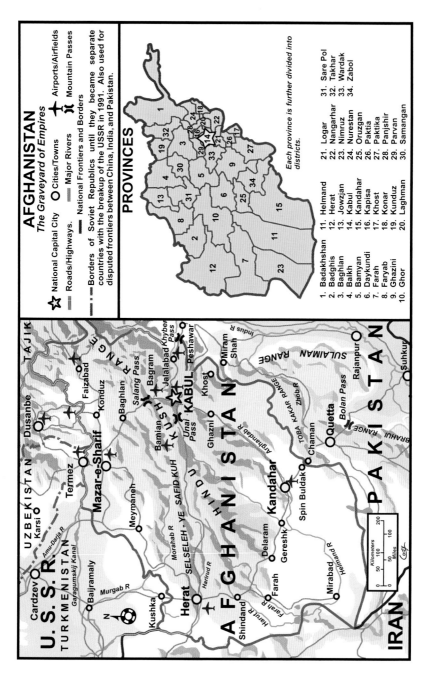

AFGHANISTAN
The Graveyard of Empires

☆ National Capital City ○ Cities/Towns ✈ Airports/Airfields

▬▬ Roads/Highways. ▬▬ Major Rivers)(Mountain Passes

▬▬▬ National Frontiers and Borders

─ ─ ─ Borders of Soviet Republics until they became separate countries with the breakup of the USSR in 1991. Also used for disputed frontiers between China, India, and Pakistan.

PROVINCES

Each province is further divided into districts.

1. Badakhshan
2. Badghis
3. Baghlan
4. Balkh
5. Bamyan
6. Daykundi
7. Farah
8. Faryab
9. Ghazni
10. Ghor
11. Helmand
12. Herat
13. Jowzjan
14. Kabul
15. Kandahar
16. Kapisa
17. Khost
18. Konar
19. Kunduz
20. Laghman
21. Logar
22. Nangarhar
23. Nimruz
24. Nurestan
25. Oruzgan
26. Paktia
27. Paktika
28. Panjshir
29. Parvan
30. Samangan
31. Sare Pol
32. Takhar
33. Wardak
34. Zabol

Map of Afghanistan showing the political breakdown of the country and its major cities, roads, and air networks. *Bill Cody* invasion, and the subsequent occupation of Afghanistan from 1979 to 1989, is the root cause of the rise of al-Qaeda and America's involvement in two Middle Eastern wars.

After ten years, 15,000 dead, and billions of rubles spent, the Soviet bear limped back over the mountain with its tail between its legs. In its wake, the war-ravaged Afghan population was inflicted with further insult to injury as murderous warlords vied for power. This rampage was then followed by the rise of Mullah Omar and the Taliban, who promised relief from the deadly cycle of violence. The movement swept the country, liberating it from the warlords except for a small slice of northern Afghanistan. The Taliban soon proved to be another form of intolerance and incapable of providing good governance. Osama bin Laden took advantage of the country's instability to train and launch his al-Qaeda operatives on their 9/11 suicide mission. In response, the United States demanded that he be ousted from the country, which the Taliban refused to do. Within days of the attack, CIA paramilitary officers were inserted into northern Afghanistan to make contact with the Northern Alliance, an eclectic assortment of former warlords brought together by a common enemy and millions of dollars in cold hard cash. The CIA was followed by U.S. Army Special Forces, supported by massive American air power and a task force of U.S. Marines. This combination made short work of the Taliban and al-Qaeda, forcing them to flee to surrounding Muslim countries, primarily Pakistan and Iran. A new government was installed, and the United States proclaimed victory.

The 2001–2002 liberation of Afghanistan was done "on the cheap." A tiny military footprint, a few million dollars to buy Afghan "loyalty," and an acceptable casualty rate, brought victory. Marine Lt. Gen. Michael DeLong remarked, "We had accomplished in eight weeks what the Russians couldn't accomplish in ten years." Unfortunately, after defeating the al-Qaeda and Taliban forces, the United States took its eye off the ball . . . Iraq became the focus of attention. The veteran CIA and Special Forces teams were pulled out to refit and prepare for the invasion of Iraq. Afghanistan was put on the back burner. As a result, the Taliban and al-Qaeda was able to refit, regroup, and return from sanctuaries in Pakistan, Syria, and Iran. The cost of this resurgence has yet to be quantified and may very well negate the sacrifice of those Americans who were the "first in."

PART I

"What an Unlucky Country"

—Hamid Karzai, after learning of
the assassination of Ahmed Shah Massoud

CHAPTER 1

The Bear Came over the Mountain

L ATE ON THE AFTERNOON OF 12 December 1979, four senior members of the Kremlin's top leadership—chief party ideologue Mikhail Suslov, KGB head Yuri Andropov, Foreign Minister Andrei Gromyko, and Defense Minister Dmitriy Ustinov—gathered in General Secretary Leonid Brezhnev's private office. The growing political crisis in Afghanistan had brought them together to discuss the latest intelligence. They concluded that the situation in Afghanistan was spiraling out of control, threatening the security of the Soviet Union's southern borders. At the time of the meeting, two bloody coups had resulted in the establishment of a communist-style government under Nur Mohammad Taraki, a brutal dictator who was strongly supported by the Kremlin. His rule brought about increasing violence by Muslim extremists. Revolts broke out across the country. The Afghan army was sent in to restore order.

General Secretary Leonid Brezhnev ordered Soviet troops to invade Afghanistan, after secretly infiltrating Spetsnaz forces to prepare the way. He was convinced that the incursion would only last three to four weeks.
National Archives and Records Administration

However, in many cases the army joined the rebels or simply melted away. Taraki begged the Soviets for emergency military assistance.

"We ask that you extend practical and technical assistance involving people and arms," Taraki implored. The Soviets responded by flying in weapons, ammunition, and additional military advisers, but refused to send in regular troops.

Ambassador Adolph Dubs

Adolph "Spike" Dubs, a career diplomat, was appointed ambassador extraordinary and plenipotentiary of the United States to Afghanistan by President Jimmy Carter on 31 May 1978. He was known as a Soviet expert, having served as the ranking charges d'affaires at the U.S. embassy in Moscow from 1973 to 1974. The Moscow assignment brought Dubs to the attention of the Kabul-based KGB (Russian internal security, intelligence, and secret police organization), which was convinced that he was closely connected to the CIA. The KGB thought that Dubs would attempt to influence the Afghan government to align with the United States. "It cannot be ruled out that in his contact with the Afghan leadership, Dubs will take advantage of his 'deep' understanding and knowledge of the situation in the USSR and Soviet foreign policy. This, in our view, is one of the most dangerous aspects of his activities." The KGB's opinion was to have a deadly consequence.

Bill Richardson, special envoy and U.S. ambassador to the UN, lays a wreath on the monument for the last U.S. ambassador to serve in Afghanistan, Adolph "Spike" Dubs, in the capital Kabul, April 1998. Dubs was kidnapped by Maoist extremists and killed during a rescue attempt by Afghan government security forces that were being advised by members of the Soviet secret police (KGB). Many in the U.S. government believed Dubs was executed on their orders.
AP photo/Zaheeruddin Abdullah

On the morning of 14 February, Spike Dubs was in the back seat of his chauffeur-driven vehicle, as it pulled up to the U.S. Cultural Center. Three men in police uniforms approached the black Chevrolet and gestured for the driver to roll down the window. When the driver complied, one of the men jammed a pistol in his face and demanded that he open the door. The three climbed in, restrained Dubs, and ordered the driver to go to the Kabul Hotel, about two

Prime Minister Alexei Kosygin stated that "if our troops were introduced, the situation would not only not improve, but would worsen." He was concerned that the soldiers would be perceived as invaders and would be opposed by the Afghan people, as well as by Afghanistan's neighbors, Pakistan and China.

* * *

miles from the Cultural Center. Upon reaching the hotel, Dubs was dragged out of the car and through the hotel lobby to a small telephone room, where his captors called the Afghan Foreign Ministry. "We've got the ambassador," they said and then demanded the release of two political prisoners. During the phone call, another man joined the group. They fired several shots in the air to clear the lobby, dragged Dubs to room 117 on the first floor, and tied him to a chair. When the American embassy staff learned of the kidnapping, they appealed to the Afghan government to negotiate his release.

Prime Minister Hafizullah Amin ordered Afghan security forces to surround the hotel. They were joined by three senior Soviet agents, including the KGB security chief, the top Russian adviser to the Afghan police, and the second secretary of the Soviet embassy. The Soviets directed the Afghans to seal off the area and stall for time. After the security forces got into position, the KGB agents "suggested" they storm the room, despite American requests to continue negotiations. The assault began shortly after 1230 with a heavy volume of automatic weapons fire. The room was riddled with bullets. Two of the captors were killed, one was captured, and one managed to escape in the confusion. Ambassador Dubs did not survive the rescue attempt. According to authors Milt Bearden and James Risen in *The Main Enemy: The Inside Story of the CIA's Showdown with the KGB*, "an autopsy showed that Dubs had been shot in the head from a distance of six inches."

The next day, according to Vasily Mitrokhin, KGB archivist, Russian agents were directed to devise a plan to justify the ambassador's death. "They [the Russians and Amin] agreed to express their condolences to the Americans, to lower flags on government buildings, and to print photographs of the four terrorists in the newspapers." They also decided to shoot the captured terrorist and to "shoot another prisoner, pretending it was the one that escaped." It was also decided to say that "the Afghan side had independently and without consultation decided to take radical action . . . and that there had been no Soviet advisers present at all." A year later the Soviets disseminated more disinformation by claiming that an Afghan investigation proved that the Americans were involved in the ambassador's death. A newspaper article titled "On Whose Conscience is the Death of Ambassador Dubs?" laid blame on the Americans. Zbigniew Brzezinski, President Carter's national security adviser, lamented Dubs' death. "It was a tragic event which involved either Soviet ineptitude or collusion."

The situation in Afghanistan had been going from bad to worse. In February 1979, the U.S. ambassador, Adolph "Spike" Dubs, a former World War II naval officer, was kidnapped by members of the Maoist extremist group Settemi-Melli posing as police. In the ensuing rescue attempt, Dubs was killed. The United States was incensed, claiming that it was "a tragic event which involved either Soviet ineptitude or collusion."

In March, anti-government religious activists took over the city of Herat. They rioted because government-mandated secular reforms—education for women, the banning of dowries, abolishment of Islamic lending institutions—threatened the power of the tribal leaders and mullahs. Land under their control was seized, threatening their livelihood. The Afghan Army's 17th Division mutinied and joined the rioters, who then plundered weapons depots and hunted down government officials and foreigners. It is estimated that over five thousand people were killed, including one hundred Soviet advisers and their families, whose heads were mounted on poles and paraded around the city. A Soviet intelligence report noted that the rebel leaders were "religious fanatics" who were motivated by ideology.

"It was under the banner of Islam that the soldiers were turning against the government." Russian defense minister Dimitri Ustinov pointed out, "The leadership of Afghanistan did not sufficiently appreciate the role of the Islamic fundamentalists in the riots." Moscow was keenly aware of the overthrow of the shah of Iran by Islamic fundamentalists, who installed a theocracy dominated by Ayatollah Khomeini. The Iranian Revolution trumpeted a *jihad* against the two superpowers—the United States and the Soviet Union—threatening the mostly Muslim Central Asian republics of the USSR.

The communist-backed Afghan government responded to the mutiny and the riots with a vengeance. Soviet-trained Afghan pilots bombed the city without mercy, killing an estimated twenty thousand residents. Other anti-government demonstrations and riots quickly followed, threatening to engulf the country in an all-out civil war. As Afghanistan disintegrated, a rift developed between President Taraki and Prime Minister Hafizullah Amin, a Columbia University graduate who the Soviets thought had close ties to the United States. An intelligence report warned Brezhnev that "Representatives of the U.S.A., on the basis of their contacts with the Afghans, are coming to a conclusion about the possibility of a change in the political line of Afghanistan in a direction which is pleasing to Washington." Brezhnev became increasingly concerned as Amin quietly gathered more and more control of the government by staffing it with relatives and supporters. The power struggle between the two Afghan leaders came to a head in September 1979, when Amin had Taraki killed. The official report stated that Taraki "had died from a serious illness, which he had been suffering for some time." The real cause of his death according to U.S. sources was "a lack of oxygen brought on by the application of fingers to the neck and pillows over the nose and mouth by three members of the presidential guard service!" Brezhnev was furious. "What a scum that Amin is!" Brezhnev was reported to have exclaimed. Moscow continued to support Amin, at least on the surface. Behind the scenes, the Kremlin's leadership was looking toward a regime change.

Amin played right into the Soviet's hands by continuing to request military assistance. In "The Take-Down of Kabul: An Effective Coup de Main," Lester W. Grau wrote, "Beginning in 1978, Soviet military and KGB advisers permeated the structure of the Afghanistan Armed Forces and Security Forces down to battalion level. In March 1979, eight Mi-8 heli-copters, a transport squadron of AN-12s, a signal center, and a paratroop battalion transferred to Bagram airbase." The men wore Afghan uniforms but were all Soviet military of the Muslim Battalion, which consisted of soldiers from the Soviet Central Asian republics, who looked and sounded like Afghan locals. Over the next several months, they conducted an "extensive reconnaissance of the country." In April 1979, a high level Russian military delegation assessed the situation. "In November," Grau reported, "a Spetsnaz battalion [154th Separate *Spetsnaz* Detachment—the "Muslim Battalion"], clad in Afghan uniforms, deployed to Afghanistan and was incorporated into the presi-dential security forces. In December, two thirty-man *Spetsnaz* units, code named '*Grom*' (Thunder) and '*Zenit*' (Zenith) deployed to Kabul, and began reconnaissance of the thirteen objectives that they would have to take out in the coming assault."

On 12 December, Brezhnev called for the meeting in his office to decide on a

The new Afghanistan President Nur Muhammed Taraki speaks at a news conference in Kabul, Afghanistan, on 6 May 1978. He was brutally murdered by henchmen a year later under orders from his prime minister Hafizullah Amin, who in turn was himself killed by the Soviets. *AP photo*

course of action. The five men settled on a two-pronged approach: to have the KGB assassinate Amin and replace him with Babrak Karmal, a Soviet stooge, and to send in troops. Brezhnev approved an order, later approved by the full Politburo, to "send several contingents of Soviet troops . . . into the territory of the Democratic Republic of Afghanistan for the purpose of rendering internationalist assistance to the friendly Afghan people [and to] create favorable conditions to prevent possible anti-Afghan actions on the part of the bordering states." A short hand-written protocol was drawn up entitled "Concerning the Situation in 'A'," which the members signed. They affixed their signatures diagonally across the text. Brezhnev scrawled his name at the bottom of the page. Major General Alexander Lyakhovsky wrote in *The Tragedy and Valor of Afghanistan* that the handwritten protocol was "kept in a special safe," and was classified as super-secret and not shown to anyone, "not even those among the highest leadership."

Russian Defense Minister Ustinov intended the operation to be a neat, surgical intervention, designed to stabilize a client regime upon which the Soviet Union had lavished twenty-five years of attention and aid. He was convinced that the military incursion would last only a short time . . . weeks or months. Indeed, Brezhnev was confident that "it'll be over in three to four weeks."

The Soviet General Staff, however, was unconvinced, and warned of a protracted insurgency. Nikolai Ogarkov, Chief of the General Staff called the decision "reckless."* He cited the warlike nature of the tribes and the mountainous terrain, which favored guerrilla warfare.

The Politburo ignored the warning and ordered the newly reconstituted 40th Army to prepare for the invasion. Its immediate objective was to secure Kabul, the capital, and the main lines of communication, especially those leading back to the Soviet border. On 7 December, Babrak Karmel, Amin's replacement, was secretly flown to Bagram air base and placed under the protection of the KGB and Soviet paratroopers. He was to assume the presidency upon Amin's removal. Thousands of Soviet troops moved to their pre-assault positions. Engineers began constructing pontoon bridges across the Amu Darya river for the use of the invasion force.

All summer the CIA monitored Soviet troop buildup until, by mid-December, the deployments had reached ominous proportions. Stansfield Turner, director of the CIA, alerted President Carter on 19 December that the Soviets had "crossed a significant threshold in their growing military

---

*It was reported that Ustinov, the Minister of Defense rebuked General Ogarkov: "Are you going to teach the Politburo? Your only duty is to carry out the orders."

Soviet Declaration to Invade Afghanistan, 12 December 1979

"Considering the military-political situation in the Middle-East, the latest appeal of the government of Afghanistan has been favorably considered. The decision has been made to introduce several contingents of Soviet troops deployed in the southern region of the country to the territory of the Democratic Republic of Afghanistan in order to give international aid to the friendly Afghan people and also to create favorable conditions to interdict possible anti-Afghan actions from neighboring countries."

involvement in Afghanistan." Three days later, Bobby Inman, the CIA's deputy head, said there was no doubt that the Soviets planned to invade the country within seventy-two hours. Inman's prediction was correct; by Christmas Eve operation "Storm 333" was ready to execute.

Storm 333

At 1500 Moscow time (1630 hours in Kabul) on 25 December, the "Limited Contingent of Soviet Troops" (LCST), two motorized rifle divisions, crossed into Afghanistan, while airborne and *Spetsnaz* forces units that had flown into Kabul prepared to seize thirteen critical points in the capital. Shortly after 1900 on 27 December, the two KGB *Spetsnaz* groups Thunder and Zenith, and the 1st Company of the 154th Separate *Spetsnaz* Detachment, attacked the Tapa-e-Tajbek palace, where Amin had taken refuge at the urging of his Soviet advisers. "We received information that something would happen," Mohammed Akbar, an Afghan Army veteran recalled. "Amin called all of his commanders to the Palace as he wanted to be prepared to command all his troops." The palace was located two miles south of the city, in an area that was not easily attacked. A winding road led up to a terraced hilltop and the palace's main entrance. The attack force faced a significant threat. A company-sized unit of bodyguards was located inside the building and in positions on the palace grounds. A 2,500-man brigade, including three tanks, twelve 100mm anti-aircraft guns, and sixteen dual-barreled DShK heavy machine guns, manned a ring of encircling and over watch positions a short distance away.

Two Soviet BTR armored personnel carriers led the assault force. "In each vehicle, we had four to five Alpha officers, the crew of the vehicle—the commander, the driver and the gunner—and in addition to that, we had

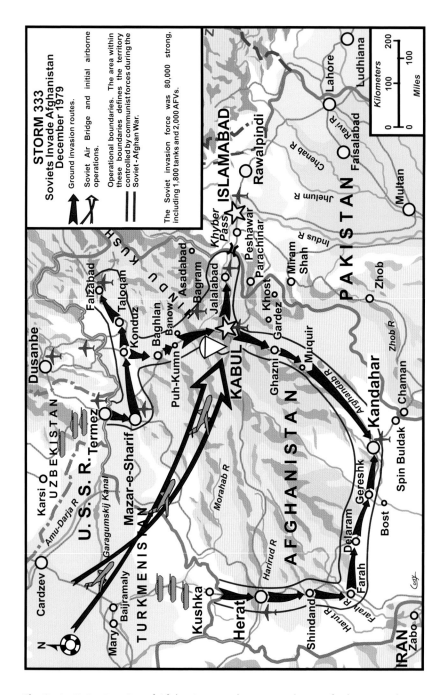

The Soviet Union invasion of Afghanistan used two ground axes of advance and an airlift that placed troops directly into Kabul. The surprise invasion was largely unopposed. All key objectives were in Soviet hands within a short period of time. *Bill Cody*

Tapa-e-Tajbek Palace where President Amin took refuge during the Soviet invasion. In a violent assault, Soviet special forces (*Spetsnaz*) overcame the Afghan troops, seized the palace, and killed Amin. *Mikhail Evstafiev*

Afghans riding with us," Commander Oleg Balashov remembered. "In my car we had the future Afghan Defense Minister. I assigned one of my men to look after him. I told him: 'Guard this man with your life. No matter what happens, he must stay alive.'" As the armored personnel carriers passed the first turn they were raked by heavy machine gun fire. The second vehicle took casualties and started burning. The Soviets returned fire, knocked out the Afghan position, and continued toward the palace, firing their on-board machine guns and cannon. Return fire was heavy, causing quite a number of personnel casualties and destroying a BMP infantry fighting vehicle. "The gunfire was terrible," Balashov exclaimed. "The enemy was shooting from the roof, from the windows, and they were protected by the walls while our fighters were on open ground and could be easily shot down."

Thunder and Zenith survivors dismounted and climbed through a window into the palace. One group cleared the bottom floor while the other charged up the stairs in a hail of gunfire.

"There were shots from everywhere," Victor Grishin recalled. "We began to gather by the entrance door leading to the corridor that opens onto the rooms on the second floor. Before we rushed forward, we had to fire our assault rifles or throw grenades." Gunfire and explosions filled the air, creating a perfect hell as the *Spetsnaz* worked their way through the building. They found Amin in one room and killed him. His body was wrapped in a carpet and taken away to be buried.

An eyewitness described his last minutes: "Amin was upstairs wandering around in shorts and an Adidas tee-shirt. He had IV drips in both arms [still recovering from the poisoning] and was dragging the IV stand with him. His terrified five-year-old son clung to his leg. Amin ordered his aide-de-camp to notify the Soviet military advisers about the attack on the palace.

KBG Assassination Attempt

On orders from the KGB, a Soviet agent, Lt. Col. Mitalin Talybov (code named Sabir) was placed on Amin's personal staff as a cook. He slipped poison into the Afghan's favorite drink, Coca-Cola. The carbonation in the liquid somehow rendered it almost harmless and Amin escaped with a minor upset stomach. However, his nephew became seriously ill and was flown to Moscow for treatment, which undoubtedly saved his life. The second poisoning attempt occurred on 27 December, the day of the Soviet invasion. Amin's cook placed the poison in the soup, which was described by one eyewitness as being "very tasty." The diners immediately fell ill. An aide to the president discovered them and called the Soviet Ambassador requesting assistance. The ambassador, unaware of the KGB plot, sent the chief surgeon of the Kabul military hospital, Anatoly Alexeev, and Victor Kuznichenko, another doctor, to help.

When the doctors arrived at the palace, they saw several government and high-raking party officials writhing in agony and immediately suspected poison. They quickly located Amin in his bedroom. He was in a deep coma and on the verge of death. The two administered first-aid by injecting him with fluids to help flush the poison from his system. After three hours of treatment, Amin responded. About this time the doctors heard shooting and assumed that Afghan rebels were attacking the palace. They helped Amin to his feet and walked him to the hallway, where he attempted to quiet his young son, who had appeared from one of the rooms. Kuznichenko, sensing more danger, urged his companion to leave with him. As they started down a hallway, gunfire erupted, and they took cover in a conference room. Suddenly a Soviet soldier burst in and opened fire, hitting Kuzinchenko in the chest, mortally wounding him. Dr. Alexeev survived the assault and was evacuated. Amin and his son were shot sometime later.

The use of poison "against the enemies of the people" had been Soviet standard procedure since the turn of the century. The first poison factory was established in 1921 at the direction of Communist party leader Vladimir Uliyanov (Lenin's party name) at the First Moscow Medical Institute. The "lab of death" was developed, according to Boris Volodarsky in *The KGB's Poison Factory, From Lenin to Litvinenko* to "find a poison devoid of any taste or smell that could not be detected in the victim's body after death…the death must appear natural." Amin was just another in a long list of "enemies of the people" who were poisoned.

His aide replied, 'The Soviets are doing the shooting!' These words upset the president, and he picked up an ashtray and threw it. 'You are lying. It cannot be.' Then he tried to call his chief of the general staff, but the communications had already been cut. Amin quietly said, 'I suspected it. I was right.' He lay down on the counter of a large wooden bar. He was still alive when the first Soviet assault troops cleared the room. When they returned later, someone had killed him."*

The "coup de main" was remarkably successful as a classic military operation employing deception, speed, and substantial force. Soviet forces gained control of Afghanistan's main cities with only minimal casualties, twenty-four men killed in action and another seventy-four wounded. However, instead of lasting a few months, the incursion lasted over nine years. Perhaps as many as five million Afghans fled during the Soviet invasion. The bulk of them, as many as three million, sought refuge in huge camps located in Balochistan, the Federally Administered Tribal Areas (FATA), and the Northwest Frontier Province (NWFP) of Pakistan. The squalid refugee camps proved to be prime recruiting grounds for the resistance groups that would become

Eugene Serge, a twenty-one-year-old Soviet armored solider from Moscow, gives a thumbs-up as he and a huge Soviet convoy begins its withdrawal from war-torn Afghanistan on 15 May 1988. He is one of several hundred thousand Soviet soldiers who served in the country during a decade of occupation that cost over fifteen thousand men killed in action and hastened the breakup of the Soviet Union. *AP photo/Liu Heung Shing*

known as the Mujahideen, which translated to "people doing *jihad*." Opposition to the take-over was quickly mounted by Afghan resistance fighters. Thousands of young men streamed back across the porous border

---

* The eyewitness description is the subject of some controversy, as another witness claims that Amin was so groggy from poison that he could not have possibly done the things that are claimed.

CHAPTER 2

Brutal-Hearted Mountain Tribes

"Allahu Akbar. Mordadbad Shuravi."
(God is great. Death to the Soviets.)
—Mujahideen Battle Cry

THE INITIAL SOVIET ASSAULT FORCE of the 40th Army—80,000 soldiers, 1,800 tanks, and 2,000 fighting vehicles—entered Afghanistan along two axes of advance. A motorized rifle division crossed the border at Kushka in Turkmenistan, while another crossed the Amu Darya river on pontoon bridges at Termez in Uzbekistan. *Spetsnaz* and airborne units were airlifted directly into the Kabul Airport and the Bagram military air base, where they assisted in isolating the city and seizing key government installations. The invasion force quickly secured their main objectives and focused on consolidating power, securing the main lines of communication, essential supply routes, and the air bases. They did not envision occupying and securing large tracts of the country. This task was to be the job of the Afghan government forces. However, the dispirited Afghan Army proved to be weak and unreliable. On several occasions, entire units went over to the Mujahideen, while individual soldiers simply took "French leave." A Soviet report admitted, "The rural areas are controlled by the rebels. Even if Soviet and Afghan forces could clear territory, they would, as a rule, return to their bases and the areas would fall back under the control of the

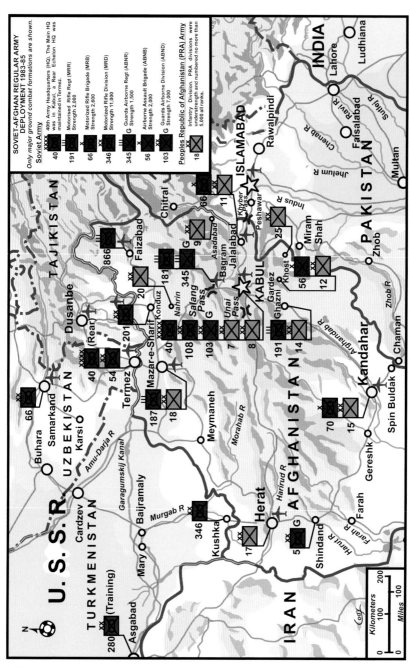

SOVIET-AFGHAN REGULAR ARMY
DEPLOYMENT 1983-85
Only major ground combat formations are shown.

Soviet Army

40	40th Army Headquarters (HQ). The Main HQ was in Kabul, a Rear Echelon HQ was maintained in Termez.
191	Motorised Rifle Regt (MRR) Strength 2,000
66	Motorized Rifle Brigade (MRB) Strength 2,600
346	Motorized Rifle Division (MRD) Strength 11,000
345 G	Guards Airborne Regt (ABNR) Strength 1,500
56	Airborne Assault Brigade (ABNB) Strength 2,000
103 G	Guards Airborne Division (ABND) Strength 7,000

Peoples Republic of Afghanistan (PRA) Army

| 18 | Infantry Division. PRA divisions were understrength and numbered no more than 5,000 all ranks. |

Bill Cody

rebels." It was estimated that the Afghan army lost an average of 20,000 men a year. By the mid-80s it was down to about 30,000 men, who were used primarily for guarding fixed installations. Of those that remained, a large percentage favored the rebels more than the government.

The success of the invasion soon wore off because the Soviets were seen as godless communists, who had ruthlessly suppressed Muslims in Central Asia. Tribal and religious leaders declared a *jihad* (holy war) against them, fueling an insurgency that kindled a unifying ideology . . . *Allahu Akhbar, Mordadbad Shuravi* (God is great. Death to the Soviets). The *jihad* became a spiritual obligation for the Muslim population. For the faithful, to fight and die in a holy war against the communist *kafirs* (infidels) was a duty that rallied support to oppose an invading army—in essence, the individual Mujahideen was fighting for his faith, his freedom, and for his family, which gave him an enormous moral ascendancy. The *jihad* was the most comprehensive in Afghan history. Thousands took to the streets in protest, only to be quashed by military force. Hundreds were killed. The educated elite, government officials, and thousands of others joined the anti-communist movement that was sweeping the country. At first, the movement lacked any sort of cohesion, but as the resistance mounted, so did international support—initially moral and diplomatic but before long material as well. Steve Coll in *Ghost Wars: The Secret History of the CIA, Afghanistan, and Bin Laden, from the Soviet Invasion to September 10, 2001* wrote, "By late 1981 the rebels roamed freely in nearly all of Afghanistan's twenty-nine provinces."

The CIA estimated that between twenty to forty thousand fighters were in the field at any one time. Thousands more were visiting family in the Pakistan refugee camps, farming, or smuggling. Brigadier General Mohammad Yusuf Khan, a Pakistani intelligence officer said, "Within every family there is a system of dividing up the military and civil responsibilities of the men-folk. Mujahideen are volunteers who receive no pay, but a man may spend only three or four months in the field, and the remainder of the year as a shopkeeper, a farmer, on contract work in Iran, or perhaps in a refugee camp caring for the womenfolk of several families. When a man feels he has had enough he goes home and is replaced, eventually, by another relative. Thus, a Commander might boast 10,000 men under his control, but in practice it is unlikely, unless there is a major offensive under way, that he could muster more than 2,000."

Many of the fighters were just "hanging around" until the weather improved. Grau noted that "combat in the mountainous regions is seasonal. In November, the snow falls, closing the mountain passes and forcing the

The Soviet military machine ran head-on into tenacious mountain warriors known as Mujahideen. The Mujahideen had a centuries-old tradition of banding together to fight invaders. *militaryphotos.net*

people down into the valleys where they winter over. Little fighting occurs, except in the low desert regions. In March and April, the snows begin to melt and combatants begin to stir. May and June are excellent months for combat. July and August are too hot and the pace of combat slows. September and October are again excellent months for combat. And in November, the snows fall." The environments of Afghanistan's mountains and deserts are physically demanding. In the summer, temperatures can reach over 130 degrees, while in the higher plateaus temperatures can fall to 26 degrees below zero. Between June to September, the "Winds of 120 Days," can have velocities up to 108 miles per hour. This wind is usually accompanied by intense heat, drought, and sand storms, which often reach several hundred feet in the air. Many of the peaks in the Hindu Kush top 20,000 feet, and are forever capped with snow and ice. Their very name means 'Hindu killer', from the time when the people of Afghanistan raided the plains of India for slaves, many whom perished on the terrible march through these unyielding mountains. The endless stretch of sand and rock in the southwest is aptly called Dasht-i-Margo—the Desert of Death.

The Afghan resistance began as a spontaneous rebellion against a common foe. Local residents took up arms and banded together under a local commander, often an influential villager. Author C. J. Dick wrote in *Mujahideen Tactics in the Soviet-Afghan War* that "*Mujahideen* commanders owed their position to social standing, leadership abilities, education and commitment to their religion. They could not rely on military discipline to gain their warriors' obedience. Rather, they led by force of personality, moral persuasion and by achieving consensus." Less than 15 percent of the Mujahideen commanders were professional military officers, but their impact proved to be significant. "They provided continuity, an understanding of military planning and issues, a modicum of uniform training and an ability to deal with outside agencies providing aid to the *Mujahideen*." For the most part they were unpaid volunteers, who "fought to protect their faith and community first and their nation next," Grau and Jalali noted. "The *Mujahideen* had to support their families, so normally all heavy weapons and 1/5th of the loot . . . went to the commander. The other 4/5ths was divided among the

Mujahideen on a captured Russion T-55 tank. Soviet armored units were road-bound and subject to ambush and mines. *AP photo*

A Mujahideen fighter with a rocket-propelled grenade fires on a road-bound Soviet convoy. *militaryimages.net*

Mujahideen combatants. Some of the *Mujahideen* would take their captured Kalashnikovs to Pakistan where they would sell them and give the money to their families to live on. Governments supporting the *Mujahideen* would buy the weapons in Pakistan's bazaars and give them [back] to the *Mujahideen* faction leaders for distribution."

Initially, the Mujahideen banded together and formed large, rather unwieldy groups to attack the Soviet and Afghan government forces. They quickly learned that this approach was useless against the overwhelming might of Soviet firepower. As the war progressed, the Mujahideen refined and diversified their tactics. They formed small highly mobile units of

Soviet Mi-24 "Hind" Attack Helicopter

The Soviet Mi-24 Hind attack helicopter, known as the "flying tank" by its crewmen, was a heavily armed gunship. The Hind made its Afghanistan combat debut in 1979, where it earned a fearsome reputation. It was called *Shaitan-Arba* (Satan's Chariot) by the Mujahideen. Its weapons system included a YaKB 12.7 four-barreled machine gun with a high rate of fire (4,000–4,500 rounds per minute) or a GSH-30K 30mm (2,000–2,500 rounds per minute) cannon. It was also armed with two to four S-8 80mm rocket pods and four 250 pound, or two 500 pound, bombs. The Hind was designed for battlefield close air support. Its thick armor protected the crew from medium to heavy machine guns, and by staying above 5,000 feet, it could remain out of reach of the Mujahideen's SA-7 (hand-held, heat-seeking) surface to air missiles. It was only when the United States introduced the "Stinger" missile that the gunship met its match.

Soviet Mi-24 Hind attack helicopter, known as the "flying tank" because of its awesome armament—machine guns, cannons, and rockets. The Hind was used in close support of convoys and infantry movements. The U.S.-made Stinger missile proved its undoing. *Department of Defense*

Up to as late as 1985, several Hind helicopters would be used in a circular pattern to engage guerrillas directly, attacking in a dive from 1,000 meters with 57mm rockets and with cluster and high-explosive 250-kilogram bombs. In 1985, Soviet use of Hinds began to change somewhat, and a wider variety of tactics began to be employed: using helicopters (either Hinds or Mi-8 Hips) as scouts; running in from 7,000 to 8,000 meters away, rising to 100 meters and drawing fire, and having other aircraft waiting behind a ridge to attack whomever opened fire; and using helicopters in mass formations.

twenty-five to thirty-five men that moved freely around the countryside, picking the time and place for attack. The mobile groups consisted mostly of young, unmarried men, who were fairly well-trained. Their operations area was much larger than that of the local Mujahideen. Often they swooped down on the road-bound Soviet armored forces from the surrounding ridges and hilltops. The Soviet army was trained for large-scale, armored operations, not for small-unit guerrilla type of combat. Author Gregory Feifer wrote that a battalion of the 201st Motorized Rifle Division was ambushed near the Pakistani border: "After *Mujahideen* attacks killed its officers and radiomen, the disorganized unit couldn't signal for help. Staying in their armored personnel carriers, the men fired until their ammunition ran out. Then the guerrillas overwhelmed them, destroying the battalion, and leaving only a few survivors."

The initial Soviet units were staffed by reservists from the Muslim Central Asian republics—Tajiks, Uzbeks, and Turkmen. The army quickly discovered that the decision was a miscalculation. "Antagonisms caused serious friction within the Soviet military," Gregory Feifer noted. "Ethnic Slavs suspected their fellow soldiers from Central Asia of sympathizing with the Afghan people. Russians and Central Asians wearing the same uniforms—even Muslims of different backgrounds and persuasions—engaged in internecine fights and beatings." The reservists were quickly replaced by the conscripts with little if any training. Brigadier General Yusuf Khan wrote that "the average Soviet had no motivation to fight in Afghanistan, other than to survive and go home." The conscript's service was miserable. He was subject to a system of bullying, which was not only tolerated but encouraged by the officers. He also received little training. "It was quite normal for a recruit to go on operations with only three weeks in the army," Yusuf Khan said. "He was merely given food and a uniform, no weapon and no training at all." The men were poorly clothed, fed, and supplied. Feifer noted that stealing became a way of life and that "the mass of Soviet soldiers throughout Afghanistan sold the Mujahideen arms and ammunition, often pilfered during combat operations, sometimes for big profit." Alcoholism and drug abuse was rampant.

The Soviets tried to improve soldier competence by placing increased emphasis on physical conditioning, mountain warfare, small-unit training, and ambush and counter-ambush techniques. They also increasingly relied on specially trained air assault and *Spetsnaz* forces. By mid-1980, they began restructuring their forces to more effectively counter guerrilla tactics. They reorganized several of their divisions to make them more flexible, and withdrew hundreds of tanks and unneeded units, such as anti-aircraft missile brigades. They increased the inventory of jet aircraft and helicopters. The introduction of the Mi-24 "Hind" attack helicopter was particularly important. The heavily armed Hind, with its fearsome appearance, symbolized the Soviet presence in Afghanistan.

The Mujahideen were hard-pressed to counter the Soviet change in tactics. They were armed with a variety of weapons from swords, to flintlock muskets, to obsolete and left-over World War II weapons, which they captured, or were brought to them by defecting soldiers of the Afghan army. Tribes often competed with each other for resources, and refused to join against a common enemy. "Tribal rivalries and blood feuds, ambitions of local chieftains, and tribal defiance," Grau and Jalali wrote in *The Other Side of the Mountain, Mujahideen Tactics in the Soviet-Afghan War*, "have kept the different parts of the land at war at different times." The Mujahideen lacked discipline and unit cohesion. "Afghanistan has, at times," Grau and Jalali noted, "been characterized as a disunited land riven by blood feuds." One Pakistani intelligence officer put it rather succinctly: "The Mujahideen have an apparently insatiable appetite for feuding amongst themselves." Howard Hart, the CIA station chief in Islamabad regarded the Afghans as "charming, martial, semi-civilized, and ungovernable . . . any two Afghans created three factions. 'Every man will be king,'" he told colleagues, Despite this proclivity for infighting, attacks against the Soviets and the communist-backed government continued.

To counter the growing resistance, the Soviets increasingly relied on a "scorched earth" policy to eliminate the Mujahideen support in the rural areas. They tried to destroy the infrastructure by bombing the villages, destroying crops, irrigation systems, and orchards, mining pastures (the Soviets scattered hundreds of thousands of mines throughout the country), and destroying livestock. This ruthless assault on the populace succeeded in driving hundreds of thousands of villagers from the countryside, separating the Mujahideen from their base of support. For example, in the strategically important Panjshir Valley, a hundred miles northeast of Kabul, the Soviets succeeded in forcing half the population of 80,000 people to abandon the valley. The rebels were forced to transport food and military supplies from fixed bases in the mountains along the Pakistani border. They used a variety of transportation methods, from pickup trucks to donkeys, mules, and camels. The primitive system became prime targets for interdiction by Soviet air and *Spetsnaz* raids and ambushes from 1985, until their withdrawal four years later.

Death by a Thousand Cuts

The often harsh climate and the rugged nature of the terrain favored the guerrilla and worked against the Soviet mechanized force, which was dependent on a road network for communications and supply. Afghanistan's land mass, almost the size of Britain and France combined, is dominated by forbidding deserts (only 22 percent of its land is arable) and towering mountains, much of which is covered by lush forests of larch, aspen, and juniper. The Hindu Kush mountains cross the center of the country and divide the northern provinces from the rest of Afghanistan. They run generally northeast to southwest and range in height from 7,000 meters above sea level in the eastern part of the country to 3,500 to 4,500

Soviet and Mujahideen Use of Mines

Soviet, Afghan government, and Mujahideen forces made extensive use of minefields. Some estimates place the number in the millions. For example, when the 40th Army withdrew, they turned over the records for 613 minefields, which could easily accommodate over a million mines. The records showed that all regions of Afghanistan were affected. The worst areas were in the southern provinces, along the eastern border with Pakistan and in the western border with Iran. The northern part of the country was somewhat less densely mined, although several extensive minefields have been discovered. The Soviet mine-laying efforts were often poorly coordinated. Former Russian officer, Timothy Gusinov, noted, "One unit often laid a minefield and marked it only on its own map without informing other units . . . convoys would place them around its bivouac and then drive away without retrieving them . . . Spetsnaz would leave them on their withdrawal route and not inform anyone . . . and the air force would deliver scatterable mines without thought for ground units." Soviet minefields were used to protect key positions—outposts, bridges, highways—and to cut rebel supply lines. Many of the major cities, including the regional capitals—Kandahar, Herat, and Kabul—were extensively mined. In Herat, the Soviets laid a barrier minefield through the western part of the city to protect them from Mujahideen attack from Iran. The Soviets also made heavy use of scatterable mines to disrupt suspected Mujahideen supply routes in remote areas.

The Mujahideen favored mines because it was a relatively inexpensive way to attack personnel and vehicles. The mines were supplied from many sources—China, Egypt, Eastern Europe, Iran—and often scattered around without rhyme or reason. The Mujahideen favored anti-tank and anti-vehicular mines to interdict convoys. It is estimated that the Soviets lost over 11,000 vehicles during the war. In one favored method, the Mujahideen stacked three anti-tank mines on top of each other, ensuring a catastrophic kill. They delighted in improvising home-made bombs. In 1986, a creative bomb-maker destroyed a government outpost by floating a 250-kilogram bomb down a river and exploding it at just the right moment. The Mujahideen often established positions to cover their mines by small arms and automatic weapons fire.

Mines are still claiming hundreds of victims each year in Afghanistan, despite massive de-mining efforts by dozens of international organizations. The United States has contributed millions of dollars to the effort.

The Mujahideen were legendary fighters, who were natural light infantry. Hardy, tough, and courageous, they were well adapted to operate in Afghanistan's rugged terrain and severe climate. *militaryphotos.net*

meters in the west. Other mountain ranges radiate westward from the Hindu Kush system. More than two hundred passes transect the mountains between Quetta, Pakistan, and the border with China. Ninety of these can be used by vehicles. Afghanistan also possesses many rivers, lakes, and river basins. The most important basins are Amu Darya, Kabul, Harirud, and Helmand. The populated "green zones" along the rivers are intersected by irrigation ditches and are thick with trees, vines, crops, and tangled vegetation. There were no railroads in the country, and there were only 18,000 kilometers of road, less than one sixth of which was paved. It is a country where the fierce Afghan guerrilla can inflict "death from a thousand cuts."

The Mujahideen were legendary fighters, from a culture in which achieving warrior status was a right of passage for young men. Afghan culture, particularly the Pashtuns, affirmed the value of a life under arms. They were natural light infantry, raised from childhood with weapons. A Pakistani intelligence officer said, "An Afghan man rarely goes unarmed, even in peacetime. To him his rifle is a part of his body, a piece of clothing without which he feels uncomfortable. A weapon to a man is like jewelry to a Western woman; he is rarely seen without it. It is a symbol of manhood." They were hardy, tough, and courageous, and superbly adapted to operate in the rugged terrain and severe climate, where they could strike suddenly at the time and place of their choosing and then melt back into the population. The ranks of the Mujahideen were filled with fighters that ranged from preadolescent boys to grizzled veterans of the Third Anglo-Afghan War of 1919. Their total numbers were difficult to estimate. *The Military Balance, 1985–1986* published a figure of 90,000, backed by about 110,000 "reserves."

Other Western estimates placed the number of men in the 200,000 to 250,000 range, while Afghan figures go as high as 744,000. Whatever their numbers, the Mujahideen fighters enjoyed the support of the local populace, who supplied them with food, shelter, and intelligence.

The Soviets were absolutely dependent on the primitive road network to keep the 40th Army supplied. The Mujahideen fell upon it like birds of prey, forcing the Soviets to deploy up to 35 percent of its force (29 battalions) to protect the lines of communications (LOC). Another 40 percent were used in various security missions—guarding fixed installations such as airfields, government facilities, and bases—leaving only a very limited number of combat troops to actively campaign. The 40th Army was stretched to the limit. Many of the front line units (56 out of 73 battalions) were continuously in action, with no stand down or troop rotation. In January and February 1981, the Soviets claimed that thirty-nine battalions conducted combat operations involving 792 battalion days. The air force at the same time carried out 12,000 sorties in support of ground troops or to drop ordnance. The Soviets claimed that almost 1,400 rebels were killed "between 25 February and 5 March."

In 1981, the Mujahideen conducted over 5,236 attacks against Soviet and Afghan government forces, an average of 436 per month. The Woodrow Wilson International Center for Scholars noted that in the same year, "they [Mujahideen] made 760 unexpected attacks, destroying 567 transport vehicles and damaging 500 administrative centers, and 4,552 members of the Sarandov [Afghan government troops] were killed." The Soviets admitted that between 60 to 90 percent of the provinces were under rebel control. The KGB reported, "The counter-revolutionary forces have managed to keep their zones of influence and to attract a considerable part of the population into the armed struggle against the existing regime." *Pravda* correspondent I. Shehedov wrote, "It is quite clear that even under the most favorable circumstances, and with the most effective strategy, the defeat of the counter-revolutionary [Mujahideen] formations will take years." The next year, the Soviets admitted that there were twice as many rebel attacks and that they were becoming more organized and better trained. "The various partisan groups were beginning to avoid battles, coordinate their actions . . . [and] change their tactics."

The ambush was the Mujahideen's favorite tactic. It had long been a key feature of their tactical playbook. C. J. Dick wrote, "The size of the ambushes varied from a few dozen men up to 350 or more, on stretches of road up to 10 kilometers or so. Determining factors were: the number of men available; the amount of cover available; the length of the column to be hit; and the importance of the target. The duration of actions varied from quick fire-and-withdraw harassing actions up to fire-fights of 1–2 hours, followed where possible by looting of the damaged vehicles and weapons collection." Most of the ambushes were against the Soviet LOCs.

Mujahideen successes were often the result of poor Soviet operational procedures, as well as adherence to stereotyped organization and tactics, incompetence, and excessive passivity. Grau and Jalali commented that "the

Kandahar Ambush

In 1982, the Soviet 70th Separate Motorized Rifle Brigade was conducting a block and sweep operation about 25 kilometers southwest of Kandahar, in the center of the Panjwayee District. The operation required the Soviets to supply its units by the road that ran through the village of Deh-Khwaja. The local Mujahideen decided to conduct a large-scale ambush—150 men in two groups, ambush force and flank security—along the road that ran between Manzel Bagh Chawk and Deh-Khwaja. In addition to AK-47 assault rifles, the ambush force was armed with a recoilless rifle, two heavy machine guns, and two rocket-propelled grenade launchers. The ambush force moved into place during darkness and took up positions in the

Destroyed vehicles and equipment littered the roads where the Mujahideen had successfully executed ambushes. They were adept at picking the place and time for their attack, knowing that the Soviets lacked the ability to pursue them into the mountains. *militaryimages.net*

Soviets or DRA [Democratic Republic of Afghanistan] seldom dismounted troops to search the area to spoil the ambush or to try to set up a counter-ambush. Air support is tardy, artillery fire is unavailable and there is no reserve to move against the ambush. Aggressive patrolling, specially-trained counter-ambush forces and priority counter-ambush intelligence are lacking." C. J. Dick noted that "morale among the Soviet forces was low, except for some elite units. Soldiers found themselves in an alien land, universally loathed as oppressive occupiers." There was little support for them at home, as the Soviet people could not understand why their sons

orchards, buildings, and ditches along the road. The commander established a roadblock and determined that when the lead convoy elements reached it, his men were to open fire.

Early in the morning, a large convoy of Soviet trucks approached the Mujahideen position. When the convoy reached the roadblock, the Mujahideen opened a heavy fire with small arms, RPGs, and machine gun and recoilless rifle fire. While surprised, the Soviets responded, indiscriminately shooting into the village and causing quite a bit of damage. Suddenly, several ammunition trucks exploded, showering the surrounding area with debris. The blasts were so powerful that burning tires were thrown some two

kilometers away. The leading vehicles in the convoy were immobilized and destroyed, their drivers either killed or wounded. Those vehicles in the rear were able to turn around and escape the ambush. The Mujahideen looted the unde-stroyed vehicles of weapons and ammunition and quickly left the area. The Soviets were not able to mount a pursuit in time to catch the attackers.

An Afghan guerrilla drops an 82mm round down the mortar tube. Mujahideen indirect-fire weapons would devastate convoys because of poor Soviet operational tactics. The Soviets seldom dismounted troops to spoil the ambush and they did not often have air or artillery support readily available. AP photo/Joe Gaal

Two Afghan guerrillas practice with AK-47 assault rifles, which they claim to have captured from Soviet troops. The Mujahideen were particularly brutal toward Soviet prisoners, often torturing and killing their captives. The Soviet soldiers were fearful of being captured. *AP photo*

were fighting in Afghanistan. Gregory Feifer noted that for one officer, "Life had turned into a mind-numbing grind . . . alleviated only by moments of absurdity and tragedy, some during long bouts of heavy drinking . . . binges lasted for days. Marijuana was easily available from locals . . . abuse was turned into a brutal form usually associated with prisons . . . Typhus, cholera, and malaria also plagued Russian troops, if not as much as the routine bouts of hepatitis."

The Mujahideen also staged raids against hard targets to obtain arms and ammunition. They worked primarily against Afghan government forces, who would often run away or give up after token resistance. In one successful operation, a Mujahideen raiding party armed with assault rifles attacked a small outpost. The raiders took advantage of the local clansmen to gather intelligence about the garrison. On the morning of the raid, the Mujahideen crept close to the outpost by using a flock of sheep as cover.

After spending the day in the middle of the flock, they launched their attack just as the garrison was eating dinner. The raiders swarmed into the compound and captured it without firing a shot. After gathering weapons, ammunition, and equipment, they left with seven prisoners. In this case the Afghan government prisoners were given a choice of joining the resistance or remaining captives. Soviet prisoners were not offered a choice and were terrified of being captured. They were often tortured and then killed. Colonel Alexander Rutskoi was shot down and captured. Knocked unconscious by an exploding hand grenade, he woke up hanging from a pole, his arms and legs tightly bound. Later he was interrogated and hung from the ceiling by his arms until he lost consciousness. He awoke to find that a rescue force had saved him from further torture.

The Mujahideen carried out extensive sabotage operations. They knocked out pipelines, cut power lines, blew up buildings, air terminals, hotels, and movie theaters. They assassinated Soviet and government officials, creating an atmosphere of widespread fear verging on terror. From 1985 through 1987, there was an average of over 600 "terrorist acts" a year. In the same time frame, the Mujahideen carried out over 23,500 rocket and mortar attacks on government installations. During one attack by fire, they inflicted an estimated 200 killed and wounded on the 66th Separate Motorized Rifle Brigade. The attackers fired over 250 82mm mortar rounds into the Soviet compound from defilade positions. The observation post was located on the high ground, giving them the opportunity to observe and adjust their fire. Local tribesmen provided them with intelligence and acted as guides. After expending all their ammunition, the Mujahideen made their way to safety. They escaped without casualties.

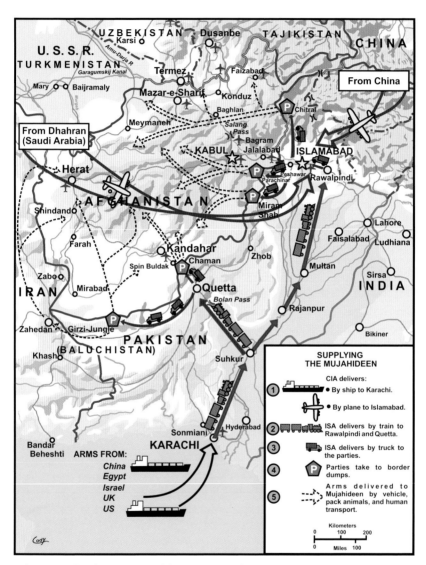

Military supplies flooded into Afghanistan, even from communist countries anxious to make a buck on the arms market. Unscrupulous arms dealers found convenient buyers for their antiquated weapons and ammunition. *Bill Cody*

CHAPTER 3

State within a State

"Pakistani Inter-Service Intelligence:
a state within a state."
—Steve Coll

IN MARCH 1979, THE CIA had sent its first proposals to support the Afghan rebels to President Carter, but it wasn't until July that it received approval to spend $500,000 for an insurgent propaganda campaign and to provide money and nonmilitary supplies. Zbigniew Brzezinski, President Jimmy Carter's national security adviser, wrote, "In my opinion this aid was going to induce a Soviet military intervention." He further stated that "we didn't push the Russians to intervene, but we knowingly increased the probability that they would." Brzezinski followed up with another memo after the invasion. "The day the Soviets officially crossed the border, I wrote to President Carter. We now have the opportunity of giving to the USSR its Vietnam War." A week later he noted, "Our ultimate goal is the withdrawal of Soviet troops from Afghanistan. Even if this is not attainable, we should make Soviet involvement as costly as possible." Anti-Soviet fever ran high in Washington. In a matter of days, the United States declared Pakistan a "frontline state" against Soviet aggression and offered to reopen aid and military assistance deliveries. President Carter also signed a top secret presidential intelligence order, called a finding (later reaffirmed by Ronald Reagan), in late December 1979, turning the CIA loose to "harass" the Soviets. The finding authorized the CIA to secretly provide military equipment, weapons, and ammunition to the Mujahideen.

The CIA's Near East Division secretly contacted its sources in Pakistan and Saudi Arabia to see how the covert aid could be placed in the hands of the anti-Soviet rebels. They learned that Pakistani president Mohammed Zia-ul-Haq had already authorized a low level of support for the Mujahideen and was willing to increase this aid, so long as the "pot did not boil over" into a major military confrontation with the Soviet Union. The Soviets did not directly attack Pakistan, but they did conduct a campaign to make the cost of its support of the Mujahideen prohibitively high. "By 1983," Brigadier General Yusuf Khan wrote, "They [the Soviets] had launched a well-coordinated campaign . . . to undermine President Zia and his policies through a massive subversion and sabotage effort." The Soviets sought to foment trouble by distributing weapons to the border tribes, infringing on Afghan airspace, shelling Pakistani border areas, and using Afghan KhAD (State Information Service, the Afghan version of the KGB) agents to set off explosives in the country.

President Zia viewed the Soviets' naked power play as a threat to Pakistan's security and bitterly condemned it. He feared that with a Soviet-backed communist government in control of Afghanistan, his country would be sandwiched between two unfriendly regimes—India on the south and east, and the Soviet Union on the north and west. He feared that Mujahideen cross-border operations would result in retaliation by the Soviets. In fact, Soviet helicopter gunships and aircraft occasionally "strayed" into Pakistani airspace, and, on more than one occasion, Pakistani civilians were injured. Finally, the Afghan refugees posed a threat to Pakistan's internal stability. Tension between the newcomers, most of whom were armed, and Pakistani citizens increased as the passage of years, and competition for scarce jobs, frayed the edges of Muslim and Pashtun hospitality. Islamabad feared that unless a way to repatriate the refugees was discovered, they might become, like the Palestinians in Jordan and Lebanon, a perpetual source of trouble. There were apprehensions that the Afghans could act as a wedge to disturb the already fragile consensus that existed among the nation's different ethnic groups.

President Zia needed American support but was determined to get as much out of it as he could from any agreement. The Carter administration regarded Pakistan as vital to U.S. interests in the Indian Ocean and the Persian Gulf and offered Zia 400 million dollars. Zia turned it down; huffily claiming it was just "peanuts." Later, the Reagan administration committed $3.2 billion in economic and military aid over a six-year period, making Pakistan the third-largest recipient of U.S. foreign aid. With the pot sufficiently sweetened, Zia jumped on board, but with an important condition. Every American dollar and gun had to pass through his primary secret service organization, the Inter-Service Intelligence, or ISI. "The ISI would retain control over contacts with Afghan rebels," Steve Coll wrote. "No American—CIA or otherwise—would be permitted to cross the border into Afghanistan. Movements of weapons within Pakistan, and their distribution to Afghan commanders, would be handled strictly by ISI officers. All training of Mujahideen would be carried out solely by ISI in camps along the Afghan frontiers." It is estimated that over 80,000 anti-Soviet fighters were trained between 1980 and 1989.

Inter-Service Intelligence (ISI)

The Inter-Service Intelligence organization was formed as a quasi-division of the army in the early days of Pakistan's independence. Its focus was largely on the military threat posed by India, and the tensions over Kashmir, which have kept the two countries on a perpetual war footing. During President Zia's administration, the ISI was used to enforce martial law and to keep Zia in power. Brigadier General Mohammad Yusuf Khan, Director of the ISI's Afghan Bureau, said that "part of the ISI's function was to keep careful watch on the generals to ensure reliability to the regime. Certainly in those days of martial law under Zia, apprehension, even fear, of what the ISI could do was very real." At the time of the Soviet invasion, Lt. Gen. Akhtar Abdur Rahman Khan, a close friend and confident of the president, was installed as director-general of the Inter-Services Intelligence with orders to take everything he could from the CIA but to keep them at arm's length. At the time of his assignment, Lieutenant General Akhtar was considered to be the most powerful man in the armed forces, with daily access to President Zia.

The ISI took on the trappings of a state within a state. It meddled in domestic politics, fomenting opposition against Benazir Bhutto, the first democratically elected Pakistani prime minister in more than a decade. It "anointed" Mujahideen commanders, deciding which would receive military aid and which would be cut out of the system. Lieutenant General Akhtar used the power of the purse to force the Mujahideen to form an alliance known as the "Peshawar Seven." Brigadier General Yusuf Khan said, "Every commander must belong to one of the seven parties; otherwise he got nothing from the ISI; no arms, no ammunition and no training." Four of the seven commanders were Islamic fundamentalists, who not

Directorate of Inter-Services Intelligence (ISI)

The Pakistani Directorate of Inter-Service Intelligence (ISI) was founded in 1948 by Major General William Cawthorne, a British army officer, who was the deputy chief of staff in the Pakistani army. The ISI is tasked with the collection of foreign and domestic intelligence; co-ordination of intelligence functions of the three military services; surveillance over its cadre, foreigners, the media, politically active segments of Pakistani society, diplomats of other countries accredited to Pakistan, Pakistani diplomats serving outside the country; the interception and monitoring communications; and the conduct of covert offensive operations. The head of the ISI is called the director general and is a serving lieutenant general in the Pakistani army. He is assisted by three deputy directors-general—DDG (Internal), which deals with counter-intelligence and political issues within the country; DDG-1 (External); and DDG-II (Analysis and Foreign relations). The ISI is further divided into lettered sections, the most notorious of which is the S wing, which manages the relationship with Islamist militant groups. The C wing liaises with foreign intelligence services, and includes a CIA-funded counter-terrorism center. Quite often, Western spies complain, the C wing says one thing while the S does another.

The nondescript headquarters of the ISI is located in Islamabad on Khayban-e-Suharwady Avenue, in the heart of the capital. Its operational offices are in the adjoining garrison town of Rawalpindi. Experts estimate that the ISI is staffed with about 10,000, which does not include informants and other personnel assets.

The ISI is organized into six divisions:

Joint Intelligence X (JIX): co-ordinates and provides administrative support, and prepares intelligence estimates and threat assessments.

Joint Intelligence Bureau (JIB): responsible for political intelligence. One of its subsections is devoted to operations against India.

Joint Counter-Intelligence Bureau (JCIB): responsible for surveillance of Pakistani diplomats abroad, as well as conducting intelligence operations in the Middle East, South Asia, China, Afghanistan, and the Muslim republics of the former Soviet Union.

Joint Intelligence/North (JIN): responsible for the proxy war in Jammu and Kashmir and the control of Afghanistan through the Taliban. It also controls all opium cultivation and heroin refining and smuggling from Pakistani and Afghan territory.

Joint Intelligence Miscellaneous (JIM): conducts espionage in foreign countries, including offensive intelligence operations and for the clandestine procurement of nuclear and missile technologies.

Joint Signal Intelligence Bureau (JSIB): operates a chain of signals intelligence collection stations along the border with India, and provides communication support to militants operating in Kashmir.

The Bank of Credit and Commerce International (BCCI): the ISI's main international financial institution.

The ISI, up to the time of the Soviet invasion, was a relatively small organization. That changed in December 1979, when it became the primary conduit for Western aid and assistance to the anti-Soviet Mujahideen. Hundreds of millions of dollars were funneled through the Pakistani intelligence agency, with little accountability. Many of its officers spent decades in the organization, growing rich on siphoned money. It became a "state within a state," answerable to neither the leadership of the army, nor to the president or the prime minister. Many Pakistanis considered the ISI to be a rogue organization because of its involvement in domestic politics.

With the Soviet defeat and the start of the civil war, the ISI support of the Taliban increased. In September 2000, Assistant Secretary of State Karl Inderfurth noted, "Pakistan [ISI] is stepping up support to the Taliban's military campaign in Afghanistan…While Pakistani support of the Taliban has been long standing, the magnitude of recent support is unprecedented…large numbers of Pakistani nationals have recently moved into Afghanistan to fight for the Taliban, apparently with the tacit acquiescence of the Pakistani government. Our reports further suggest that direct Pakistani involvement in Taliban military operations has increased in the past few months." Recently leaked classified military reports indicate that some elements of the ISI continue to support the Taliban with weapons, safety, and operational planning.

Support for the Taliban, as well as other militant groups, is coordinated by operatives in the shadowy S Wing. Little is publicly known about the S Wing, which officials say directs intelligence operations outside of Pakistan. American officials said that the S Wing provides direct support to three major groups carrying out attacks in Afghanistan: the Taliban based in Quetta, Pakistan, commanded by Mullah Muhammad Omar; the militant network run by Gulbuddin Hekmatyar; and a different group run by the guerrilla leader Jalaluddin Haqqani. Ambassador Peter Tomsen told *Frontline* in 2006 that the ISI knows exactly where they are, even that "the Taliban leaders wander around in Pakistan clearly organizing offensives into Afghanistan."

only hated the Soviets but held the United States in great disdain. The ISI operations officer, according to Steve Coll, was "an ardent Islamist, much more religious than the typical Pakistani army officer, his CIA colleagues believed." Brigadier General Yusuf Khan admitted, "Relations between the CIA and ourselves were always strained. There was never really a feeling of mutual trust. I resorted to avoid contact with the local CIA staff as much as possible." The ISI played a two-handed game, professing to rid Afghanistan of the Soviets, while pushing their own agenda. They were determined to install a friendly government that would give them "breathing room" on their western border.

The United States provided billions of dollars in aid to the Mujahideen during the 1980s, most of which passed through ISI hands. Saudi Arabia matched the American contribution dollar for dollar, under an agreement with President Ronald Reagan. The United Kingdom, Egypt, China, and Iran also provided aid to the various rebel factions. As the war progressed, the Mujahideen's antiquated weaponry was replaced with new and more potent weapons—Soviet-made AK-47s, RPG-7s, 60mm mortars, and 12.7mm heavy machine guns—which allowed the donor countries to remain anonymous. Some communist countries jumped on board just to make a buck selling weapons and equipment even though it was going to be used against their Soviet ally. "Dissident Polish army officers accepted payoffs to sell surplus Soviet weapons in secret to the CIA," Steve Coll wrote. "The Chinese communists cleared huge profit margins on weapons they sold in deals with the CIA. The Egyptians were selling the CIA junky stores of weapons previously sold to them by the Soviets." There was so much cash flowing through the international arms suppliers that anyone with communist-made weapons could reap a bonanza.

Coll said it was hard for the CIA to determine who was making a reasonable profit and who was ripping off the agency. The CIA station chief knew the ISI was stealing, but he considered their "theft" modest and reasonable. With billions of dollars going through its hands, the Pakistani intelligence agency grew immensely powerful. "The ISI inducted hundreds of army officers to monitor not just Afghanistan, but India and all of Pakistan's foreign intelligence as well as domestic politics, the economy, the media, and every aspect of social and cultural life in the country . . . by 1989 it was the most powerful political and foreign policy force in Pakistan," Ahmed Rashid wrote, "repeatedly overriding civilian governments and parliament in policy areas." However, in 1979 President Zia used the ISI's double-dealing skills to his advantage. His country was no longer an outcast on the world's stage; Pakistan was now on the front line in the fight against Soviet aggression.

The Afghan Bureau's nondescript operational headquarters was located at Camp Okhri on the northern outskirts of Rawalpindi, approximately twelve kilometers from the capital. It was a large complex of some seventy to eighty acres, surrounded by high brick walls. The compound contained offices, warehouses, garage facilities, a large training area, mess halls, and barracks for five hundred men. The compound was situated on the main road that ran from Rawalpindi to Islamabad. A Pakistani army camp was across the road, while civilian houses lined the other side, marking the outskirts of the city. Brigadier General Yusuf Khan said that "international jet airliners flew directly overhead as they made their approach to Islamabad airport. Its very location within the confines of a major town made it inconspicuous. Of the countless thousands of passers-by none suspected it for what it was—the command post for the war in Afghanistan." Weapons, ammunition, and military supplies of all types were stored at the site, waiting to be trans-shipped to Afghanistan. "On my first day I was taken round the offices, and to see the main warehouse, where I received my first shock," Yusuf Khan recalled. "Lying in the open, in piles under an arched roof, were all types of small arms, mortars, rocket launchers, and recoilless rifles, together with their ammunition. Just about every safety rule I had ever been taught for arms storage was being broken, and this within a densely populated area. The logistics officer's response to my concern was, 'Sir, we are fighting a secret war; you will soon get used to it.' "

The Afghan Bureau had three branches. The Operations Branch was headed by a colonel, who was responsible for the day-to-day operational planning, and the selection of Mujahideen targets. This branch also coordinated intelligence collection and dissemination and supervised Mujahideen training. The Logistics Branch was also headed by a colonel. Its mission was to allocate and ship weapons and ammunition. The third branch, headed by a lieutenant colonel, dealt with psychological warfare—the operation of three radio stations, distribution of leaflets, and interrogation of prisoners. Brigadier General Yusuf Khan said, "From 1984, through to 1987, over 80,000 Mujahideen went through our training camps, hundreds of thousands of tons of weapons and ammunition were distributed, while active operations were being planned and carried out in all of the 29 provinces in Afghanistan. I eventually had an establishment of some 60 officers, 100 Junior Commissioned Officers (JCOs), and 300 NCOs."

The bureau had two forward headquarters: a major facility at Peshawar, the provincial capital of the NWFP, and a smaller depot at Quetta in southern Pakistan. Both facilities were located close to the main routes into Afghanistan. The ISI headquarters in Peshawar was located close to the "Peshawar Seven's" complexes of offices, warehouses, and ammunition dumps. "It is Peshawar that attracts the journalists and the spies as a magnet attracts metal. For the latest gossip, rumor, report or whisper, you must start in Peshawar," Yusuf Khan wrote. Quetta, the capital of Baloshistan Province, was also a garrison town, located approximately 100 kilometers from the Afghan border. Its headquarters was smaller than Peshawar, but had its own warehouses that enabled supplies to be shipped directly from the docks in Karachi, instead of via the main warehouses in Rawalpindi. Peshawar was the center of the supply organization, with Quetta the secondary one in the south. The ISI transported the supplies from the two headquarters to the Mujahideen warehouses, where it was distributed to each guerrilla commander. Brigadier General Yusuf Khan said, "Each party had its own method of deciding allocations. If some commanders failed to receive their supply, there was little I could do about it."

Once the distribution was made, the supplies had to be transported to hundreds of small operational bases scattered all over Afghanistan. "It was one of the most complicated, chaotic and time-consuming operations of the war," Yusuf Khan wrote. "Trucks, and tractors, carts and camels, mules, and horses all played their part, as did the backs of the Mujahideen themselves." In 1984, it was estimated that 10,000 tons of arms and ammunition went through this pipeline. Three years later, that tonnage had increased seven fold. The Mujahideen were being supplied with modern weapons and equipment, upgraded RPGs, the latest version of the assault rifle, tons of plastic explosive, hundreds of long-range sniper rifles, and pallets of night-vision goggles . . . and the most up-to-date American anti-aircraft missile, the FIM-92 Stinger.

The downing of three helicopters marked a new chapter in the war. No longer could Soviet pilots fly with relative impunity at low levels. They now had to stay above the Stingers' effective ceiling of 12,000 feet, which severely diminished their capacity to provide close air support. The CIA station chief cabled headquarters that the introduction of the Stinger was "the most significant battlefield development" of the war.

FIM-92 Stinger

The FIM-92 Stinger is a shoulder-fired portable infrared-homing surface-to-air missile that is capable of engaging low-altitude, high-speed aircraft. It is classified as a Man-Portable Air-Defense System (MANPADS). It has a range of up to 15,700 feet and can target aircraft at altitudes between 600 and 12,500 feet. The missile is 1.52 meters long, 70mm in diameter, and weighs 33 pounds, complete. The Stinger is launched by a small ejection motor that pushes it a safe distance from the operator before engaging the main two-stage solid-fuel sustainer, which accelerates it to a maximum speed of Mach 2.2 (750 meters a second). The warhead is a 3kg penetrating hit-to-kill warhead type with an impact fuse and a self-destruct timer.

The Stinger, manufactured by Raytheon Missile Systems, saw its first combat during the Falklands war between Great Britain and Argentina. On 30 May 1982 an Argentine SA-300 Puma helicopter carrying fourteen members of the National Gendarmerie Special Forces and two crew members was shot down by "D" Squadron of the Special Air Service. Six passengers were killed and eight injured. In 1986, the Stinger was provided to the Mujahideen, which marked a turning point in the war. It is estimated that the Soviets lost on average, one helicopter a day, with over 270 claimed kills.

After the war, the United States attempted to buy back the unused missiles for $80,000 to $150,000 per missile, which cost the U.S. Treasury approximately $55 million. In 1996, the CIA estimated that 600 Stingers were still unaccounted for.

The introduction of the FIM-92 Stinger shoulder-fired missile in 1986 had a significant impact on the war. It forced the Soviets to change their air support tactics. They could no longer fly at low levels with relative impunity. *USMC*

Stinging the Bear

Commander Engineer Ghaffar and his thirty-five Mujahideen commandos crept through the scrub growth until they reached a small knoll overlooking the airfield. At a signal from Ghaffar, the men deployed among the rocks, careful to conceal themselves from the air. As they waited in the hot sun, three of the men busied themselves with several objects that looked, at first glance, to be Rocket Propelled Grenade launchers. Suddenly the unmistakable sound of helicopter blades slicing through the super-heated air reached them. Within seconds, eight of the fearsome Mi-24 Hind gunships appeared. The three men stood, placed the launchers on their shoulders, sighted, and pulled the triggers. Missiles leaped from the launchers. One, instead of heading skyward, fizzled into the rocks a few hundred yards away. The other two missiles flew true, striking two of the Hinds and sending them crashing to the ground in flames. Two more missiles were launched, and another Hind was blown out of the air. The remaining Hinds scattered like a covey of quail. One of the Mujahideen filmed the event with a video camera. Steve Coll described the scene: "'*Allahu Akhbar! Allahu Akhbar!*' the shooters cried as they fired the Afghan war's first Stingers. By the time . . . the third helicopter [was hit], the videotape looked 'like some kid at a football game,' . . . 'everybody is jumping up and down.'"

By sheer coincidence, a U.S. KH-11 spy satellite passed over the site and took photographs showing three charred balls of steel scrap, lying side by side on the active runway. The highly classified photographs and video were viewed

First Sting, by Stuart Brown. The painting depicts the first operational use of the Stinger missile in Afghanistan. *Collection of the Central Intelligence Agency*

at the highest levels of the U.S. government, including a special screening for President Reagan. The decision to supply the Mujahideen with the FIM-92 Stinger was made only after a long and emotional debate between the CIA and the State Department. The debate centered on introducing a readily identifiable U.S. weapon system into the war, and possibly sparking Soviet retaliation. It was decided that the risk was worth the benefit. Between 1986 and 1989, approximately 2,000 to 2,500 Stinger missiles were given to the Mujahideen.

The Bear Limped (Back) over the Mountain

"The troop withdrawal is not a defeat. It is the completion of an international mission."

—Lt. Gen. Boris Gromov,
Limited Contingent of Armed Forces
of the Soviet Union

On 11 March 1985, Mikhail Gorbachev assumed the office of general secretary of the Communist Party of the Soviet Union. He came into power with a reformist agenda, which called for the restructuring of the Soviet political and economic system (*Perestroika*) and giving more freedom to the Soviet people (*Glasnost*). He also tried to improve relations and trade with the West and reduce Cold War tensions. Seven months after taking office, Gorbachev moved to settle the Afghan issue, which he characterized as a "bleeding wound." He met with Babrak Karmal and told him that "by the summer of 1986, you'll have to have found out how to defend your cause on your own. We'll help you, but with arms only, not troops." Gorbachev said that Karmal "was dumfounded" by the news. The Afghan had expected the Soviet Union to support his government for "a long time—if not forever." The general secretary went on to offer Karmal guidance. "If you want to survive . . . broaden your base of support. Make a deal with truly influential forces . . . and leaders of now-hostile organizations . . . show the people some tangible benefits . . . and get your army in shape for the survival of your regime." Gorbachev's prophetic guidance remains just as valid today as the United States struggles to resolve its own Afghan problem.

On 13 November 1986, fifteen members of the Politburo's inner circle sat quietly in Mikhail Gorbachev's private office as the army's chief of staff explained that the Soviet Union was no closer to a victory in Afghanistan

Stinger Training

ISI's Afghan Bureau established a Stinger training school, complete with simulator, at its Okhri camp in Rawalpindi. All the Mujahideen were taught there by the ISI, ten of whom had gone through an eight-week course in the United States. Brigadier General Mohammad Yusuf Khan personally selected the first two Mujahideen for the Stinger mission; a military engineer trained in the Soviet Union, named Engineer Ghaffar, and Adel Darwesh. "For us it was a moment we had been anticipating for four years, a chance to confront our most hated opponent of the war on equal terms," Yusuf Khan explained. "These two Commanders had been entrusted to attack the helicopter gunship, or indeed any aircraft, with the U.S. Stinger anti-aircraft missile. On this first occasion it had developed into an outright competition between these two Commanders. Back at Rawalpindi, where they and their teams had been trained, they had challenged each other as to who would get the first kill." The Afghans selected for training were generally those with a proven combat record, particularly those who had done well with the Russian SA-7 Grail surface to air missile.

The Mujahideen were put through a three-week training program, twenty men at a time. The trainees were taught to ambush Soviet helicopters. One method was to attack an outpost and wait for the helicopters to respond. Another was to deliberately drive vehicles along dirt roads to create dust and then ambush any helicopter that tried to destroy them. Many of the Stinger teams were deployed around airfields, which gained the Mujahideen a tremendous psychological advantage when Soviet aircraft were destroyed over their own runways. The first Stingers were deployed at Jalalabad, Kabul, and Bagram, followed by the airfields at Mazar-e Sharif, Faisabad, Kunduz, and Maimana. Pakistani records showed that the Mujahideen achieved a success rate between 70 to 75 percent, 10 percent higher than the U.S. standard for qualification. Yusuf Khan attributed it to "the high standard of training imparted, the determination of the trainees to succeed, the natural

than when the 40th Army forded the pontoon bridges across the Amu Darya river seven years earlier. After the bemedaled general concluded, Gorbachev posed the question, "What are we doing there?" Not one of the members had a ready answer. He asked another, "Will we be there endlessly? Or should we end this war?" The questions hung in the air. Gorbachev went on. "The strategic goal is to finish the war in one, maximum two years, and withdraw the troops," he said with finality. "We have set a clear goal: Help speed up the process so we have a friendly neutral country, and get out of there." Andrei Gromyko interjected and proposed modifications. One attendee described Gorbachev's glare as "truly withering." He further stated, "Those looks said it all: 'You ass, what are you battling about, affinity of the Mujahideen for weapons and the aggressive anti-aircraft tactics we employed with Stingers."

The introduction of the Stinger missile put the Soviets on the defensive. Yusuf Khan said, "They became reluctant to fly low to push home attacks, while every transport aircraft at Kabul airport and elsewhere had its landing and take-off protected by flare-dispersing helicopters. Even civil airliners, which we did not attack, adopted a tight corkscrew descent to the runway, causing much nervousness and vomiting by the passengers." It was reported that, on one occasion, two Hinds were strafing a village when one was hit by a Stinger. The pilot of the other aircraft immediately bailed out.

Mujahideen atop a downed Soviet helicopter. It was estimated that the Soviets lost on average one helicopter a day after the introduction of the Stinger.
AP photo

giving us advice? You got us into this dirty business [Afghanistan], and now you're pretending that we're all responsible!" By this time, the Soviet people were sick to death of a war they didn't understand and were openly questioning the Politburo's decision to continue it. The war was costing over two billion rubles a year, and the country's economy was teetering on the verge of collapse. Hundreds of thousands of Afghan veterans had returned, bringing home stories of low morale, drug and alcohol abuse, and criticism of the war. The decision was made. Gorbachev announced, "In the course of two years, effect the withdrawal of our troops from Afghanistan." Steve Coll described it as "one of the most significant Politburo discussions of the late Cold War."

Shortly after that Politburo meeting, Soviet Foreign Minister Eduard Shevrdnadze was in Washington and met privately with Secretary of State George Schultz. "We will leave Afghanistan," Shevrdnadze told the startled American. "It may be five months or a year, but it is not a question of it happening in the remote future. I say with all responsibility that a political decision to leave has been made." Schultz was quite taken aback. None of the U.S. intelligence estimates even hinted that the Soviets were thinking of pulling out. Schultz, according to Coll, "kept the news under his hat" for several weeks. Other top-level Soviet officials alerted their American counterparts, but it wasn't until Gorbachev personally told Ronald Reagan that the Soviet withdrawal was taken seriously.

In February 1988, Gorbachev declared that Soviet forces would begin pulling out of Afghanistan, half by 15 May, and the other half nine months later. The major players—Pakistan, Afghanistan, Soviet Union, and the United States, but not the Mujahideen commanders—met in Geneva, Switzerland, to codify the agreement. The bilateral agreement between Pakistan and Afghanistan, with the United States and the Soviet Union acting as guarantors, was known as the Geneva Accords. It was signed on 14 April 1988.

Brigadier-General Yusuf Khan wrote, "The Soviets withdrew a battalion at a time, usually at night, overloaded with Panasonic TV sets and other Western electric goods unobtainable at home. They wore their medals and some took their pet dogs. It was more or less a dignified departure." Ten months after signing the accords, at 1155 a.m. local time on 15 February 1989, five hundred men of the 201st Reconnaissance Division rolled across the wrought iron "Friendship" Bridge at Termez. Forty-five-year-old Lt. Gen. Boris Gromov, the trim, handsome commander of the 40th Army, was the last soldier across.

"Gromov stopped his tank halfway across the bridge," Coll wrote, "climbed out of the hatch, and walked toward Uzbekistan as one of his teenage sons approached him with a bouquet of carnations."

The father and son embraced and walked the last fifty yards together, toward an arch decorated with bunting and regimental flags. A military band played, while a crowd of military families, who had been flown in for the ceremony, looked on. A Russian television crew filmed the elaborately staged event, which was designed to look like a victory parade. Some of the returning troops were feted with a banquet, serenaded by a military band as they sat at a long linen-draped table. The cameras did not catch the sight of the last Soviet soldier killed in action. The paratrooper had been shot by a sniper during the withdrawal. His remains were wrapped in a military blanket and strapped on the back of a tank. Gromov himself was criticized by the defense minister. "Why are you leaving last, and not first, as a commander should?" the minister complained. Gromov responded assertively, "I consider that five and one half years service in Afghanistan gives me the right!" It was reported that the 40th Army commander did not

The last Soviet to leave Afghanistan, Lt. Gen. Boris Gromov, commander of the Soviet 40th Army, with his son Maxin, at the bridge over the Amy Darya River, at Termez, on 15 February 1989. The Soviet commander had crossed from the Afghan town of Khairaton. *AP photo/Tass*

look back as he stepped into Soviet territory. He later admitted, "The war was a huge and in many respects irreparable political mistake."

Bribery, Bluff, and Butchery

No one expected the Soviets' hand-picked proxy President Mohammed Najibullah to last more than a few months after their withdrawal. The CIA produced a classified National Intelligence Estimate (NIE) that confirmed his early demise. Titled "USSR: Withdrawal from Afghanistan," the secret report stated, "We judge that the Najibullah regime will not long survive the completion of Soviet withdrawal, even with continued Soviet assistance." It further postulated that "the regime may fall before withdrawal is complete." Instead, Najibullah managed to sustain his tenuous grip on power for another three years, despite the efforts of the United States and Pakistan. The United States wanted a "stable" moderate regime, while Pakistan sought a friendly Islamic regime to give them "strategic depth" against the threat posed by India.

Najibullah was able to survive, according to Nikolas K. Gvosdev in *The Soviet Victory that Never Was*, because he "recognized the futility of the earlier Soviet strategy in Afghanistan. Afghans, he knew, would not fight and die for the Soviet Union. But, he realized, Afghans could be co-opted to work with the government to defend local and clan interests. Najibullah allowed regional leaders—and, in some cases, former Mujahideen commanders—to form their own militias and, with mixed results, to join the regular army." The first test of his strategy came from the Mujahideen attack on Jalalabad, the third largest city in the country, only fifty kilometers from Kabul. Major General Hamid Gul, who replaced Lieutenant General Akhtar as director of ISI, pushed the warlords to abandon their guerrilla campaign in favor of a post-Soviet conventional warfare strategy. He promised that "the city will fall like a ripe apple."

By March 1989, nine warlords had assembled up to 10,000 fighters in the hills surrounding Jalalabad. In four months of heavy fighting, the Mujahideen forces suffered over 3,000 casualties and were forced to concede defeat. The battle for Jalalabad represented a great psychological as well as military victory for Najibullah's forces. The warlords and the ISI had underestimated the Afghan government's soldiers fighting spirit. "They had to fight to survive," Brig. Gen. Mohammad Yusuf Khan wrote. "Some early killings by the Mujahideen of prisoners confirmed in their minds

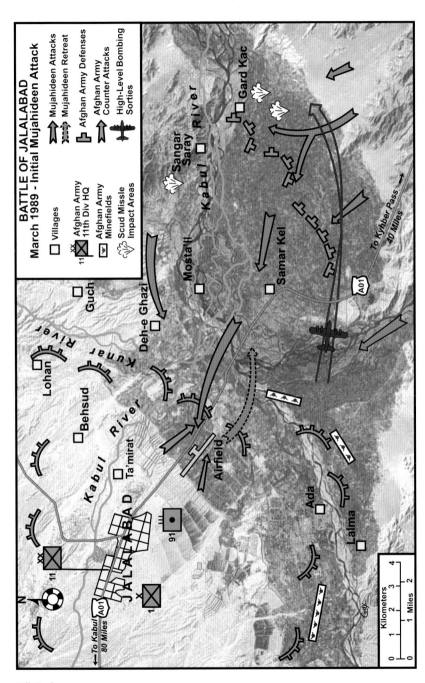

BATTLE OF JALALABAD
March 1989 - Initial Mujahideen Attack

Legend:
- Villages
- 11 Afghan Army 11th Div HQ
- Afghan Army Minefields
- Scud Missile Impact Areas
- Mujahideen Attacks
- Mujahideen Retreat
- Afghan Army Defenses
- Afghan Army Counter Attacks
- High-Level Bombing Sorties

Bill Cody

that surrender was no option." The Jalalabad defenders were protected by extensive defensive positions that included belts of barbed wire and minefields. They were well supplied with ammunition and supplies that were left by the Soviets. The defenders were supported by the Afghan air force, which launched over 100 sorties a day, using modified AN-12 transport planes to drop anti-personnel cluster bombs on the Mujahideen positions. In addition, three R-11 "Scud-B" surface to surface missile batteries, manned by Soviet personnel, fired over 400 rockets from positions near Kabul.

Jon Lee Anderson observed the battle first hand, after being escorted to the area by a plainclothes "Pakistani agent from the Inter-Services Intelligence... [who] was assisting the Mujahideen." He described how fields of poppies and wheat were burning after being set ablaze from the heavy shelling. He wrote, in *The Lion's Grave, Dispatches from Afghanistan*, "The front lines nearest the enemy positions—around the Jalalabad airport at the eastern edge of the city—were exposed to enemy fire and manned for the most part by untrained fourteen- and fifteen-year-old boys who had been recruited only weeks earlier from madrassas in Pakistan's Afghan refugee camps, and they were dying in droves." Despite thousands of casualties, the Mujahideen could not break through the formidable government defenses and withdrew in an atmosphere of bickering and recriminations among their commanders. Ahmad Shah Massoud complained, "The damage caused by our lack of a unified command is obvious. There is a total lack of coordination, which means we are not launching simultaneous offensives on different fronts. As a result the government can concentrate its resources and pick us off one by one. And that is what has happened at Jalalabad."

The victory gave President Najibullah a much needed morale boost, while the confidence of the Mujahideen nose-dived, causing several of the warlords to agree to a truce. With the immediate threat eliminated, Najibullah sought to buy off influential commanders and drive a wedge between the various warlords. He dispensed billions of rubles (US$300 million a month) provided by the Soviet Union as bribes. At one point, Najibullah bragged that twenty thousand mullahs were on his payroll, an extraordinarily expensive program that only lasted as long as the money kept flowing. In December 1991, the Soviet Union collapsed, eliminating the gravy train that had enabled Najibullah to buy loyalties across the country. A series of defections soon followed. One of the most important Uzbek militia leaders, Abdul Rashid Dostum, joined forces with Ahmed Shah Masoud in January 1992. The alliance created a formidable opposition and caused Najibullah's regime to lose control in most of northern

President Mohammed Najibullah was handpicked by the Soviet Union to run the country. His regime collapsed after the fall of the Soviet Union, and Najibullah was killed. *U.S. government*

Afghanistan. Two months later, Najibullah agreed to step down if the United Nations could broker an agreement.

The United Nations attempted to mediate between the parties but could not bring them together. When the UN plan failed, Najibullah's regime collapsed entirely, setting the stage for a confrontation between the two main contenders for power, Masoud and Gulbuddin Hekmatyar, a ruthless Mujahideen Islamist, who was strongly supported by the ISI. The two were implacable enemies as a result of a long-standing vendetta. One of Hekmatyar's senior commanders ambushed and killed thirty-six of Masoud's men, including seven of his best leaders and friends. Several of the men were brutally tortured before being killed. Masoud sought revenge and eventually caught and hanged the perpetrators. The two rivals vied for control of Kabul, with Masoud eventually prevailing, but not before the city was ravaged by heavy fighting. Kabul was so dangerous that the American embassy was closed.

Retribution was swift among the warring tribes. Hundreds of thousands were killed, maimed, and displaced during the civil war. *militaryphotos.com*

Brigadier General Yusuf Khan wrote, "I found it a bit odd, seeing the Americans pulling out at this moment. It seemed as though it was the Soviets that had been protecting them all these years, and now they feared for their safety, just as the Mujahideen appeared about to win the war. We were supposed to be their allies. The eleven staff, including four Marines, watched somberly in a biting wind as the national flag was hauled slowly down before hurrying to the airport." The embassy remained closed for nearly a decade, until the autumn of 2001.

On August 19, 1991, an attempted coup by Soviet hard-liners and KGB operatives to overthrow Gorbachev failed, but the Communist Party of the Soviet Union collapsed within weeks. With the Soviet Union in the midst of imploding, the United States searched for ways to support Gorbachev's embattled government. Newly elected President George H. W. Bush agreed with the Kremlin to stop all aid to the warring Afghan parties . . . but the cutoff did not end the fighting. While the two warlords fought over Kabul, "local commanders jostled for power," William Maley wrote in *The Afghanistan Wars*. "There was a sharp increase in predatory warlordism . . . particularly in southern Afghanistan." Various commanders carved out "a piece of the action" in the Kandahar region. "Any group of young Pashtun fighters with a few Kalashnikovs and rocket propelled grenade launchers could set up a checkpoint and extort payments on the highways," Steve Coll wrote. "By 1994, the main road from Quetta in Pakistan through Kandahar and on toward Herat and Iran, was choked by hundreds of extra-legal road-blocks." The local population was subject to unchecked violence. Coll noted that "reports of unchecked rape and abduction, including child rape, fueled a local atmosphere of fear and smoldering anger."

CHAPTER 4

Commander of the Faithful (*Amir-ul Momineen*)

*"The Taliban will fight until there is no blood
in Afghanistan left to be shed . . . ."*
—Mullah Mohammed Omar

AS THE WARLORDS BATTLED FOR power, Afghanistan fell into chaos. Kabul, Jalalabad, Kandahar, and other cities were shelled into ruins; thousands of their citizens were killed in the crossfire or suffered from starvation, deprivation, and extortion. Hundreds of thousands fled the war-ravaged country. Murder and banditry reigned supreme. For the *jihadists* who had triumphed over the Soviets, the conditions in the country were particularly galling. They searched desperately for an end to the wanton violence. A former Mujahideen commander asserted, "Whenever we got together, we would discuss the terrible plight of our people living under these bandits. We were people of the same opinions and we got on with each other very well, so it was easy to come to a decision to do something." That something occurred near the city of Kandahar in the summer of 1994, when a new movement appeared. Supposedly a religious teacher had a dream in which a woman told him, "We need your help; you must rise. You must end the chaos. God will help you." He went to a local businessman for help and was given money, vehicles, arms, and ammunition. He raised a small force of religious students and confronted a local thug.

The most common story of the confrontation involved two teenage girls that were abducted and raped by a Mujahideen commander. Hearing of the girl's plight, the group attacked the thug's base camp, freed the girls, and captured the commander, who was then hanged from the barrel of a tank. The teacher is reported to have said, "We were fighting Muslims who had gone wrong. How could we remain quiet when we could see crimes being committed against women and the poor?"

Pakistani journalist Rahimullah Yousufzai interviewed the teacher known as Mullah Omar. "We took up arms to achieve the aims of the Afghan *jihad* and save our people from further suffering at the hands of the so-called Mujahideen."

Mullah Omar

Cheers swept through the throng in the courtyard as the tall, well-built man with a long black beard stepped out on the roof of the old mosque. He held a cloak in his hands, allowing it to flutter open in the early morning breeze. With great solemnity, he carefully wrapped it around his body. The assembly of over 1,000 Afghan mullahs roared, "*Amir-ul Momineen,*" (Commander of the Faithful), proclaiming their unqualified support for him. The carefully staged event, the largest gathering of mullahs in modern Afghan history, was meant to consolidate and legitimize one Talibani as the undisputed leader of the organization. Mullah Mohammed Omar, by the simple wearing of the cloak purported to be the Prophet Muhammad's ancient robe, confirmed his leadership of the Taliban that April day in 1996. Correspondent Ahmed Rashid in *Taliban: Militant Islam, Oil and Fundamentalism in Central Asia*, wrote that "It was a political master-stroke, for by cloaking himself with the Prophet's mantle, Mullah Omar had assumed the right to lead not just Afghans, but all Muslims." A declassified U.S. State Department memo confirmed Rashid's opinion. "Mullah Mohammad Omar was proclaimed *Amir-ul Momineen* by a gathering of Afghan *Ulema* [Islamic scholars]. [He] is generally viewed as the final voice of authority within the loosely organized Taliban hierarchy."

Mullah Mohammed Omar, known simply in the Western world as Mullah Omar, is shrouded in mystery and myth. He has been the subject of intense interest for the world's intelligence agencies. Despite a multi-million dollar price on his head, and a massive manhunt by the U.S. military and Coalition partners, he has eluded capture. Not much is publicly known about him. Middle Eastern expert Peter Marsden wrote in *The Taliban, War*

Mullah Omar

Up to $10 Million Reward

Height: Tall
Hair: Black
Nationality: Afghan
Scars/Distinguishing Characteristics: Mullah Omar has a shrapnel wound to his right eye and is bearded.

WANTED

Mullah Omar's Taliban regime in Afghanistan sheltered Usama Bin Ladin and his al-Qa'ida network in the years before the 11 September attacks. Although Operation Enduring Freedom removed the Taliban regime from power, Mullah Omar remains at large and represents a continuing threat to the United States and its allies.

REWARD

If you have any information concerning this person, please contact your local FBI office if you are in the United States, or the nearest US Embassy or Consulate. If you prefer to use E-mail, send your information to rfj@state.gov. If you prefer to use the telephone, please call 1-800-US REWARDS.
www.rewardsforjustice.net

Mullah Mohammed Omar, the reclusive leader of the Taliban. Very few photos of him exist and those that do show a light complexioned, thin-faced man with a bushy black beard and mustache. His most distinguishing feature is a missing right eye, the result of a wound. *The National Counterterrorism Center*

and Religion in Afghanistan, "Omar is rarely seen in public or by visiting dignitaries. He limits his contacts to a few close associates . . . and leaves the tasks associated with the outside world . . . to his subordinates." The few photographs in existence that purport to depict him show a light complexioned, thin-faced man, with a bushy black beard and mustache. Even this physical appearance is disputed. He is alternately described as being either tall and well built, or small and frail. Author David Loyn claimed to have seen him, calling him "tall, with a fair complexion for an Afghan and a Grecian nose, prominent above his unkempt black beard." Journalist Rahimullah Yusufazi, who has interviewed Omar, described him as "a very simple man, a village clergyman: heavily built, not very articulate, a shy person who seemed to know little about the world."

All reports agree that Omar's most distinguishing feature is a missing right eye, lost as a result of a shrapnel wound received during a 1989 skirmish with Russian forces near Sangisar. Taliban legend claims that after being wounded, Omar removed his own eye and sewed the eyelid shut. Another tale had Omar "taking hold of his eye, yanking it out, and throwing it away." A more credible report indicated that his eye was surgically removed at a Red Cross hospital in Pakistan. The shrapnel also reportedly scarred his cheek and forehead.

It is commonly accepted that Mullah Omar was born in the late 1950s or early 1960s in Nodeh, a small village near Kandahar in southeast Afghanistan. His family was poor and landless. He grew up in a mud hut, not an uncommon situation for the majority of Afghans. According to Ahmed Rashid, Omar was a member of "the Hotak tribe, the Ghilzai branch of Pashtuns [the largest ethnic group in Afghanistan]." According to his very brief biography, Omar's father died when he was a young man, leaving support of the family on his shoulders. His limited "formal" education consisted of memorizing the Koran at one of the small religious schools (madrassas) that populated the countryside.

Steve Coll wrote in *Ghost Wars* that "from the religious texts he learned to read and write in Arabic and Pashto only shakily. He never roamed far from Kandahar."

Vahid Majdeh, a Taliban official, said that Omar, as well as other Taliban leaders "had no knowledge beyond a few religious books and their worldly perspective was limited to a couple of provinces in Afghanistan. The majority of these leaders had no desire to study anything but the Holy Koran, and religious texts." Omar's studies were interrupted by the Russian invasion in 1979. He became a guerrilla with the anti-Soviet *Harakat-i-Inqilab-i Islami* (Islamic Revolutionary Movement) faction of the Mujahideen. Stories abound that he was "a crack marksman who destroyed many Soviet tanks with RPGs during the Afghan War."

During the anti-Soviet *jihad*, Omar moved up in the ranks until he achieved deputy commander status. Author Neamatollah Nojumi wrote in *The Rise of the Taliban in Afghanistan, Mass Mobilization, Civil War, and the Future of the Region* that "Mullah Omar became a commander in the Arghestan district in the province of Kandahar. He commanded a group of local *Mujahideen* over the control of the strategic location north of the Kandahar-Chaman Highway." Contemporary reports state that he was wounded at least four times, but neglect to note the nature and extent of the wounds, except for the loss of an eye. There is little documentation regarding his service in the war, except for a brief account by Abdul Salam Zaeef in *My Life in the Taliban*. Zaeef described how a Soviet unit attacked his unit, which included Mullah Omar, near Sangisar. The fighting was intense. The Russians were able to get within a hundred meters of their position. "Hand to hand, grenades flying over our heads," Zaeef related, "the ground was littered with bodies." Zaeef said that Mullah Omar seized a light machine gun and used it against the Russians. "Twenty paces from me, Mullah Omar took cover behind a wall. As he looked around the corner, a shard of metal scrap hit him the face and took out his eye." Zaeef went on to describe how Omar, despite the wound, wanted to stay with the unit when it moved out. "We urged him not to go . . . and in the end he didn't come. He went to Pakistan for treatment." Mullah Omar's time with the Mujahideen made him a combat-hardened veteran, skilled in guerrilla warfare.

Rocket Propelled Grenade

The Rocket Propelled Grenade (RPG-7) was the weapon of choice for the Taliban during the Soviet-Afghan war. The RPG-7, a shoulder-fired, muzzle-loaded, anti-tank and anti-personnel grenade launcher, is a descendent of the World War II German Panzerfaust. The launcher fires a fin-stabilized, oversized grenade from a 40mm tube that has an effective range of 300 meters against moving point targets and 500 meters against stationary point targets. Its anti-tank round has a maximum range of 920 meters, while the anti-personnel round can reach out to 1100 meters. The anti-tank round can penetrate up to 600mm of rolled homogeneous steel.

The Mujahideen effectively used the RPG-7 against the Soviet T-62 main battle tank, armored personnel carriers, trucks, and even helicopters. The guerrillas found that they needed to get close and "hug" the Soviets because of the Russian superiority in artillery and air support. Afghanistan's rugged terrain favored the Mujahideen who formed small highly mobile units of ten to thirty men that launched surprise attacks and ambushes on the ponderous Soviet road-bound convoys. Roads often followed the narrow valley floors, allowing the Mujahideen to set up ambushes on the ridgelines and fire down on the road-bound convoys. The guerrillas selected the RPG positions so that their launch signature was camouflaged as much as possible. They would often soak the ground behind the position to prevent a tell-tale cloud of dust. However, the battle-wise fighter knew to immediately switch positions because the flash of the missile launch and the whitish blue-gray smoke was a dead giveaway.

The Mujahideen placed heavy reliance on RPGs by forming special armored-vehicle hunter-killer teams. The teams found the best way to knock out a T-62 was to volley-fire RPGs at a range of 20–50 meters, an extremely dangerous range, not for the faint of heart. Mullah Omar, having knocked out three Russian tanks with RPGs, earned himself a reputation for bravery among his followers.

Declassified U.S. Department of State Message: Taliban Decision-making and Leadership Structure

Summary: Mullah Omar plays the key role in Taliban decision-making, while his advisers…are believed to play key roles in policy implementation. Although they do not seriously rival Omar for influence, several Taliban leaders, including Taliban deputy leader Mullah Rabbani, reportedly maintain an independent power base. Because of Omar's highly personalized leadership style, Taliban institutions, such as the "inner" Shura, have weakened from disuse, although the "Ulema" Shura is believed to maintain some authority. While the movement is under the sway of Omar, it does not appear reliant on his survival. Afghanistan's mullahs are mobilized and the Taliban will probably remain the leading force in the Pashtun community into the foreseeable future."

The Taliban leadership structure is opaque. It is extremely difficult to understand what goes on within the walls in Kandahar or how the Taliban relate to one another. What is known is that the Taliban have created four major institutional structures:

The predominantly Durrani Pashtun 23-member "inner Shura" or governing authority, located in Kandahar is composed of the Taliban's collective leadership. It consists of seven committees: military, finance, ideology, administrative, political, propaganda and intelligence. Its decisions are based on the group consensus, within Mullah Omar's guidance.

The "Outer Shura" is composed of over 100 members and is meant to advise the Inner Shura. It includes many religious figures and provincial notables but is relatively unimportant.

The "Caretaker Council's" primary role is to implement policy and issue directives to Taliban "government" ministries.

The "Ulema Shura" influences social policies and has a key role in advising Omar on Islamic law.

In general, influence in the movement can basically be judged by one's closeness to Omar.

Following the humiliating Soviet withdrawal in 1989, Omar moved to Singesar, a poor village of some twenty-five families near Kandahar, where he became a teacher and prayer leader in a small religious school funded by a local businessman. Coll noted that "in exchange for religious instruction, villagers provided him with food. He apparently had no other reliable source of income. He shuttled between the village's small mud-brick religious school and its small mud-brick mosque. He lived in a modest house about two hundred yards from the village *madrassa*." *New York Times* correspondent Dexter Filkins visited Singesar accompanied by one of its residents.

"Hassan pointed to a mud-brick house next to the mosque," Filkins said. "'He [Omar] lived in a simple hut,' the guide recalled. 'He would come early in the morning and lead prayers and then take tea and sit in that room until noon studying the Koran alone. He didn't talk much, only to his friends.'" Ahmed Rashid claimed that Omar has three wives and five children that were still living in the village in 2000.

Omar emerged as a populist figure because of his willingness to assist the downtrodden against the brutality of the local thugs. As his reputation and success grew, more and more students from the Islamic madrassas (religious schools) joined his fledging band. "Many people were searching for a solution," Mullah Mohammed Abbas recalled. "With a group of friends we spent time discussing what we should do. The Mujahideen leadership had utterly failed to bring peace . . . so we came to Kandahar to talk with Mullah Omar and [then] joined him." It is interesting to note that Omar was not a charismatic leader, nor a great orator. Steve Coll wrote that "he [Omar] spoke in Pashto in a peasant's provincial accent. In meetings he would often sit silently for long periods. When he spoke, his voice was often no louder than a whisper. He sometimes talked about himself in the third person, as if he were a character in someone else's story." Omar was chosen, according to many Taliban, because of his "piety and unswerving belief in Islam, not for his political or military ability." Mullah Hassan explained, "We selected Mullah Omar to lead this movement. He was the first amongst equals and we gave him the power to lead us and he has given us the power and authority to deal with people's problems." Omar himself told a Pakistani journalist, "We took up arms to achieve the aims of the Afghan *jihad* and save our people from further suffering at the hands of the so-called *Mujahideen*."

Rahimullah Yusufazi, one of the few who personally interviewed Mullah Omar before 2001, said that he is "a man of few words and not very knowledgeable about international affairs [however] his reputed humility, his legend as a ferocious fighter against Soviet invaders in the 1980s, and his success in ending the lawlessness and bloody warlords' feuds of the early 1990s cemented his power." Yusufazi went on to say, "His followers adore him, believe in him and are willing to die for him."

CHAPTER 5

Warriors of God

THE FIRST FOOT-SOLDIERS TO JOIN Mullah Omar's band according to popular narrative were teenage religious students called Taliban, meaning "seekers of knowledge." Ahmed Rashid wrote that the students chose the name because it "distanced themselves from the party politics of the Mujahideen and signaled that they were a movement for cleansing society rather than a party trying to grab power." They broadcast their intent to restore order and justice by punishing robbers, murderers, rapists, and restoring an Islamic way of life, which struck a popular chord with a country sick of war and yearning for a return to peaceful normalcy. Within two years, the Taliban had gained control of most of the country, a remarkable achievement, considering that the bulk of their force was largely an army of Islamic school students. The students were mostly young—fourteen to twenty-four years old—Pashtun refugees who had fled Afghanistan in the 1980s and joined religious schools along the border in Pakistan. The schools, many of whom were funded by Saudi Arabia, Pakistan, and the Gulf States, provided free room and board and a source of income for the students by which to support their families. The curricula of the madrassas varied from school to school but generally followed a similar pattern. "They studied the Koran, the sayings of the Prophet Mohammed and the basics of Islamic law as interpreted by their barely literate teachers," Rashid noted. "Neither teachers nor students had any formal grounding in math, science, history or geography."

In addition to Islamic law, the students were indoctrinated with the concept of *jihad* (holy war) and *shahadah* (self-sacrifice). Neamatollah

A convoy carrying firewood, gas, and food is stopped by Taliban militia on a highway leading to Kabul in October 1995. After capturing Kargha and Buthak in different directions from the city, the Taliban claimed strategic military gains against the Afghan government in the battle for Kabul. *AP photo/Haider Shah*

Nojumi wrote in *The Rise and Fall of the Taliban*, "What they [the Taliban] learned was a highly charged and politicized version of Islam that spoke of the expectation of a holy war around the world." They were taught that fighting in a *jihad* was the highest form of bravery and personal salvation. Nojumi noted that "Islamic belief in *shahadah* and *jihad* made these students fearless fighters on the battlefield." It also made them ruthless adversaries, who showed little mercy to those who thought, dressed, or behaved differently from how they had been trained. Rashid characterized them as "the orphans of war, the rootless, and the restless, the jobless and the economically deprived with little self-knowledge. They admired war because it was the only occupation they could possibly adapt to." William Maley wrote in *The Afghanistan Wars*, "The Taliban were not simply an example of villagers coming to the cities. Their values were not the values of the village, but the values of the village as interpreted by refugee camp dwellers or *madrassa* students who typically had not known normal village life. They were a pathogenic force, whose view of the world conspicuously omitted the pragmatic moderation which historically had muted the application of tribal and religious codes in Afghan society."

Declassified U.S. Department of State Message: Pakistan Involvement in Afghanistan

The mullahs convince these young boys at the Madrassas to go to the war and fight this holy jihad. Their parents know nothing of this until their bodies are brought back to Pakistan. There mullahs are compelling their young teenagers to go on this holy jihad against the Kafirs...the Talib students go to Kandahar or Herat for approximately 15–20 days of military training. Individuals providing the training are personnel from Pakistan's Frontier Corps.

The students believed fervently in their teachers' recitation of primitive Islamic injunctions, one of which prohibited women from participating in normal society; they were ejected from the workplace, schools, and markets, required to wear veils and burqas while moving about the community, forced to live behind blackened windows within the home, and even obliged to choose their children's names from a sanctioned list. In addition, men were prohibited from wearing Western style clothes, sporting stylish haircuts, or even trimming their beards. In 1996 the Taliban issued a formal decree: "In the areas under the Taliban government every kind of wickedness and immorality, cruelty, murder, robbery, songs and music, TV, VCR, satellite dish, immodesty, traveling [women] without an immediate blood related person, shaving-of or trimming the beard, pictures and photographs, have all been totally banned." The Taliban ruled that the punishment for murder was a public execution by a male member of the victim's family. Thieves were subject to surgical amputation of their hands and arms, while adultery was punishable by public stoning.

In early October 1994 the Taliban seized the Pasha Arms depot, a large weapons and ammunition dump near Spin Buldak from the forces of Gulbuddin Hekmatyar, a former Mujahideen warlord, and chief benefi-ciary of ISI support. The cache, which was stored in seventeen underground tunnels, included 18,000 Kalashnikov assault rifles, artillery pieces, tons of ammunition, and a large number of vehicles. William Maley wrote that a source told him that "they [the Taliban] have sufficient stocks to run their affairs for quite some time, for years even!" The capture of the weapons at Spin Buldak put the Taliban on the map, and it is generally accepted that it was a milestone in their rise to power.

The Taliban did not waste any time in firming up their relationship and support from the Pakistanis. "There was a meeting at ISI headquarters with some of the leaders of the Taliban—not Mullah Omar," Steve Coll reported, "but some of his aides—and the ISI chief in late autumn of 1994. It was a get-to-know-you, introductory meeting. From that beginning, the ISI became more and more involved with the Taliban. . . ." As the Taliban gained more power, this relationship changed character. The ISI became more involved in military operations by supplying technical, logistical, and tactical advice from undercover Pakistani intelligence operatives. The American ambassador to Pakistan, Peter Tomsen, noted that "throughout this whole period, the ISI played the major role in military matters, from organizing offenses to equipping the forces that were fighting, and even putting out public statements. There was a colonel ['Colonel Imam'] in Herat [who] was coaching Mullah Omar and other Taliban, who were for the most part semiliterate, on how to administer their areas and how to proceed militarily."

Two weeks after the Spin Buldak incident, Pakistan sent a thirty-vehicle convoy loaded with medicines, consumer goods, and food along the

Taliban Punishment

The July 29, 2010, Time magazine cover showed a young Afghan woman who had been brutally disfigured on orders of a Taliban commander for running away from an abusive husband. A Taliban gang dragged her from a house in the dead of night and hauled her in front of a vengeful mob. "Shivering in the cold air and blinded by the flashlights trained on her by her husband's family, she faced her spouse and accuser," Aryn Baker wrote in the article. "The commander gave his verdict, and men moved in to deliver the punishment. Aisha's brother-in-law held her down while her husband pulled out a knife." The girl's face was horribly mutilated, and then she was left to die. This incident highlights the incredible brutality of the Taliban regime and its supporters. The commander's decision, while incomprehensible to most Westerners, was completely in line with the Taliban's strict interpretation of Islamic (Sharia) law, an inflexible code of rules and penalties that are rigorously enforced. The Taliban introduced a host of prohibited activities that were enforced by the General Department for the Preservation for Virtue and the Elimination of Vice. The enforcers were members of the organization who, according to Neamatollah Nojumi, "patrol the street with long sticks, making sure that people go to mosque at the time of daily prayers, women are covered from head-to-toe with a garment, and men have not shaved their beards."

Spin Buldak-Kandahar road to test the feasibility of sending goods from Pakistan through Afghanistan to Central Asia. The vehicles were from the Pakistani Army's National Logistics Cell, which had been set up by the ISI in the 1980s to transport supplies to the Mujahideen. The convoy carried among others, two Taliban commanders, and Amir Sultan Tarar, a senior ISI field officer known by his *nom de guerre*, "Colonel Imam." Twelve miles outside Kandahar, the convoy was stopped by four former Mujahideen commanders, who controlled the area. They demanded money, a portion of the goods, and a pledge that the ISI would stop supporting the Taliban. Colonel Imam attempted to negotiate the convoy's release but was unsuccessful. The Pakistanis considered several military options, including the use of its own special forces but decided instead to ask the Taliban for help. On 3 November, a force of Taliban launched an attack, which succeeded in routing the bandits and freeing the convoy. One of the bandit leaders was chased into the desert and killed, along with ten of his bodyguards.

Spin Buldak

Spin Buldak was a sprawling, run-down truck stop located in southeastern Afghanistan on the Pakistani border. It was an important transshipment and refueling stop for the "transport mafia," a joint Pakistani military and civilian venture to ship goods from Pakistan to Central Asia via Afghanistan. Retired General Nasirullah Babar, the Pakistani interior minister, with the concurrence of Prime Minister Benazir Bhutto, established the Afghan Trade Developing Cell within the government to facilitate the venture. Ahmed Rashid wrote that "for the transport mafia, control of the town was critical. They had donated several hundred thousand Pakistani Rupees to Mullah Omar and promised a monthly stipend to the Taliban, if they would clear the roads of bandits and guarantee the security for truck traffic." The truck stop and the large weapons and ammunition dump were guarded by gunmen from Hekmatyar's *Hizb-e-Islami* party. On 12 October, 200 of Omar's Taliban moved in secret to within striking distance of the Pasha Arms depot. They divided into three groups and assaulted the surprised defenders, who quickly ran away. A declassified U.S. State Department report stated that "the seizure was preceded by artillery shelling of the base, from Pakistani Frontier Corps positions and was coordinated by Pakistani officers on the scene." Anthony Davis wrote in *How the Taliban became a Military Force* that "some independent analysts question whether the Taliban did actually capture such stocks there, arguing that the Pasha dump had been systematically looted long before...implying that the story provided a thick smoke-screen behind which such supplies might flow" to Pakistan's ISI.

Colonel Imam

"Colonel Imam," whose real name is Amir Sultan Tarar, was a prominent intelligence officer in the ISI and a special warfare expert who received training at Fort Bragg, North Carolina, by U.S. Army Special Forces. Anthony Davis noted that he was a "Pashtun with extensive experience in cross-border liaison with the southern Afghan Mujahideen, 'Imam' was to play an important role in the rise of the Taliban and subsequently served as Pakistan's Consul-General in Herat." During the Soviet-Afghan War, Imam ran the ISI's Afghan Bureau operation in Peshawar, where he developed close ties with Gulbadin Hekmatyar. It was during this time that the CIA became aware that he was a fervent Islamist, with a deep hatred of the west. Despite his politics, he was invited to the White House by President George Bush Sr. and was given a piece of the Berlin Wall with a brass plaque inscribed: "To the one who dealt the first blow." After the war, he was instrumental in helping to train the Taliban and is, according to many, the "Father of the Taliban." Tarar claims to know Mullah Omar but does not know where he is. In a recent interview, he claimed that he has not seen Mullah Omar since the 2001 U.S. bombing of the Taliban.

He was later hung from a tank barrel, as a mute reminder to others who might challenge the Taliban.

Immediately after freeing the convoy, the Taliban swept into Kandahar, Afghanistan's second largest city. In only two days of sporadic fighting, they captured the city and a large quantity of military equipment, including six MiG-21 aircraft (only one was operational), six Mi-17 transport helicopters, and dozens of tanks and Soviet-made BMP infantry fighting vehicles. The commander of the city's most powerful defenders surrendered without resistance in what became a Taliban hallmark, bribery of the opposition. It was rumored that Colonel Imam had a hand in the skullduggery. General Nasirullah Khan Babar told journalists that the city's captors were "our boys." The capture of Kandahar marked a remarkable series of military successes for the Taliban. In less than two years (1994 to 1996) they grew from a force of less than a hundred men to one of several thousands, and succeeded in capturing Kabul and occupying over two-thirds of the country.

"It is a significant reflection on this campaign that in seventeen years of war," Anthony Davis wrote, "no Afghan force, neither government or opposition, had ever carried out such a swift and complex series of operations over such a wide operational area. This was mobile warfare at its most effective."

It defies belief that the ill-trained Taliban, whose expertise up to this time was in hit-and-run tactics, could organize, plan, and execute brigade and division sized attacks supported by artillery, armor, and aircraft. Anthony Davis noted that "the organizational skills and logistical where-withal required to assemble from scratch, expand, and maintain such an integrated fighting machine during a period of continuous hostilities are simply not to be found in Pakistani *madrassas* or Afghan villages." It is common belief that the ISI was instrumental in providing logistical support in the form of fuel, ammunition, spare parts, vehicles, operational training, and planning. "As has been extensively documented in a range of foreign and Pakistani publications," Davis asserted, "Pakistan's military intelligence has been deeply and aggressively embroiled in covert support to armed Afghan opposition movements."

The Pakistanis were not the only ones who supported the Taliban. Steve Coll noted, "Saudi charities, religious ministries, and wealthy Saudi indi-viduals also aided the Taliban's rise during 1995 and 1996." Prince Turki al-Faisal, director of the Saudi General Intelligence Directorate (GID)

Followers of Mullah Omar were called Taliban, meaning "seekers of knowledge." They were mostly young Pashtun students, who grew up during the civil war in refugee camps along the border, such as this camp near Miram Shah, Pakistan, where the tents of thousands of Afghan refugees cover a plain in 1989. *AP photo*

provided indirect support through the ISI. "The scale of Saudi payments and subsidies to Pakistan's army and intelligence service during the 1990s has never been disclosed," according to Coll, "[but] probably amounted in some years to at least several hundred million dollars." Saudi money enabled the ISI to continue supplying the Taliban, even as money from the United States dried up. Finally, after the Taliban captured the northern city of Mazar-e Sharif, in May 1997, Saudi Arabia, Pakistan, and the United Arab Emirates recognized the Taliban as the official government of Afghanistan. Their recognition was premature because the Taliban was unable to defeat the Northern Alliance, the last force between it and total control of the country.

The Northern Alliance, originally known as the United Front, or Supreme Council for the Defense of the Motherland, was a coalition of northern ethnic militias under the command of former Mujahideen commanders— Ahmad Shah Massoud, Abdul Shah Dostum, Ismael Khan, and Shia Muslims (Hazara) from central Afghanistan. The commanders led an estimated 40,000 men and controlled nine to ten northern provinces from

Taliban militia stand on their tank with a pile of used shell casings at a Taliban frontline post at Gumharan, south of Kabul, September 1995. *AP photo/Haider Shah*

Saudi General Intelligence Directorate

The Saudi Arabian General Intelligence Directorate (GID) was established by royal decree in 1957. The GID was loosely modeled after the CIA. Its charter made it responsible for security, anti-terrorism, and foreign liaison. The organization was built around family connections, which did nothing to inspire professionalism in its ranks. For many years, it had a reputation for being weak and unprofessional, according to Steve Coll. In the mid-1970s, Prince Turki al-Faisal took the reins and held them for two decades, becoming, according to Coll, "one of the longest-serving and most influential intelligence operatives on the world stage." Under Prince Turki, the GID used Saudi Arabia's oil revenue to buy information and allies. Turki was described by Coll as "A champion of Saudi Arabia's austere Islam, a promoter of women's rights, a multimillionaire, a workaholic, a pious man, a sipper of banana daiquiris, an intriguer, an intellectual, a loyal prince, a sincere friend of Americans, a generous funder of anti-American causes, Prince Turki embodied Saudi Arabia's cascading contradictions."

The Soviet invasion of Afghanistan brought the GID quickly to the forefront, as Saudi Arabia used the spy service to channel funds to Pakistan's ISI in support of the Afghan rebels. The Saudi royal family, viewing the Soviet's attempt to extend its influence in the region as a threat to its oil resources in the Persian Gulf, opened its purse strings. Representatives of the GID hand-delivered wooden boxes stuffed with cash to the ISI headquarters. After the U.S. decision to support the Mujahideen, the Saudis formalized an agreement with the CIA to match congressional funding. The Saudi government wrote checks to the tune of hundreds of millions of dollars—and that did not include the further millions of dollars from religious charities. Much of that money was used to support hundreds of madrassas along the Afghan-Pakistani border.

Despite GID and CIA collaboration, the two agencies pursued separate political agendas, even as they cooperated in supplying tens of thousands of tons of weapons and ammunition to the Afghan rebels. Prince Turki funneled money to favored commanders outside CIA or ISI control. It is generally accepted that Osama bin Laden had a substantial relationship with the GID during the early to mid-1980s. Coll wrote that "some CIA officers concluded that bin Laden operated as a semiofficial liaison between the GID, the international Islamist religious networks and the leading Saudi-backed Afghan commanders." That relationship quickly soured when bin Laden railed against the Saudi rulers. Prince Turki alleged that he attempted to convince Mullah Omar to oust bin Laden from Afghanistan, but was unsuccessful. The CIA was not convinced, but, at the time, it needed the GID to support the covert Afghan war.

Ahmad Shah Massoud—leader of the Northern Alliance until he was assassinated two days before 9/11—repairs a captured Soviet assault rifle in 1986. Massoud, known as the Lion of Panjshir, was one of the most successful Afghan guerrilla leaders, credited with a string of victories against Soviet and Afghan troops. *AP photo/Masood Khalili*

1996 to 2001. The core group was mainly non-Pashtun Tajiks and Uzbeks, fierce fighters who were able to keep the Taliban at bay. Massoud gradually assumed overall leadership of the Northern Alliance. He was a brilliant commander who had fought the Soviet Army to a standstill. His successful defense of the Panjshir Valley against six Soviet attacks earned him the nickname "Lion of the Panjshir." The Northern Alliance was supported by Russia, Iran, and India, while the Taliban received money from Saudi Arabia, the Gulf States, and Pakistan. The United States, under the terms of the 1988 Geneva Accords, was not supporting either side . . . and had, in fact, lost interest in Afghanistan altogether.

CHAPTER 6

Al-Qaeda, The Base

"The reality is you had to make do with the strategic situation you found in Afghanistan."
—Robert Gates, 1993

THE DEPARTURE OF THE SOVIETS was cause for celebration in the halls of the CIA headquarters in Langley, Virginia. Steve Coll reported that the new director, William Webster, hosted a champagne party, and the U.S. embassy in Islamabad sent a congratulatory two-word cable to him: "We won!" With that declaration, the United States quickly folded its tent and faded into the sunset. The United States saw little strategic value in Afghanistan, and it became a backwater for American policy. Robert Gates, then director of Central Intelligence, summed up the withdrawal thusly: "Afghanistan was a battlefield between the United States and the Soviet Union, now that the battle is ended, we have other agendas and other countries in mind and Afghanistan is not one of them." The U.S. withdrawal created a political vacuum, which was quickly filled by regional players with their own agendas. Pakistan and Saudi Arabia wanted a malleable Afghan government to act as a foil against India and Iran, and vice versa, while Russia and the Central Asian States preferred the status quo. The support they provided the warring Afghan factions intensified the civil war and created a recipe for the growth of the Taliban.

Zalmay Khalilzad, a senior analyst for the Rand Corporation, laid the Afghan problem squarely at the feet of the United States. In a 1996 article for the *Washington Post* he said, "After the fall of the Soviet Union we stopped paying attention. This was a bad decision. Instability and war in Afghanistan provided fertile ground for terrorist groups to train and hide."

The Taliban's capture of Kabul in September 1996, and its imposition of harsh penalties, did not unduly alarm Washington. Glyn Davies, a State Department spokesman, said, "The United States finds nothing objectionable in the policy statements of the new government, including its move to impose Islamic law." Despite increasing evidence of the Taliban's savagery

Osama bin Laden

Osama bin Laden (most American government agencies, including the FBI and CIA, use either "Usama bin Laden" or "Usama bin Ladin", both of which are often abbreviated to UBL) was born on 10 March 1957 in Riyadh, Saudi Arabia. His father was a billionaire entrepreneur with close ties to the Saudi royal family. Bin Laden was raised as a Wahabist Muslim, but, while in high school, he became involved in religious studies taught by members of the Muslim Brotherhood, an Egyptian-based Islamic organization whose aim was to replace secular and nationalist Arab leaders with Islamic governments. Throughout his school years, he continued to pursue a deepening religious faith. In 1979, just after the Soviet invasion, he made his first trip to Afghanistan, where he saw, first-hand, conditions inside the country and the plight of the refugees. Upon returning to Saudi Arabia, he raised money to establish several training camps in Afghanistan and attracted a number of senior Arab ex-military men from Syria and Egypt to fight under his command. His first major fight with the Soviets occurred at the battle of Jaji, where he earned a battlefield reputation as a fighter after being wounded in the leg. Bin Laden returned to Saudi Arabia after the Soviet withdrawal.

The 1991 Iraqi invasion of Kuwait caused bin Laden to break with the Saudi government after it invited Western troops into the kingdom. He began making inflammatory remarks about the Saudi royal family. As a result, he was forbidden to leave the country and closely watched. Under the guise of a business trip, Bin Laden fled the country, first to Sudan and then to Afghanistan. For several years, he stayed one step ahead of various Saudis plots to kill or capture him. In 1996, after his citizenship was publicly withdrawn, he began actively politicking against the kingdom and the United States. The 1996 bombing of the Khobar Towers in Saudi Arabia, in which nineteen Americans were killed, was attributed to his handiwork. When the Taliban swept into Jalalabad, he left Sudan and returned to Afghanistan after Mullah Omar promised him protection. In 1998, he issued a *fatwa* (a religious edict) declaring that the killing of North Americans and their allies was an "individual duty for every Muslim." In July, his confederates bombed the U.S. Embassies in Kenya and Tanzania, killing over 200 people. Two years later, he was identified as being behind the suicide bombing of the against non-Pashtuns, and the repression of women, Washington initially considered the "seekers of knowledge" to be acceptable, because they were anti-Iranian, anti-Shia, and apparently pro-Western. In addition, Taliban success on the battlefield seemed to herald a period of relative calm after decades of war, which boded well for the building of a long-cherished oil pipeline across Afghanistan. In December 1997, three senior members of the Taliban visited the United States under the auspices of the Union Oil Company of California (Unocal), which was seeking to build the pipeline.

USS *Cole*. Finally, the 9/11 attacks were laid at his feet. The U.S. government offered a $25 million dollar reward for information leading to his capture or death. Nearly ten years after the attacks on the World Trade Center and the Pentagon, he was killed during a U.S. special ops team raid on his compound in Abbottabad, Pakistan, on 2 May 2011. His body was buried at sea.

Usama Bin Ladin

Up to $25 Million Reward

Aliases/Name Variants: Usama bin Muhammad bin Ladin, Shaykh Usama bin Ladin, the Prince, the Emir, Abu Abdallah Mujahid Shaykh, Haj, the Director; also known as UBL, OBL
Place of Birth: Saudi Arabia
Height: 6'4" – 6'6" (193-198 cm)
Weight: 160 lbs (73kg)
Hair: Brown
Eyes: Brown
Nationality: Saudi Arabian (citizenship revoked)
Scars/Distinguishing Characteristics: Bin Ladin has a full beard, a mustache, and walks with a cane
Status: Fugitive

WANTED
Usama Bin Ladin is wanted in connection with the 11 September 2001 attacks on the World Trade Center and the Pentagon and for the 7 August 1998 bombings of the US embassies in Dar es Salaam, Tanzania, and Nairobi, Kenya. More than 3,000 people were killed in these attacks. The embassy bombings killed 224 civilians and wounded more than 5,000 others. Usama Bin Ladin and other terrorists—specifically Ayman al-Zawahiri, Fazul Abdullah Mohammed, Abdullah Ahmed Abdullah, Saif al-Adel, Anas al-Liby, Ahmed Mohamed Hamed Ali, and others already in custody—are members of al'Qaida, the international terrorist network headed by Bin Ladin.

REWARD
If you have any information concerning this person, please contact your local FBI office if you are in the United States, or the nearest US Embassay or Consulate. If you prefer to use E-mail, send your information to rfj@state.gov. If you prefer to use the telephone, please call 1-800-US REWARDS.
www.rewardsforjustice.net

Osama bin Laden, leader of al-Qaeda and mastermind of the 9/11 attacks. *The National Counterterrorism Center*

During the visit, the group was met by Karl Inderfurth, assistant secretary of state for South Asian Affairs, who according to Coll, "expressed his strongest concerns about the condition of Afghan women, tolerance for drug trafficking, and desire to get the peace process moving along.

At one point, Inderfurth had to break away for another meeting. Michael E. Malinowski, director of the Pakistani, Afghanistan and Bangladesh Bureau (PAB) took over. He questioned the Taliban on their pledge that Afghanistan would not be used by terrorists as a base for operations. Malinowski specifically pointed out a Saudi terrorist financier named Osama bin Laden that had "damaged the image of Afghanistan to the world." At this point, bin Laden was not a high value target. According to Coll, bin Laden was considered by the CIA to be a "blowhard, a dangerous and wealthy egomaniac and a financier of other radicals, but was isolated in Afghanistan." The Taliban representatives assured Malinowski that they would keep their commitment. They indicated that bin Laden was simply a guest and would not cause trouble. The meeting ended with the Taliban saying they were pleased with the opportunity to meet with representatives of the U.S. government and assured Malinowski that bin Laden's movements were being restricted.

As early as January 1996, the CIA's Counterterrorism Center started to track bin Laden, when they realized he was "one of the most significant financial sponsors of Islamic extremist activities in the world." They established a special twelve-person unit in a suburban Virginia office park known as the "bin Laden Issue Station," code named "Alex." Their message traffic referred to bin Laden as UBL (Usama bin Laden), and the station's first assignment was to gather intelligence about his activities. Steve Coll noted that "the National Security Agency [NSA] tapped into bin Laden's satellite telephone and kept track of his international conversations." At one point, the station began drafting plans to capture him, but, before they could be implemented, bin Laden slipped out of their reach into Afghanistan, where he sought refuge, first in Jalalabad and then in Kandahar.

"I want to come to your areas," bin Laden wrote in a letter to Mullah Omar, "but I need a promise from you that you are going to protect me . . . "

Omar wrote back, "You are most welcome. We will never give you up to anyone who wants you." Bin Laden's bodyguard said the Saudi flew to Jalalabad in a small plane with two of his sons, a small security detachment, and a former Egyptian special forces officer, Ayman al Zahwiri, who became al-Qaeda's military commander.

Mullah Omar encouraged Bin Laden to "come to Kandahar because it is our stronghold and main headquarters." Bin Laden quickly ingratiated himself to the Taliban leader by giving him money and military support. In the 1997–1998 northern offensives, he sent several hundred al-Qaeda jihadist volunteers, called "Brigade 55," to fight alongside the Taliban. It was also reported that bin Laden married one of Omar's daughters, which further cemented their relationship. While in Kandahar, bin Laden called for *jihad* against the Saudi royal family and raged against American

Osama bin Laden poster retrieved from a building in Kandahar. *defenseimagery.mil*

policy in the Middle East. Three months after returning to Afghanistan, bin Laden declared war on the United States in a call to arms titled, "The Declaration of Jihad on the Americans Occupying the Country of the Two Sacred Places." His pronouncements raised his standing on the CIA's "kill or capture" list and earned him the enmity of the Saudis. A great deal of pressure was applied to Mullah Omar by both nations to expel him. Omar told Rahimullah Yusufazi, a Pakistani newsman, "I will never deliver bin Laden . . . I don't want to go down in history as someone who betrayed his guest. I am willing to give up my life, my regime; since we had given him refuge, I cannot throw him out now." The CIA's Counterterrorism Center determined that one of bin Laden's many residences (Tarnak Farm) offered "a good location for a snatch," but the operation was never approved.

In June 1998, Saudi Prince Turki flew to Kandahar to convince Mullah Omar to give up bin Laden. "We made it plain," Turki said, "that if they [the Taliban] wanted to have good relations with Saudi Arabia, they have to get bin Laden out of Afghanistan." Turki reported that Omar agreed. "Assure the king and the crown prince that this is my view," Omar is reported to have said. American intelligence analysts were skeptical of Turki's version of the meeting. They remained convinced that Saudi Arabia was unwilling to cut their ties with bin Laden. When al-Qaeda launched two devastating attacks on the U.S. embassies in Kenya and Tanzaniaon on 7 August 1998, the U.S. was caught flat-footed and scrambled to determine which terrorist group was responsible. The attacks left two hundred and twenty-four dead and thousands wounded.

The deputy director of the Counterintelligence Center said, "Intelligence from a variety of human and technical sources, statements of arrested suspects, and public statements from bin Laden's organization left no doubt about its responsibilities." Thirteen days after the attack, President Clinton authorized a cruise missile strike on al-Qaeda training bases in eastern Afghanistan and the al-Shifa Pharmaceutical Plant near Khartoum, Sudan, an alleged chemical weapons plant.

On 20 August, seventy-five Block III "Tomahawk" land attack cruise missiles (TLAMs), valued at three quarters of a billion dollars, were launched against the Zawhar Kili training camp, seven miles south of the

Al-Qaeda—The Base

Al-Qaeda, meaning "the base" in Arabic, was formed by Osama bin Laden and a small group of associates in 1988 to "Lift the word of God, to make His religion victorious." Bin Laden did not attach any particular meaning to the name. "Brother Abu-Ubaydah al-Banshiri—God rest his soul—formed a camp to train youth to fight against the oppressive, atheist, and truly terrorist Soviet Union," bin Laden stated. "We called that place al-Qaeda— in the sense that it was a training base—and that is where the name came from." According to the minutes of the first meeting, membership requirements included:

- Members of the open duration (the top graduates of a training program)
- Listening and obedient
- Good manners
- Referred from a trusted source
- Obeying statutes and instructions of al-Qaeda

The members were required to take an oath. "The pledge of God and this covenant is upon me, to energetically listen and obey the superiors who are doing this work, rising early in times of difficulty and ease." The minutes noted that, "Work of al-Qaeda commenced on 9/10/1988." Unmarried recruits received $1,000 a month, while married men received $1,500. All recruits were given a round-trip ticket home and thirty days vacation. There was a health-care plan and even a buy-out option. For a poor, unemployed Arab, the salary and benefits were an extremely attractive package.

city of Khost in eastern Afghanistan. An intelligence report had indicated that al-Qaeda's top leadership was going to meet there, including bin Laden. U.S. Marine Corps General Anthony Zinni was not convinced. "The intelligence was not that solid . . . it was a long shot, very iffy." The missiles struck a nearly empty camp.

Abu Jandal, Osama's chief bodyguard, described the attack as "a concentrated bombardment. Each house was hit by a missile, but they did not destroy the camps entirely. They hit the kitchen of the camp, the mosque, and some bathrooms. Six men were killed." Jandal only counted al-Qaeda casualties. More than a dozen Pakistani volunteers were also killed, some of whom were ISI officers, according to Richard Clarke. However, the strike missed bin Laden; the al-Qaeda leader was in Kabul at the time. Another thirteen missiles hit the pharmaceutical plant, destroying the facility and igniting a major political firestorm for the administration. Several investigations proved that the plant was manufacturing pharmaceuticals, not the chemical weapons the United States claimed.

After the attack, Clinton addressed the country. "Today I ordered our armed forces to strike at terrorist-related facilities in Afghanistan and Sudan because of the imminent threat they presented to our national security." However, the missile strike failed to achieve its objective of eliminating al-Qaeda's leadership. On the contrary, the strike raised the stature of Osama bin Laden.

A well-respected Pakistani cleric said the attack made him "a symbol for the whole Islamic world. He is a hero to us, but it is America that first made him a hero." Steve Coll wrote, "The missile strikes were his biggest publicity payoff to date." In September 1998, under increasing pressure from the United States, Saudi Arabia sent Prince Turki to meet with Mullah Omar and remind him of his promise to hand over bin Laden. The meeting did not go well. Turki was angrily berated. "Why are you persecuting and harassing this courageous, valiant Muslim?" Omar demanded. He continued to rant against the Saudi Kingdom and the United States until the Saudi interrupted him, saying, "I'm not going to take any more of this," and left the meeting. Within days, Saudi Arabia withdrew its ambassador from Kabul.

Bin Laden continued to plot against the United States, despite reports that the Taliban had ordered him to refrain from "engaging in political or press activities." Abdul Hakim Mujahid, a Taliban spokesman, said that "while bin Laden could remain in Afghanistan he could not use Afghan soil for military operations." Fed up with Taliban's intransigence, President Clinton signed an executive order imposing a number of unilateral economic restrictions on the Taliban, freezing all their assets in the United States, and banning all commercial and financial ties between the Taliban and the United States. The United Nations Security Council also took action, passing Resolution 1333, which imposed a complete arms ban. However, Pakistan evaded the ban and continued to covertly supply weapons to the Taliban. The United States was reluctant to pressure the Pakistanis, because it was thought they might use their influence to moderate the Taliban. The U. S. and U.N. sanctions only hardened Omar's resolve. "I will never deliver bin Laden . . . since we have given him refuge, I cannot throw him out now. I am willing to give my life [and] my regime."

On 7 October 2000, two al-Qaeda suicide bombers using a skiff struck the USS *Cole* as the ship was refueling in the Yemeni port of Aden, killing seventeen American sailors and wounding forty-two. The first U.S. military to arrive was a detachment from the Interim Marine Corps Security Force Company that was flown in aboard a P-3 Orion from Bahrain. A platoon from the 2nd Fleet Antiterrorism Security Team (FAST) Company out of Yorktown, Virginia, and another platoon arrived on the 13th from Doha, Qatar. The Marines secured the *Cole* and a nearby hotel that housed the U.S. Ambassador to Yemen. Al-Qaeda's commander in the Arabian Peninsula, Abdal Rahim al Nashiri, was arrested for his role in the bombing. During interrogation, he admitted that, in late 1998, he met bin Laden and proposed mounting an attack against a U.S. ship. Bin Laden approved and provided money for the operation. Nashiri said that he reported directly to bin Laden with the details of the operation. After the attack, bin Laden celebrated with a poem:

> A destroyer, even the brave might fear,
> She inspires horror in the harbor and the open sea,
> She goes into the waves flanked by arrogance, haughtiness
> and fake might,
> To her doom she progresses slowly, clothed in a huge illusion,
> Awaiting her is a dinghy, bobbing in the waves.

Abu Janal described the operation's decision-making process: "The planning for the *Cole* operation was carried out by the people [on the ground]. The idea formed, and the target was set, and then it was referred to a higher military control committed in al-Qaeda called the Military Affairs Committee, which does not plan, but gives the green light, the support,

On 12 October 2000, USS *Cole* (DDG 67) was badly damaged by two al-Qaeda suicide bombers, while refueling in the Yemeni port of Aden. Seventeen American sailors were killed and forty-two wounded. *U.S. Navy*

and the funds for these operations." Bin Laden told the Al Jazeera news channel's Pakistan bureau chief, "We did the *Cole* attack and we wanted the United States to react."

The Clinton administration viewed al-Qaeda's attacks as separate occurrences rather than as part of a larger conspiracy. Clinton's counterterrorism director and the CIA's Counterterrorism Center were consistently at loggerheads over the nature of the threat posed by bin Laden's al-Qaeda. The CIA viewed al-Qaeda as "a threat to be managed, not solved." Terrorism was just part of the global environment and could be "reduced, attenuated, and to some degree controlled," but it "was a war that could not be 'won.'" The counterterrorism director, on the other hand, had "his hair on fire" worrying about al-Qaeda's next strike. Other constituencies within the administration had varying viewpoints. The White House was concerned about the political ramifications of a failed attack on bin Laden or al-Qaeda a la the pharmaceutical plant. The State Department did not want its diplomatic relations with Pakistan and Saudi Arabia jeopardized. And, finally, the Justice Department's lawyers warned of legal issues with an unprovoked strike. The end result was that various offensive plans were developed but never acted upon by the Clinton administration.

CHAPTER 7

The Big Wedding
(*Al Ourush al-Kabir*)

*—Al-Qaeda code name for the September 11, 2001,
attack on the World Trade Center.*

THE BUSH ADMINISTRATION TOOK OFFICE focused on issues totally unrelated to terrorism—missile defense, trade, stronger economic and political relationship with Latin America, reduction in nation building, and small scale military engagements—and displayed little interest in al-Qaeda. Steve Coll wrote that "CIA briefers sensed that Bush's national security cabinet viewed terrorism as the kind of phenomenon it had been during the 1980s: potent, but limited, a theatrical sort of threat that could produce episodic public crises but did not jeopardize the fundamental security of the United States." The director of Central Intelligence, George Tenet, issued a warning to the White House that there were "strong indications that bin Laden was planning new operations and was now capable of mounting multiple attacks with little or no warning." In early spring 2001, the CIA received threat warnings about bin Laden and al-Qaeda that were "off the page." Coll noted that "Between 1 January and 19 September, the FBI issued 216 classified threat warnings, including 6 that specifically mentioned airplanes or airports. The FAA issued 15 notices of possible terrorist threats against American airlines."

The Pentagon after American Airlines flight 77 crashed into the west wing. All 64 people aboard—58 passengers (including the 5 hijackers), 4 flight attendants, and 2 pilots—were killed, as well as 125 occupants of the Pentagon. *U.S. Navy*

The badly damaged quadrant of the Pentagon after the fires were extinguished. *Department of Defense*

As recovery efforts continued after the 9/11 attack, a huge American flag is unfurled over the side of the Pentagon by rescue workers. *U.S. Navy photo by Petty Officer 1st Class Michael W. Pendergrass*

At 8:46 a.m., American Airlines Flight 11 flew into the World Trade Center's North Tower, followed by United Airlines Flight 175, which hit the South Tower at 9:03 a.m. Among the 2,752 victims who died in the attacks were 343 firefighters and 60 police officers from New York City and the Port Authority. *U.S. Navy*

On 6 August, Tenet set up a briefing for Bush at his Crawford, Texas, ranch. According to Professor Geoffrey Wawro of the University of North Texas, the subject was titled "Bin Laden determined to strike in the U.S." Wawro wrote that after the brief, Bush jokingly told the briefer, "All right, you've covered your ass now," and moved to other topics. Five weeks later, at 0846 on 11 September, Mohamed Atta, the al-Qaeda operations commander, flew American Airlines Flight 11 into the north tower of the World Trade Center (WTC). Seventeen minutes later, United Airlines Flight 175 crashed into the south tower. One hour and thirteen minutes after being struck, the north tower collapsed, followed twenty-nine minutes later by the south tower. A third aircraft, American Airlines Flight 77, flew into the Pentagon, and a fourth airliner, United Airlines Flight 93, crashed into a field near Shanksville, Pennsylvania, after the passengers and crew attempted to retake control of the aircraft from the hijackers. The attacks left almost 3,000 people dead. It was determined that Khalid Sheikh Mohammed and Ramzi bin al-Shibh masterminded the operation, but that bin Laden was the ultimate commander. The 9/11 Commission concluded that the Saudi was "very much in charge of the operation." Professor Wawro noted that bin Laden spent $400,000 funding the operation, which inflicted $30 billion in direct costs and hundreds of billions in indirect costs to the U.S. economy.

On 13 December 2001, the Defense Department released a translation of a bin Laden video tape that U.S. forces had recovered from a house in Jalalabad. In it, he and another unidentified man discussed the 9/11 attack. "We calculated in advance the number of casualties from the enemy who would be killed based on the position of the tower. We calculated that the floors that would be hit would be three or four floors. I was most optimistic of them all . . . I was thinking that the fire from the gas in the plane would melt the iron structure of the building and collapse the area where the plane hit and all the floors above it only." Bin Laden talked about the hijackers: "The brothers, who conducted the operation, all they knew was that they have a martyrdom operation and we asked each of them to go to America but they didn't know anything about the operation, not even one letter. But they were trained and we did not reveal the operation to them until they are there and just before they boarded the planes."

PART II

Boots on the Ground, Northern Afghanistan

CHAPTER 8

First In

"Terrorism against our nation will not stand."
—George W. Bush

T HE TELEVISION CAMERAS WERE ROLLING on the morning of 11 September 2001, as the president read to an elementary school class in Sarasota, Florida. Andrew H. Card, Bush's chief of staff, entered the camera's field of view, bent over, and whispered into the president's ear. "A second plane hit the second tower [of the World Trade Center]," he exclaimed. "America is under attack!" Card's electrifying message was indelibly etched on the president's face.

Bush recalled that at that moment, "I made up my mind . . . that we were going to war." Within minutes of the attack, Secretary of Defense Donald Rumsfeld ordered U.S. commands throughout the world to go to Force Threat Condition Delta (FTCD). The increased threat level was designed to bring U.S. forces to a heightened state of alert "when a terrorist attack is taking place or has just occurred." It is the armed forces' highest terrorist alert. Central Command (CentCom), located at MacDill Air Force Base, Tampa, Florida, is responsible for the Middle East, including Egypt and Central Asia.

Its commander, General Tommy Franks, suspected that al-Qaeda was behind the attacks—"Only al-Qaeda and Osama bin Laden have the capacity to launch an operation of this magnitude," he said—and ordered his staff to prepare lists of missile targets in Afghanistan. At the time, the United States did not have any Tomahawk missiles available in the area but

President Bush gathers information about the terrorist attacks on a secure phone set up in Emma E. Booker Elementary School in Sarasota, Florida, where he was reading to schoolchildren when the second aircraft crashed into the World Trade Center. *White House photo by Eric Draper*

would have eighty within twenty-four hours and two hundred within forty-eight hours. At an afternoon meeting with the president, Tenet echoed Frank's theory, stating that "the whole operation looked, smelled, and tasted like bin Laden."

Marine Corps Lieutenant General Michael DeLong, Franks' deputy, immediately convened CentCom's Crisis Action Team (CAT) to monitor the situation (Franks was in Crete at the time). He also ordered all the regional commanders to "lock down their bases." They immediately responded by erecting physical barriers, restricting entry to the facilities, and doubling the guard. Those granted entrance were surprised to see the security force turned out in flak jackets and helmets and carrying weapons with live ammunition. In some locations, machine gun positions were established to provide extra firepower. In reviewing CentCom's "off-the-shelf" operational plans, DeLong discovered that the cupboard was bare.

"CentCom had not developed a plan for conventional ground operations in Afghanistan," Franks admitted. "Nor had diplomatic arrangements for basing, staging, overflight and access been made with Afghanistan's neighbors." CentCom went on a "day on, stay on" work schedule. "Twenty-four hours a day, even through a hurricane," DeLong noted. Frank's staff came up with three options. The first was a cruise missile strike, the second added manned bombers to the missiles, and the third included the first two plus "boots on the ground." The first two options were nonstarters. Bush demanded a more lethal response. *Washington Post* Assistant Managing Editor Bob Woodward wrote in *Bush at War* that Colin Powell told him, "Bush was tired of rhetoric. The President wanted to kill somebody." Later Bush exclaimed, "I don't want to put a million-dollar missile on a five-dollar tent!"

On Saturday, 15 September, Tenet formally briefed Bush and his war cabinet in the wood-paneled conference room in Laurel Lodge at Camp David, the presidential retreat in Maryland's Catoctin Mountains. He directed their attention to a "TOP SECRET" briefing book titled "Initial Hook: Destroying al-Qaeda and Closing the Safe Haven." Woodward wrote, "In the upper-left-hand corner was a picture of bin Laden inside a circle with a slash superimposed over his face, the CIA's adaptation of the universal symbol of prohibition." The book outlined a strategy to take the fight to al-Qaeda and the Taliban. One of its precepts was to deploy covert CIA paramilitary operatives to work alongside U.S. Special Forces to support anti-Taliban warlords.

"The agency has some contacts in Afghanistan [with various tribal warlords] and we have people in place," Tenet announced. "I think we can handle this thing." He claimed that the CIA had "more than one hundred

Cabinet meeting on 12 September to discuss the terrorist attack. From left, Secretary of State Colin Powell, President George W. Bush, Vice President Dick Chaney, and Chairman of the Joint Chiefs of Staff, Dick Myers. *White House photo*

Director of Central Intelligence George J. Tenet developed a plan to introduce paramilitary officers into Afghanistan to work alongside U.S. Army Special Forces to support anti-Taliban Northern Alliance leaders. *U.S. Government*

Secretary of Defense Donald H. Rumsfeld speaks at a December 2006 Pentagon town hall meeting. Rumsfeld was noted for his unhappiness with the military for its slow deployment into Afghanistan. *Department of Defense*

sources and subsources, and relationships with eight tribal networks spread across Afghanistan." However, their strongest ties were with Ahmed Shah Massoud's "United Islamic Front for the Salvation of Afghanistan," known in the Western and Pakistani media as the Northern Alliance, a loose confederation of tribes composed primarily of ethnic Tajiks, Hazaras, Turkmen, Pashtuns, and Uzbeks.

Rumsfeld was not happy that Tenet had "stolen a march" on the Pentagon, which had yet to develop a viable operational plan. "This needs to be a military operation," he interjected. "And if it's going to be a military op, then it has to be run by the military, not the CIA." Tenet wrote that Rumsfeld continued to press the issue until "the Vice President intervened by saying, 'Don, just let the CIA do their job.'"

Later, at the behest of the secretary of defense, Franks called on Tenet at his headquarters to try and change the director's mind. "I want you to subordinate your officers in Afghanistan under me," the general stated.

"It ain't gonna happen, Tommy," Tenet responded. Franks passed the rebuff to Rumsfeld, who did not take it kindly. Ron Susskind, in a *Frontline* interview, said, "I think it's a bitter pill for the Pentagon [Rumsfeld] in this great historical moment. . . . In some ways, they wait their whole life to be called to duty at a moment like this. And the Pentagon is largely on the sidelines, watching—and watching, of all people, the CIA. Oh!"

However, Tenet and Franks had a good working relationship, and agreed on a Memorandum of Understanding (MOU), which spelled out the command relationships between the two organizations. Tenet ensured the memo did not tie the CIA's hands. "Go dumb early," Tenet joked, "and that is exactly what we did with the MOU: drafted it, coordinated it with CentCom, and put it on the shelf," effectively pulling an end run around Rumsfeld. At the operational level, "the CIA and Special Forces personnel on the ground melded together immediately," Tenet noted. "They did not worry about who was in charge."

CIA officer Gary Berntsen wrote in *Jawbreaker* that "I understood immediately that the coordination process . . . between us and the military would be complex." However, he added, "If you want to win in this tough place [Afghanistan], we'd better be ready to do a lot of things differently. We fight together, or we die separately," he empha-sized. The agreement, Rumsfeld noted, was that "operational control of the joint Defense-CIA efforts would migrate over time from CIA to Defense once our special operators were on the ground with the Afghan anti-Taliban militias."

President Bush was excited about Tenet's proposal and declared, "I want the CIA to be the first on the ground." Tenet wrote, "The gloves came off," in his book *At the Center of the Storm: My Years at the CIA.* Bush authorized the agency an extra $1 billion in funding to carry out its mission. On 17 September, Bush signed a finding that authorized the CIA to engage al-Qaeda and other terrorist organizations anywhere in the world and to assassinate individuals designated as terrorists. It was the broadest and most lethal authority in its history. In essence, the agency was given a free hand in Afghanistan. The CIA's war plan envisioned the deployment of teams into different parts of the country to work with the Northern Alliance and Special Forces. Each team had a leader who spoke either Farsi or Dari and a Special Activities Division officer as the second in command.

Berntsen noted, "The teams would be filled out with a combination of case officers (most with previous military training) and SAD officers, who had served as combat soldiers with the U.S. Special Forces, Navy SEALS, or Marine Corps Force Recon."

The president pushed Tenet to insert the teams as soon as possible. "Go, go, go," Bush told him. "I want the CIA to be the first on the ground, preparing the way for the military with both intelligence officers and paramilitary officers." Nine days later, the first of seven Special Activities Division teams was inserted into northern Afghanistan. The Northern Afghanistan Liaison Team (NALT), code named "Jawbreaker," was a ten-man unit—seven field officers and a three-man aircrew—led by the veteran CIA field officer Gary C. Schroen, the former station chief in Kabul. Author Steve Coll said that Schroen was "a career CIA officer in the Directorate of Operations who had developed an expertise on Afghanistan and in particular had gotten to know the Northern Alliance leaders quite well from previous trips into Afghanistan and from his work during the anti-Soviet war in the 1980s."

Schroen was actually in the process of retiring when he was called in to meet with Cofer Black, the director of Counterintelligence Center (CTC), and offered the assignment. According to Schroen it was a very short meeting— just a couple of questions. "Will you take a team into Afghanistan, leaving within three to five days," and "Can you get it together?"

Schroen did not blink and immediately agreed. "I wanted to get in the fight," he said. The mission that Schroen accepted was risky at best. His team could be cut off and be on their own, without the possibility of American help. There was also some uncertainty about the reception they would receive from the Northern Alliance. Its leader, Ahmed Shah Massoud, had been assassinated by al-Qaeda two days prior to 9/11, and the organization was in considerable disarray. Nevertheless, the mission was a go.

The team was inserted near the town of Barak, a collection of stone-walled houses in the Panjshir Valley, north of Kabul. Schroen wrote in

Gary C. Schroen, the veteran CIA field officer who was picked to lead Team Jawbreaker, the first paramilitary team into Afghanistan. *Getty Images*

First In, an Insider's Account of How the CIA Spearheaded the War on Terror in Afghanistan, "It was 2:45 p.m. on 26 September 2001, and we were deep in the Panjshir Valley in northeast Afghanistan." The team was inserted by an American flight crew piloting a Russian-made Mi-17 helicopter. The flight path took them through a 14,500 foot-high pass in the Hindu Kush mountains, an adventure in itself. Schroen noted that "even though our helicopter had been extensively reconditioned and upgraded by expert mechanics, this flight over the pass was straining the limits of the aircraft."

Team Jawbreaker's mission was to link up with the Northern Alliance (NA), prepare the battlefield, and to pave the way for the insertion of Special Forces. "Once the Taliban defenses are broken, your job is to find bin Laden, kill him and bring his head back on ice," Schroen said after a meeting with his boss. "That's about the clearest, most direct order I've ever received as a CIA officer," Schroen lightheartedly recalled. "The team went in light, except for three cardboard boxes packed with three million dollars in cold hard cash that was to be given to the leaders of the Northern Alliance. "I was passing out large sums of money . . . $200,000 here, $250,000 [there] . . . to generate the impression that we weren't going to talk; we were going to actually help them get ready to fight," Schroen explained. "I was authorized full personal discretion in how the funds . . . were disbursed. I

The CIA's Team Jawbreaker was inserted by a Russian-made Mi-17 helicopter like this one descending during a resupply mission in Nurristan province in 2011. The Russian helicopters were at their maximum flight limitations in the Hindu Kush mountains. *U.S. Navy photo by Vladimir Potapenko*

Special Activities Division

The Special Activities Division (SAD) is a section of the CIA's National Clandestine Service. SAD provides the president of the United States with an option when overt military and/or diplomatic actions are not viable or politically feasible. The highly secretive organization can be directly tasked by the president or the National Security Council, at the president's direction, to conduct direct military action by Paramilitary Operations Officers of the Special Operations Group (SOG), an element within SAD. Members of SOG are typically former military who have special operations experience in sabotage, personnel, and material recovery, kidnapping, bomb damage assessment, hostage rescue, and counter-terrorism. Their primary strengths are agility, adaptability, and deniability. They operate clandestinely in remote locations behind enemy lines to carry out direct action (including raids, assassinations, and sabotage), support of espionage, counter-intelligence, sabotage, hostage rescue missions, and guerilla or unconventional warfare.

The Special Operations Group is organized into three branches: Air, Maritime, and Ground, and is thought to have around 150 paramilitary personnel. They are trained at Camp Perry, Virginia, (known as "The Farm") and at privately owned training centers around the United States. Their training encompasses weapons, explosives, hand-to-hand combat, high performance driving, parachuting, SCUBA and closed circuit diving, foreign language, Survival, Evasion, Resistance and Escape (SERE), combat first-aid, and tactical communications. They are normally deployed in six-man teams. The teams often work with U.S. Special Operations forces.

The authority to conduct covert action is derived from the National Security Act of 1947. President Ronald Reagan, in his 1984 Executive Order 12333 titled "United States Intelligence Activities," defined covert action as "special activities," both political and military, which the U.S. government could legally deny. The CIA was designated as the sole authority in 1991 to conduct special activities but only after receiving a "Presidential Finding," issued by the president of the United States. These findings are monitored by an oversight committee composed of members of the Senate Select Committee on Intelligence, and the House Permanent Select Committee on Intelligence.

decided who to pay and how much . . . I did not require advance approval from headquarters."

Despite many Washington naysayers—"Why are we paying this money? How can you trust these guys?"—Schroen and his team continued working hard to secure Alliance support. "We were busy," he recalled. "My role primarily was to interface with the leadership of the Northern Alliance, the general, now Marshal [Mohammed Qasim] Fahim, who had taken over command of the Northern Alliance; with their intelligence chief; with their foreign minister, Dr. Abdullah . . . trying to convince them that we were deadly serious about coming in and really providing them with assistance." The Afghans were concerned; America had left them in the lurch before. Schroen reasoned with them. "What you guys have never had is the kind of tactical support that the U.S. Air Force and U.S. Navy are going to be able to put on the ground," he said. "The Taliban have never experienced . . . one percent of the terror that they're going to feel when we start dropping bombs on them." He explained his mission: "What our job is here is to get Americans on the ground that can help bring those bombs right on top of the Taliban." The Alliance leadership finally came on board after the promise of air support.

> "We're not running out of [fixed] targets, Afghanistan is."
> —Donald Rumsfeld

At approximately 1630 UTC (Coordinated Universal Time, the time standard by which the world regulates clocks and time) on Sunday 7 October 2001, the United States and Great Britain started their limited bombing campaign. Feroz Ali Abbasi, a Ugandan Briton and member of the Taliban, was captured in Pakistan. "I had expected the bombing on Tuesday because I had heard nearly a month previous that a fax had been sent to bin Laden from [an individual] in America warning him of the attack," he said. "Bin Laden had warned the people at a mosque that America was going to bomb in one month's time." Abdul Salam Zaeef tried to convince Omar that the United States was going to launch an attack. "Omar was unwilling to believe the details," he said. "He reasoned that America couldn't launch an offensive without a valid reason . . . and there was no incontrovertible proof incriminating bin Laden on the attack. In Mullah Mohammed Omar's mind there was less than a ten percent chance that America would resort to anything beyond threats . . . ."

The bombing focused primarily on "Taliban air defenses, facilities physically and symbolically associated with Mullah Omar and UBL [Osama bin Laden], and al-Qaeda training camps," according to General DeLong. Strikes were reported in the capital, Kabul (where electricity was cut off), at the airport and military nerve center of Kandahar (home of the Taliban's Supreme Leader Mullah Omar), and also in the city of Jalalabad (military/terrorist training camps).

General DeLong explained, "Coming up with a target list was having us all scratching our heads. We had to put our hopes in 'targets of opportunity,'

Mohammad Abdul Karim Khalili, vice president of Afghanistan, gives a speech during the April 2004 re-opening of Bamiyan University. The Taliban closed and occupied the university in 1998; consequently the buildings were heavily damaged during Operation Enduring Freedom. *USMC photo by Lance Cpl. James Patrick Douglas*

First Vice President Mohammad Qasim Fahim talks to media in May 2009. Fahim was defense minister of the Northern Alliance, succeeding Ahmad Shah Massoud, who had been assassinated by al-Qaeda operatives posing as journalists. In October 2001, Fahim marched on Kabul together with U.S. Coalition Forces to attack the Taliban *AP photo/Musadeq Sadeq*

hitting the enemy when they moved, especially when they fled the early air campaign." The limited air campaign was designed to avoid alienating the south's large Pashtun ethnic group, which formed the basis of the Taliban's support. It was hoped that the bombing would cause a split in the ranks of the Taliban and cause the moderates to turn over bin Laden.

The Taliban troops were not initially targeted because they had a great deal of support in the Pakistani army, particularly the ISI. It was thought that a move against them might destabilize President Pervez Musharaff's government. It had taken strong pressure to bring him around. "You're either with us or against us," Bush told the international community. Musharraf said in an interview on CBS' *60 Minutes* that Richard Armitage, the number two man at the State Department, had threatened Mahmoud Ahmed, the Pakistani intelligence chief, to "bomb Pakistan back to the stone age," if the country didn't agree to U.S. demands. Musharraf quickly agreed to become an ally in the war against terror.

Barnett Rubin, Senior Fellow at New York University's Center on International Co-operation said, "It was a huge shock to them [Pakistan], but they had seen it coming to some extent because they knew that the presence of al Qaeda in Afghanistan was going to create problems for them, and how to deal with that had already become a rather contentious issue within the Pakistani military. They did not have full control over the Taliban by any means. There were lots of tensions between the Taliban and Pakistan." In return for Pakistan's support, the United States pledged to offer, among other things, assistance in reducing the country's $6 billion foreign debt and forgive $800 million in direct aid.

Fifty Tomahawk land-attack missiles (TLAMs) were fired in the first wave against fixed high-priority targets by two Aegis destroyers, USS *McFaul* (DDG-74) and USS *John Paul Jones* (DDG-53); a *Spruance*-class destroyer, USS *O'Brien* (DD-975); and an Aegis cruiser, USS *Philippine Sea* (CG-58), as well as two U.S. and British nuclear attack submarines. Britain's Royal Air Force (RAF) also provided Tristar and VC-10 tankers to help supplement U.S. Air Force KC-135s and KC-10s in providing in-flight refueling for navy aircraft aboard carriers in the North Arabian Sea. The USS *Enterprise* (CVN-65) and USS *Carl Vinson* (CVN-70) launched F-14 and F/A-18 fighters over 600 nautical miles from their targets. Each carrier air wing provided air support for a twelve-hour shift; *Enterprise* was designated the night carrier, while *Vinson* handled daylight sorties. The average flight lasted more than four and a half hours, with a minimum of two in-flight refuelings per fighter each way to complete the mission.

USS *John Paul Jones* (DDG-53) launching the first Tomahawk Land Attack Missile (TLAM) against al-Qaeda and Taliban training camps and military installations on 7 October 2001, in support of Operation Enduring Freedom. *U.S. Navy*

Commander. Anthony Giaini, Executive Officer of VF-213, led a strike into western Afghanistan. "The strike I led on the first night of the war reflected both on the realities imposed on us by the limited number of assets we could support (particularly with tankers), the ranges involved, and the kind of enemy we faced. Unless, and until, we could eliminate the air defenses in Afghanistan, the tankers would not be going in-country."

The U.S. Navy's attack plan called for gaining air superiority, after which the strikes would attack key Taliban and al-Qaeda targets— SAM (Surface to Air Missile) sites, AAA (Anti-Aircraft Artilley) batteries, barracks, ammunition dumps, tank/APC/truck parks, and terrorist training camps—in and around Herat, Shindand, Shibarghan, Mazar-e Sharif, and the southern Taliban stronghold area of Kandahar. The plan also called for providing close air support to anti-Taliban forces. Commander Giaini was involved in the planning.

"The target list eliminated not only the limited command and control nodes of the Taliban and al-Qaeda, but just about every piece of military gear and potential military site in the country," Lt. Cmdr. Bill Lind recalled. However, in order to proceed, there were some political considerations that had to come together. "The plan itself reflected some of the hard political realities, as for OEF [Operation Enduring Freedom] to succeed," he said. "We would require the support of everyone from very shaky friends to our traditional and closest allies. The key nations for us were Pakistan (whose territory we would have to cross) and Britain, who luckily for us, had an exercise underway in Oman at the time, and the RAF had big wing tankers already in-theatre. Frankly, we couldn't have fought Operation Enduring Freedom without the help of both nations."

The navy's heavily laden aircraft carried laser-guided bombs (LGBs), JDAMs (Joint Direct Attack Munitions), the AGM-84 SLAM-ER (Standoff Land Attack Missile—Extended Range), and the AGM-154 JSOW (Joint Standoff Weapon), the last of which had been used in combat for the first time only recently before in Iraq in early 2001 during Operation Southern Watch. U.S. Navy ordnance specialist Chief Warrant Officer grade 3 Michael Lavoie said, "We uploaded bombs in quantities that we had never previously hung on a VF-213 aircraft—two of the Tomcats carried pairs of 1000-pound GBU [Guided Bomb Unit]-16s, and the remaining jets were armed with 500-pound GBU-12s. I truly wondered whether these aircraft were going to get off the deck." Lieutenant Commander Michael Peterson of VF-213 was in the raid on a SAM site. "The Taliban may not have had more than one radar-guided SAM guarding Kabul, but these guys had a shitload of AAA! It looked like you could get out of the jet and walk across it."

Five Air Force B-1B Lancer bombers ("Bones") and 10 B-52 ("Buff")* heavy bombers operating out of the U.S. Navy Support Facility on Diego Garcia in the Indian Ocean and two Air Force B-2 ("Spirit") stealth bombers from Whiteman AFB, Missouri, each carrying sixteen 2,000 pound satellite-aided GBU-31 JDAMs, were directed against Taliban early warning radars and military headquarters buildings. The B-2 flights were the longest-duration combat sortie in history—forty-eight straight hours and more than 14,000 miles. The heaviest bombing that night by far was conducted by Air Force B-52s from the 28th Air Expeditionary Wing, based on Diego Garcia, who rained both JDAMs and hundreds of 500-pound Mk 82 unguided bombs on al Qaeda terrorist training camps in the valleys of eastern Afghanistan.

CentCom kept a tight leash on the bombing because of a fear of collateral damage. Targets that involved a high risk of harm to civilians or to mosques had to be personally cleared at the highest level, sometimes by Rumsfeld and even the president. In one case, a Predator unmanned aerial vehicle (UAV) spotted what was thought to be a convoy suspected of containing Mullah Omar. The strike was not approved because it could not be conclusively proved that Omar or other Taliban leaders were in the vehicles. The bombing continued, with little discernable results. Lieutenant Comander David Lobdell of VF-41 was frustrated with bombing the same target time after time. "We attacked the key Afghan airfields several times over in the early stages . . .

*The B-1 Lancer is commonly called a Bone, after a newsman neglected to hyphenate "B-One" and wrote "Bone." The B-52 is affectionately known by its crewmen as "Big Ugly Fat Fellow" or "Buff."

An F-14 Tomcat of Fighter Squadron 211 ("Checkmates") prepares for launch to conduct aerial reconnaissance over Afghanistan on 31 December 2001. The Checkmates were attached to Carrier Air Wing 9 aboard the USS *John C. Stennis*. *U.S. Navy*

every third night I was bombing the air base on the outskirts of Kabul, despite video showing that the aircraft on the ground had not been flown in a number of years." The Northern Alliance looked on the bombing as a waste of time and questioned whether the United States was really in the fight.

Schroen was also extremely frustrated. He strongly urged CentCom to "bomb the front-line troops here in Kabul and in other places around where the Northern Alliance forces can then take advantage of that and move forward." He was convinced the Northern Alliance could break through the Taliban lines with the help of American air power. His recommendation was ignored and the deep strikes continued. They had little impact on the Taliban. In fact, Schroen reported, "The Taliban were encouraged and their morale was high, because there was so little bomb damage and casualties."

Jalaluddin Haqqani, the Taliban's military commander, said, "The military strikes have failed to inflict any serious or crippling damage. Mullah Omar, Osama bin Laden, and all other commanders are safe and sound and carrying out their duties."

On 16 October, a second CIA eight-man team, Team Alpha, was inserted by U.S. Special Operations helicopters and successfully linked up with General Rashid Dostum's Uzbek forces south of Mazar-e Sharif. The team's support of Dostum did not sit well with the Northern Alliance leadership. Dostum was a legendary Uzbek warlord with a nasty, ruthless reputation. He was known as the "Butcher of the North" and was notorious for shifting allegiance and for making deals to support his own interests. However, he was an effective battlefield commander, with a well-trained and equipped force of between 10,000 to 15,000 men. The team soon found itself astride Afghan ponies in a desperate cavalry charge against the Taliban, who were armed with automatic weapons and cannon. Dostum threw six hundred cavalrymen into the fight, a hundred men in each wave.

"[A]n officer in the middle of the line stood in his stirrups and raised a sword into the air," Schroen wrote. "A shouted command could be heard above the firing, and the line of horsemen surged forward almost as one." The charge went home, piercing the Taliban line and sending them fleeing from the battlefield. One of Dostum's men "raised both arms toward the sky—his AK-47 in his right hand and the severed head of a Taliban fighter held by its hair in his left—and he shouted in a clear, ringing voice, 'Allahu Akbar!' The fight was over."

CHAPTER 9

Task Force Dagger

De Oppresso Liber ("To Liberate the Oppressed")
—Motto, U.S. Special Forces

THE 5TH SPECIAL FORCES GROUP (Airborne), under the command of Colonel John Mulholland, was located on the sprawling U.S. Army base at Fort Campbell, Kentucky. It comprised a headquarters company, four operational battalions, and one general support battalion. Its area of responsibility included the twenty-five nations located in the Horn of Africa, the northern Red Sea, the Arabian Peninsula, Iraq, and South and Central Asia, including Afghanistan. Mulholland knew immediately after 9/11 that his soldiers "would be players" in any retaliatory strike because his soldiers were trained and equipped to operate in that area of the world. Mulholland was notified that he was to be part of the "expedition to Afghanistan," as the theater of operations was initially known. "By the 13th [September] a decision had been made to stand up what's

Special Forces crest. *U.S. Army*

called a Joint Special Operations Task Force headquarters," Mulholland said. "It was apparent we'd be going into Afghanistan," after it was learned that al-Qaeda and Osama bin Laden were behind the attack. "I was going to be [heading] a joint headquarters, meaning U.S Army, Air Force, Navy, and other forces working jointly. [It] was the first time I would have done that, [so I was] coming to grips with who those other players are going to be and how we were going to work together."

Mulholland's command was designated Joint Special Operations Task Force North (JSOTF-N), code-named "Task Force Dagger." Its mission was to provide command and control over the Special Forces teams that were to be inserted into Afghanistan. Task Force Dagger deviated from Special Operation Force doctrine by initially reporting directly to CENTCOM rather than through Special Operations Command-Central (SOCCENT). Task Force Dagger was composed of the 5th Special Forces Group, the 160th Special Operations Aviation Regiment (Airborne), and the 720th Special Tactics Group of the Air Force Special Operations Command. The 1st Battalion, 87th Infantry, 10th Mountain Division, would furnish base security and would serve as a quick reaction force (QRF).

Mulholland's staff immediately began the planning process. However, he explained, "Afghanistan was new to the 5th Group as an area of

Colonel John Mulholland (right), commanding officer 5th Special Forces Group (Airborne) briefs General Franks (left) at Bagram airbase on 1 November 2001. Mulholland was selected to lead Joint Special Forces Task Force North, code named Task Force Dagger. His command was composed of 5th Special Forces Group, the 160th Special Operations Aviation Regiment (Airborne), and the 720th Special Tactics Group. *defenseimagery.mil*

operations [and] I was concerned about our lack of precise cultural and tribal knowledge. Our soldiers spend a great deal of time learning the language and culture and background of the people they will work with to better understand them, and in order to work successfully with them to achieve both our objectives as well as our counterparts' objectives." He pressed hard to gather information about the Afghan commanders his force would be dealing with. "We did work to get a better grip on who the various players were on the ground. Some of the prime personalities came to light very quickly . . . but by the time we put teams on the ground there was still a great deal of uncertainty . . . because we did not know from first-hand experience what we were dealing with. Certainly in those early days there was a great deal of concern and worry as we put people on the ground of just what we were putting them into." Mulholland found the Afghan commanders to be a mixed bag. "Some of those fellows had histories that were not necessarily consistent with the kind of guys you would want to work with," he pointed out. "Some of them had pretty strong radical Islamic leanings that would put them potentially in a category of being anti-American or anti-Western." In several cases, he strongly recommended that "we should not put American soldiers on the ground with these leaders."

Based on the initial intelligence, Mulholland identified two senior Afghan leaders in the north—Fahim Khan and Rashid Dostum. Detailed personal information about the two was not available during the early planning sessions, and it was assumed they had political as well as military influence. "It was going to be important to put a senior level of leadership to help influence the political as well as the military," Mulholland said. He planned on using two of his battalion commanders as liaison officers with the warlords to provide an "extra level of experience and expertise."

Early in the planning process, he divided Afghanistan into two sections based on a north-south orientation. *Weapons of Choice—ARSOF in Afghanistan*, from the U.S. Army's Combat Studies Institute, noted that "the northern sector included the vast Hindu Kush mountain range, itself the size of Kentucky, and all the lands to the north and northwest. The southern sector was the area south of the Hindu Kush, which also had formidable chains of mountains as well as arid high deserts." The 5th Special Forces Group was tasked with the northern sector, roughly above the 34th parallel along the east-west highway that ran between the cities of Herat and Kabul. The southern sector would come under the control of JSOTF-S (South), which was to be staffed from the U.S. Navy Sea-Air-Land (SEAL) teams.

Operation Detachment Alpha

Operation Detachment Alpha (ODA) is the primary operational element of a Special Forces company. The detachment consists of twelve men: two officers and ten sergeants, who are all Special Forces qualified and cross-trained in five functional areas: weapons, engineer, medical, communications, and operations and intelligence. The cross-training allows the team to operate in two six-man elements. ODAs can perform the full range of Special Forces missions, including long-term unconventional warfare and foreign internal defense missions that involve direct contact with indigenous military or paramilitary forces. They can also be tailored to execute short-term direction action and special reconnaissance missions.

Lieutenant Colonel David Fox, a former Special Forces battalion commander, said that, "The ODA is the heart and soul of Special Forces. I like to say that they're the tip of the spear. You have this huge support structure behind every A-team that goes out. But the guys that are on the ground make things happen. They are the individuals that build the rapport. They are the guys that are the tactical experts. They organize the indigenous force, if you will, and prepare them for combat. They bring in a tremendous amount of skills, experience and maturity. That's why I call them the heart and soul—they're the guys that are making things happen."

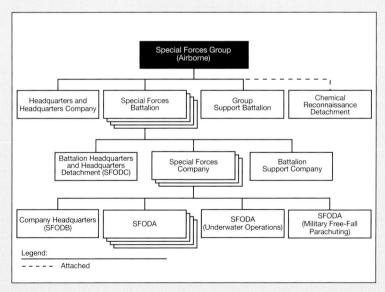

Special Forces Group (Airborne) organizational chart. *Department of Defense*

Upon notification of the mission, Mulholland ordered four Operational Detachment Alphas (ODAs) to stand by for immediate deployment. Linda Robinson wrote in *Master of Chaos: The Secret History of the Special Forces*, "The men of 5th Group gathered in the conference room, which doubled as the group's museum. Gas masks, Soviet-made rifles, land mines, battalion flags, and other mementos of Desert Storm, Somalia, Operation Southern Watch, and the Vietnam era were crammed into glass cases in the anteroom. The memorabilia overflowed into the conference room, where uniformed mannequins and a DShK anti-aircraft gun sat in the left corner of a stage area, where the group's commander stood in front of a screen. A handful of team leaders were seated in a semicircle before him, around a three-inch-thick varnished blond wooden table the size of a pool table . . . Colonel John Mulholland, who had just assumed command of 5th Group over the summer, gave his men a one-sentence brief: 'Gentlemen, you have been selected to infiltrate Afghanistan.'"

The selected teams entered Fort Campbell's Isolation Facility (ISOFAC), where they pored over all the available classified information on Afghanistan—geography, population, culture, enemies, and allies. Doug Stanton wrote in *Horse Soldiers, the Extraordinary Story of a Band of U.S. Soldiers who Rode to Victory in Afghanistan* that "ISOFAC was a closed world within the tightly held universe . . . guards manned the gate in the chain-link fence, tipped with concertina-wire. From the outside, it was window-less jumble of metal-gray blocks." Protocol called for each team's mission to remain secret from the others. The men remained isolated until the mission was called away for the C-17 Globemaster flight to Uzbekistan. On 10 October, just shy of four weeks after al-Qaeda's attack, Mulholland and his soldiers touched down on a crumbling Soviet-era airbase at Karshi-Khanabad ("K-2" or "Camp Stronghold Freedom") in south-central Uzbekistan, just 120 miles from the Afghan border. The ODA soldiers were taken to the base isolation area, a handful of tents surrounded by a single strand of concertina-wire. One team suffered through a seventy-two hour downpour, which left them struggling in ankle deep mud. Without exception, the soldiers were happy to leave when their turn came to be inserted.

Major Roger Crombie, Alpha Company, 1st Battalion, 87th Infantry, recalled landing at K-2. "We were landing blacked out. The aircrew was putting on their body armor and loading their sidearms. We came off the aircraft thinking we were going straight into a patrol base. We didn't really know what we were getting into." His company quickly took over security for one end of the runway from the air force. Creature comforts were few

Karshi-Khanabad, headquarters of the American effort in Afghanistan. The crumbling facility had been a Soviet-era airbase in Uzbekistan. It was located 120 miles from the Afghan border. *defenseimagery.mil*

and far between. Many of the men had to sleep under the stars and then were able to move into several old, filthy Russian bunkers that were infested with bats, whose droppings were toxic. They finally moved into tents, where they stayed for much of their deployment.

According to Master Sgt. Dale G. Aaknes, Task Force Dagger's J-4 noncommissioned officer in charge (NCOIC), it took more than seventy-two flights of C-17 transport aircraft to deploy the entire force, which was completed the first week in October. A local resident was quoted as saying, "Every hour, night and day, one plane comes in or flies out, sometimes even two. This has been going on for a week and every day there are more planes." A commercial pilot said, "Every time we fly in or out there are several U.S. Air Force planes and helicopters on the tarmac. Today, one C-141 Starlifter [a long-range, heavy lift transport plane] landed right in front of us."

Within minutes of arriving at K-2, Mulholland was whisked away to his headquarters, which operated out of twenty heavy green vinyl tents that were joined end to end to create a long florescent-lit tunnel. The Joint Operations Center (JOC), as it was known, was crammed with state-of-the-art computers and communications equipment that would keep him in touch with his deployed teams. A key component of Task Force Dagger's headquarters was the coordination of close air support (CAS) with the Special Operations Forces teams (SOF) on the ground.

Air Force Lt. Col. George Bochain, on loan to SOF to help coordinate air-ground attacks said, "Colonel Mulholland did not have a centralized planner in his staff that would be able to tie [CAS and SOF] together . . . he needed somebody to dedicate his entire time to managing that piece for him . . . it is what guys like me do for a living." Bochain worked hard to establish a functional Air Support Operations Center (ASOC). "There was a targeting cell that had been set up, and there was a fire support cell," he recalled, "however, there were many things that needed to be fixed." He immediately streamlined the air support request process by directing the SOF to go through Task Force Dagger's ASOC instead of going through the theater-level air operations center. He also instituted an "instant messenger" type online chat protocol to track CAS requests, which replaced sticky notes that adorned computer screens.

Mulholland was under considerable pressure from the secretary of defense to deploy his teams. The president was pushing Rumsfeld. Bob Woodward wrote that Bush "was growing a little impatient." The frustration "rolled down hill" to CentCom. "When is something going to happen?" Rumsfeld demanded. "What is the situation with those teams?"

General Franks wrote that "Rumsfeld was never personally abusive. But he was not what you would call 'user-friendly.' His questions continued relentlessly. His chronic impatience had never been so obvious." In one memo, Rumsfeld ended with "You must figure out a way for us to get the job done!" Mulholland had the teams standing by, but severe weather in the mountains and the difficulty of obtaining flight clearances forced postponement after postponement. Schroen was very concerned about the clearances because "without official coordination with the appropriate governments [Uzbekistan and Tajikistan], an unannounced, unauthorized flight over their borders could result in the aircraft being fired upon." President Imomali Rakhmonov of Tajikistan was under considerable pressure from Russia to avoid cooperating with the United States. "We didn't have accurate information about the American plans," he said. "It wasn't clear to us."

Robin Moore, in *The Hunt for Bin Laden: Task Force Dagger, On the Ground with the Special Forces in Afghanistan*, credits Maj. David Brigham, the popular defense attaché in Tajikistan, with acquiring the clearances. "The NA [Northern Alliance] leaders threw in a last minute glitch by insisting that the soldiers be in civilian clothing, not U.S. Army uniforms." Colonel Mulholland vehemently opposed this restriction. "The colonel exploded

160th Special Operations Aviation Regiment (Airborne) "Night Stalkers"

Originally created as Task Force 160, the unit was formed from soldiers of the 101st Airborne Division at Fort Campbell, Kentucky. In October 1981, the unit was officially designated the 160th Aviation Battalion. The regiment then became an airborne unit in October 1986 and was redesignated the 160th Special Operations Aviation Group (Airborne). The modern-day 160th Special Operations Aviation Regiment (Airborne) was officially activated in June 1990. Soldiers of the 160th pioneered the army's nighttime flying techniques. The unit became known as the "Night Stalkers" because of its capability to strike undetected during the hours of darkness and its unprecedented combat successes. "Night Stalkers Don't Quit," was its motto.

The regiment is organized into four battalions, each of which has a strategic composition of light, medium, and heavy helicopters, all highly modified and designed to meet the unit's unique mission requirements. The 1st Battalion has one AH-6 Little Bird helicopter company, one MH-6 Little Bird helicopter company, and three companies of MH-60 Black Hawk helicopters; the 2nd Battalion has two MH-47 Chinook helicopter companies; and the 3rd and 4th Battalions each have two MH-47 Chinook helicopter companies and one MH-60 Black Hawk helicopter company. Each battalion also has a Headquarters, Headquarters Company, and a maintenance company.

The Chinook MH-47E is the work-horse of the regiment. It can accommodate a Humvee or up to forty-four fully equipped personnel plus its five man crew—pilot, co-pilot, crew chief, and two side gunners. The engines generate more than 8,000 shaft horsepower, permitting the Chinook to lift up to 28,000 pounds—more than its 25,000-pound empty weight—and cruise at nearly 150 mph. Tandem rotors make the Chinook very maneuverable and impervious to most cross winds. Sixty-foot diameter rotors with three composite blades overlap, so the CH-47 has a surprisingly small footprint and can take off and land more steeply than conventional helicopters. It is jammed with millions of dollars worth of equipment, including

in anger," Schroen recalled. Despite the Northern Alliance's request, the Special Forces soldiers wore U.S. Army tan fatigues with the insignia and name tags removed. Once the Northern Alliance leadership found out that they were there to direct the bombing, the subject of uniforms never came up, and the Special Forces adopted Afghani dress. They also grew beards and let their hair grow to blend in with the locals.

Finally, the weather finally cleared over the mountains, and Colonel Mulholland gave approval for the insertion of two twelve-man teams from electronic countermeasure equipment, forward-looking infrared scanners, and terrain-following radar, which allows the aircraft to fly "nap of the earth" at night, in adverse weather, and in high-threat environments. Estimates of the MH-47E's cost are as high as $40 million per helicopter.

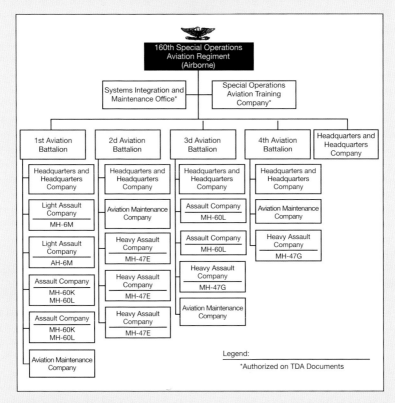

160th Special Operations Aviation Regiment (Airborne) organizational chart. *Department of Defense*

the 5th Special Forces Group. They were flown in by specially configured twin-rotor MH-47E Chinook helicopters from the 2nd Battalion, 160th Special Operations Aviation Regiment (Airborne), nicknamed the "Night Stalkers," and U.S. Air Force Special Operations Command MH-53J Pave Low helicopters—the eighty four-foot behemoth is the largest helicopter in its inventory. The rugged Hindu Kush mountains (nicknamed "The Bear") presented extremely difficult flying conditions. The U.S. Army's *Weapons on Choice—ARSOF in Afghanistan* noted that "the mountain ranges created rapidly changing weather systems that were extremely difficult to forecast . . .

In order to fit in better with local forces, combined with austere living conditions, grooming standards for Special Forces in combat are relaxed, as shown by the long hair and beard sported by this member of ODA 342 who is pulling security with a .50-caliber machine gun. *U.S. Army photo by Sergeant First Class Fred Gurwell*

An MH-47E Chinook from the 160th Special Operations Aviation Regiment. *defenseimagery.mil*

there were times when the weather changed significantly by the hour. The terrain soared from 6,000 to more than 16,000 feet mean sea level. Narrow mountainous valleys intensified and channelized the weather . . . the pilots were forced to fly in zero-visibility conditions for long hours, testing the endurance and mettle of the aircrews and the performance and capability limits of the aircraft." The weather was so bad; two of MH-60 Black Hawk helicopter escorts had to turn back, leaving the troop birds to go it alone.

CHAPTER 10

Operational Detachment Alpha 555 Tiger 01

JUST AFTER MIDNIGHT ON 19 October, two MH-53J Pave Low helicopters with ODA [Operational Detachment Alpha] 555 (Triple Nickel), call sign Tiger 01, aboard, threaded their way through the Hindu Kush mountains toward a landing zone in the Panjshir Valley. The team's mission was to support Gen. Mohammad Fahim Khan, Massoud's successor in the Panjshir Valley. But first they had to get there. Rain pelted the helicopters, reducing visibility to near zero and forcing the pilots to rely solely on instruments. Shortly after takeoff, one of the birds lost its electronics and was literally flying blind. At one point, a crewman spotted a jagged pinnacle ahead. "Pull up! Pull up!" he shouted. The pilot reacted by pulling back hard on the stick, causing the aircraft to surge upward. The abrupt movement caught the men in the troop compartment by surprise.

Air Force Master Sergeant William C. Markham took off his head-phones. "If I was about to impact the side of a mountain, I decided I'd rather not know about it," he recalled mumbling. The helicopters flew onward until they reached their destination. *Washington Post* staffer Dana Priest wrote in *'Team 555' Shaped a New Way of War*, "Both choppers had landed in the wrong place. On a moonless night, the two halves of ODA 555 (Triple Nickel) were separated by several miles and one small mountain."

MH-53J Pave Low helicopter, as seen through night vision goggles, on a mission to insert a team of Special Forces into a landing zone somewhere in Afghanistan. *U.S. Army*

Two CIA operatives, Hal and Phil (pseudonyms), waited patiently in the dark, moonless night for Triple Nickel to arrive. They had been on the ground for several weeks working with the Northern Alliance commanders, promising them that U.S. forces were coming to help them defeat the Taliban. Tonight was finally the night—two other insertion attempts had been scrubbed because of bad weather. They watched incredulously as one of the helicopters over-flew the landing zone and disappeared into the darkness. A second aircraft touched down in a blinding cloud of dust, and the six members of ODA 555 rushed down the ramp, weapons at the ready. They crouched down and scanned the area for signs of danger.

"They told us that where we were landing was a secure spot," a team member recalled. "But whether they meant the spot where the helicopter touched down . . . we really didn't know."

As the aircraft lifted off and the dust settled, the team spotted bobbing flashlights. They leveled their weapons, fingers tightening on the triggers, and prepared to kill the intruders. Suddenly a huge figure stepped out of the darkness and said cheerfully, "Hey, guys, I'm Hal. Welcome to Afghanistan."

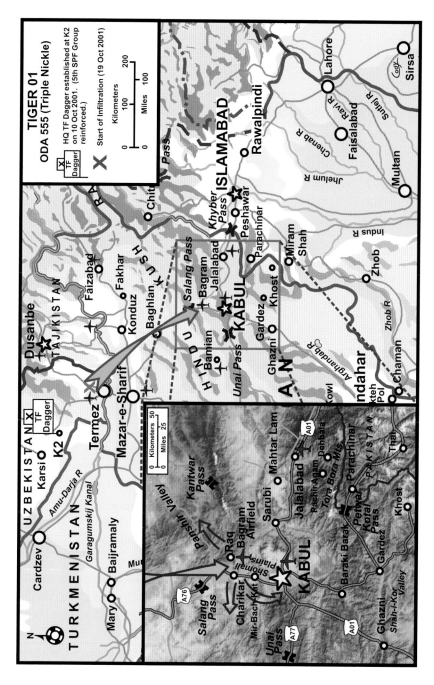

Tiger 01, Operational Detachment Alpha 555 (Triple Nickel) was assigned to support Gen. Mohammed Fahim Khan in the Panjshir Valley, north of Kabul. Inserted by helicopter just prior to midnight on 19 October, it was the first ODA team on the ground. *Bill Cody*

Chief Warrant Officer David Diaz, the team leader, was miffed. The flashlights gave away their position, and he wasted little time in chewing out the CIA operatives for carelessly exposing them.

Hal was unrepentant. "Relax, you're in friendly territory," he said good-naturedly. Hal was a former SEAL and now a veteran member of SAD. He was no stranger to covert operations. The Panjshir Valley had long been under the control of Ahmad Shah Massoud's Northern Alliance fighters. Neither the Soviets nor the Taliban had been able to wrest control of this strategic terrain. The team shouldered its equipment and moved out. After finding the missing team members, Hal led the team—eleven Special Forces soldiers and one air force combat controller—to a safe house in the tiny village of Astana, in the north-central Panjshir Valley. Diaz reported their safe arrival to Task Force Dagger, who forwarded the welcome news to General Franks.

"CentCom was elated," Lt. Gen. Michael DeLong reported. "Franks called the Chairman of the Joint Chiefs of Staff. 'Tell the secretary [Rumsfeld] that we've got Special Forces troopers on the ground and more are on the way.'"

One team member recalled, "The first day we got in, they [Hal and Phil] took us to a house, where they fed us and we got a briefing on the mission." They were told they would work with Gen. Bismullah Khan, the Northern Alliance Deputy Minister of Defense and an ally of Fahim. Bismullah Khan was a top commander during the Soviet war, as well as in the fight against the Taliban. Early the next morning Phil led the team to another safe house where he introduced them to the Afghan leader.

Moore wrote, "Flanked by bodyguards in Panshir tiger stripes, an Afghan with a long beard and a crooked nose stepped forward to shake Phil's hand. 'Here are the American Special Forces warriors I've been promising you,' Phil said.

'Okay,' Bismullah responded, 'show us what you can do.'" The Afghan commander was somewhat reserved because he knew that the only reason the Americans were there was because of 9/11.

"I wouldn't say they mistrusted us initially," Markham recalled, "but there was a certain sense they weren't sure how we could help them."

Diaz looked Bismullah in the eye and replied confidently, "All you have to do is show me where to start."

The next night the Special Forces soldiers, the CIA operatives, and their Afghan escort moved closer to the bitterly contested Bagram airfield, which was littered with debris going back to the Soviet invasion. "We stayed there for a day," a team member said. "From there, we went forward to survey the front line." The position was too far away for the team to be effective. "Look, we need to move close," they urged, but Fahim would not allow it.

"They didn't want us on the battlefield because the Taliban and al-Qaeda were hunting us and figured we'd be safer if they moved us some place where his [Fahim] trusted guys could watch us," Sergeant 1st Class Frank (pseudonym) complained. "So we'd go from there, move up to a certain part

Bagram airfield was littered with the wreckage of Soviet-era aircraft and vehicles, as well as thousands of mines. *USMC*

of the battlefield, do what we needed to do, and then we'd move back . . . The front lines were too porous and they didn't feel that it was secure enough." Finally, a four-man survey team was able to get close to the Taliban lines, into the control tower that overlooked the enemy positions.

"The view was startling," one of the survey team recalled. "We could see Taliban tanks, artillery, troops, command posts, vehicles and ammunition bunkers." The survey team identified more than fifty targets. They called back with the report and an urgent request to "Bring the CAS equipment, fast!"

Master Sergeant Markham, combat controller with the 23rd Special Tactics Squadron, hurriedly joined them, along with Gen. Abdul Wahid Baba Jan, known simply as "General Babajan," a Northern Alliance sub-commander. "General Babajan starts pointing out all the enemy positions," Frank recalled. "We were like, 'You mean that's al-Qaeda right there, and that's Taliban?' He knew. 'Yes, General so-and-so lives in that house. This is where his lines are.' So we said, 'Wait a minute,' and got on the radio. 'Hey, are there any aircraft coming this way?' 'Yes, it'll be there in two hours.' So we'd call back up and have the guys bring down some laser equipment and we started dropping bombs."

Author Linda Robinson wrote, in *Masters of Chaos, The Secret History of the Special Forces,* "The Afghans watched in wonder as the Special Forces soldiers set up their secret weapon, a dark gray box called a laser target designator, and pointed its lens toward the Soviet-made tanks and artillery. Its laser marked the target and the range finder calculated the distance." Markham contacted a navy F/A-18 Hornet, lazed the target with his AN/PEQ-1 Special Operations Forces Laser Marker (SOFLAM), and watched as a five-hundred-pound bomb obliterated a bunker.

"We hit a Taliban commander and a C2 [command and control] element that was controlling the Bagram air field," Frank said. "The Northern Alliance owned three quarters of it, but the southern eastern end was covered by the Taliban and the al-Qaeda. They were all set up in what used to be a village, but they had moved all the civilians out. They'd made it in to a military garrison, and that's where they covered it." General Babajan and his men erupted with cheers as the explosion threw debris into the air.

The Taliban hit back. Large-caliber artillery shells bracketed the American position, sending them scrambling for cover. Chief Warrant Officer Diaz stopped them. "Everybody stop where you're at," he yelled, "and get back here! We will not be effective if we leave. The Taliban are bad shots, don't even bother to duck."

Markham recalled, "We were on top of a two-story building when they began attacking. The gunfire was intense. Then, they turned the guns on us.

It was like large, flaming footballs flying at our position. The buttons on my uniform were getting in the way of me getting low enough. All I kept thinking was I needed aircraft. I grabbed the radio and called for immediate CAS."

"Send everything!" he pleaded. "The exchange of fire was tremendous. It was the heaviest amount of fire I've seen for that amount of time. I was putting aircraft in holding patterns," he said. "I was putting B-52s in timed strike patterns. When they rolled in, my fighters were out, and they could drop their bombs from 30,000 feet. Once those bombs hit, my fighters were rolling in and putting bombs right on. It was like the B-52 was marking the target for them."

The Taliban continued to attack. "We knew that if we didn't get something on the ground quick, we were probably going to be overrun," Markham said. A B-52 reported in carrying a full load of 2,000-pound "dumb" bombs. "It was not the ideal situation," he said. "On a training mission with inert bombs, you have to be five miles away [from the target]. And now we're talking 500 meters. My teammates had to have full confidence in me," he explained. "I looked at them, they looked at me, and we sat there for what seemed like hours, but it was a couple of seconds. We asked: 'Is this what we want to do? Is this good with everybody? Does everybody agree?'" He established a "kill box," the four coordinates that encompass the enemy, and radioed them to the B-52's pilot. The pilot hesitated, and then asked Markham if he were sure he wanted to go through with it. "I told him that if we didn't, we were going to be dead anyway," Markham said matter-of-factly. "We needed every bomb they had, and we needed them in that box."

On the first pass, Markham waved off the bomber. "We re-verified everything again," he said. Markham was reassured by the confidence he heard in the aircraft commander's voice, and made the call: "Cleared hot." The bombs fell, and Markham looked one last time into the clear blue sky. "It was one of the most beautiful things I've ever seen. That B-52 at 30,000 feet, leaving four big contrails," he said. It would take the bombs four and a half minutes to arrive—the longest minutes of their lives. "I thought about family," Markham said, as he stared at the red beret in his hands, "the lives of my teammates, the lives of the Northern Alliance soldiers."

The Americans sent word down the line: "Get down! Get down!" Markham drew a deep breath and hugged earth. Moments later, the ground began to shake beneath him as 2,000-pound bombs detonated every thousand feet along a mile-long line. The deep explosions were "the most horrific feeling I ever felt in my gut," Markham said. "It seemed like it went on for hours." Dirt, rocks, and shrapnel filled the skies. Northern Alliance soldiers began screaming in fear, though they barely could be heard above the monstrous roar of the explosions. The building beneath the A-team started

A Rockwell B-1 Lancer (Bone) responding to a request from an air force combat controller. Its load of 500-pound bombs would absolutely devastate Taliban defenses. *U.S. Air Force*

to buckle amid the concussions. Then there was a deafening silence. The Taliban radio chatter had ceased and their guns were silent. There were no more explosions. The Americans raised their heads and looked downrange. The Taliban front line was decimated. Hulks of tanks and vehicles lay smoldering. Pieces of rifles and boots were strewn among massive craters. An occasional secondary explosion erupted amid the rubble.

The team stayed seven hours, until dusk, directing a continuous flow of warplanes onto the Taliban front lines until there were no more aircraft available. Markham remarked, "The mindset is to get aircraft on the scene to eliminate that target. That's everything you train for, it come down to that moment. You've got to eliminate that threat so they don't have it anymore." That night, back at the safe house, the Afghans honored the Americans with a huge feast and a long list of targets for the next day. "Once they saw that we were a definite asset for them, there was an immediate rapport," Markham said. "The one and only mission some Northern Alliance soldiers had was to protect us from dying and, unfortunately, some of those soldiers gave their lives to do that," he said, visibly moved by the recollection. "I take my hat off to the soldiers that were assigned to us. They maybe were not the best technically or the most knowledgeable . . . but for their cause, probably some of the bravest."

For nearly a week, ODA 555 was one of only two Special Forces teams inside Afghanistan, so it had the entire range of air force and navy planes at its call; F-18, F-14, and F-15 fighters, B-52 and B-1 bombers, and Spectre AC-130H gunships. Frank said, "When we started hitting pinpoint targets only a kilometer in front of us, the Afghans were like, 'All right, this is for real.'"

Another teammate, Staff Sergeant Russell (pseudonym) explained, "The Afghan soldiers would leave their fighting positions to come watch the Americans do their magic—bring the bombs in on enemy targets. They had these little walkie-talkies that worked basically on a repeater system. They had all the same frequencies that the Taliban had. I'm sure that they talked back and forth to each other, and probably cussed each other out on the radio from time to time."

The Northern Alliance soldiers used the radios to trick the Taliban into revealing their positions. "They did it," Russell said, "by asking them questions. They sounded just like a Talibani soldier and after we dropped a bomb, they'd ask how close it was." Often the Taliban would respond with information that the Northern Alliance would pass to the combat controller. "Then the next thing you know, that guy who was basically saying how far we missed them by would no longer be there," Russell explained. "You'd hear people on the other end of the radio complaining or [being] upset about a friend he'd lost on the radio. I was just amazed. I couldn't believe that they were able to do that for us; helped us in a very big way."

The elimination of the Taliban's defensive positions around the airfield cleared the way for an advance on Kabul. However, General Franks did not want the Northern Alliance to move on the city until there was a power-sharing agreement among Afghanistan's ethnic blocs, who were meeting in Bonn, Germany, trying to work out a deal. According to Gary Berntsen, Franks met with Fahim in Dushanbe, Tajikistan, in mid-October to hammer out a strategy. "Franks set out his priorities: have the NA forces of Dostum take Mazar-e Sharif, use it as a staging area to make a joint attack with Uzbek forces under Berryelah Khan to make a joint attack on Taloquan," Berntsen said. Once the northern cities were taken, Franks wanted Fahim's forces to move west and cut off the escape of the Taliban in the north. Fahim agreed not to enter Kabul without Franks's permission.

"We had known there was an agreement between Fahim and General Franks that he [Fahim] was going to stop short of Kabul," one of the Triple Nickel team recalled. Fahim let it be known however, that, despite the agreement, he was not going to stop.

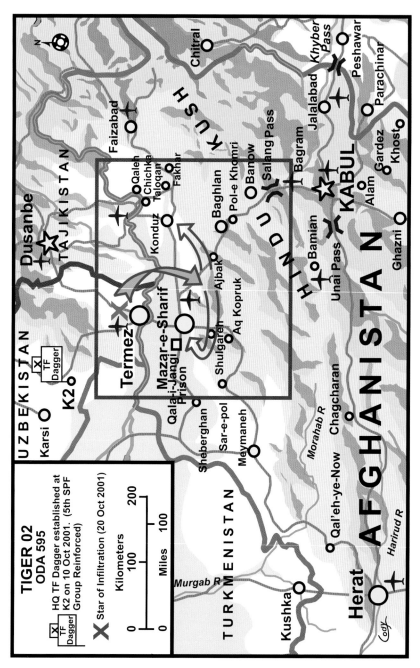

Tiger 02, Operational Detachment Alpha 595, was assigned to support Gen. Abdul Rashid Dostum's attack on Mazar-e Sharif, a strategically important city because of its cultural, economic, and religious importance in northern Afghanistan. *Bill Cody*

CHAPTER 11

Operational Detachment 595 Tiger 02

"I asked for a few Americans.
They brought with them the courage of a whole army."
—Gen. Abdul Rashid Dostum

AT 0200 ON THE MORNING of the twentieth (October 2001), Operational Detachment Alpha 595 (ODA-595), under the command of Capt. Mark D. Nutsch, was safely inserted into the Dari-a-Souf Valley (Valley of the River of the Caves), sixty-eight miles south of the strategically important city of Mazar-e Sharif in the Hindu Kush mountains.

"We're flying blacked out in this MH-47E helicopter [and] they're doing this at a very low altitude, using night-vision goggles," Nutsch explained. "We drop down to a low altitude at a screaming air speed . . . and we hit a surprise sand storm and heavy fog which created near-zero visibility conditions. The armed escort had to turn back, and we flew alone through the mountains for the remainder of the trip." Despite the terrible flying conditions, the pilot put them down in the exact landing zone, a dry riverbed. "It was the perfect infiltration," Nutsch exclaimed.

Chief Warrant Officer Cal Spencer, assistant team leader, described their arrival. "We came out the back of the helicopter through the dust and clouds," he said. "You saw the Afghans coming out to lead us. It was a tense time, and very eerie, because they wear robes with AK-47s coming out of them. It was like the sand people from *Star Wars*."

The most lethal item of equipment the soldiers brought with them was the SOFLAM, which gave them the ability to locate and designate targets for aircraft by using laser technology. The SOFLAM shot a laser beam to mark the target so that a laser-guided bomb could lock on and destroy it. Gary Berntsen described the equipment as looking "like a giant pair of elongated binoculars mounted on a small tripod with a trigger attached to a coiled length of cable." Once a target was located, air force combat controllers contacted the aircraft via satellite radio, gave them their position, and pointed out geographic features to assist in orienting the aircrew. Most of the ordnance that was dropped were 500-pound, and an occasional 2,000-pound BLU-109 "bunker buster" JDAM. The bombs were programmed to hit within a radius of forty feet. With the introduction of Special Forces teams, CentCom's Combined Air Operations Center (CAOC) divided Afghanistan into thirty engagement zones ("kill boxes") to facilitate the quick vectoring of aviation assets. The CAOC, which controlled all aircraft in the region, was located at Prince Sultan Air Base in Saudi Arabia.

Fortunately ODA 595's team only had to walk a few hundred meters to their destination—a mud fort nicknamed "The Alamo" by the CIA. Doug Stanton wrote in *Horse Soldiers, the Extraordinary Story of a Band of U.S. Soldiers who Rode to Victory in Afghanistan*, "The fort looked like something out of the American Old West. Each of its walls was made of smooth mud. They measured about 200 feet long and stood eight feet high. Five wooden doors were spaced along the front. In the middle stood a wooden gate, wide enough for a team of oxen and a wagon—or a tank—to roll through. A hitching post for horses stood outside the gate."

Nutsch remembered that their accommodations were "the finest caves and buildings that the Afghans could provide. We were sleeping in a cleaned-out cattle stable [in which] they had laid some carpets down on the ground. We had two or three pet mice and rats that were running around the area. That was our home for the next several days."

Within minutes of their arrival, the Special Forces soldiers met the eight members of Team Alpha, the CIA paramilitary unit that had been inserted on the evening of 16 October to make the initial liaison with Dostum. Team Alpha was led by R. J. (pseudonym), a former Army Ranger, who, according to Schroen, "was well versed in the tribal situation, having worked with several Mujahideen commanders in the past." He spoke excellent Dari and "would be a valuable addition in the field . . . [and] had the military background to fit in perfectly with Dostum and his Soviet-trained commanders." The CIA operators quickly briefed the soldiers on what they could expect from Dostum's soldiers. They also worked out who was going to do what to whom without worrying about who was in charge. Each team had its own strengths and areas of expertise.

Early the next morning, the team found out why there was a hitching post. Spencer was standing outside when "he suddenly heard the beat of hooves . . . a vibration in the warm ground." Several horsemen thundered up shouting, "He is coming! The general is coming!"

Nutsch recalled, "First about twenty horsemen came galloping up. They were armed to the teeth . . . your typical Soviet small arms, RPGs, AK-47s and light machine guns. About ten minutes behind them, another thirty horsemen arrived . . . ."

Stanton wrote, "A white horse emerged from a curtain of dust. The man in the saddle, immense, strong-shouldered, holding the reins in one hand while the other resting gently on his leg, looked straight ahead, the horse churning beneath him while the man floated atop."

Special Forces soldier using the AN/PEQ-1 Special Operations Forces Laser Marker (SOFLAM). This sophisticated equipment is a lightweight integrated laser designator and rangefinder that provides Special Forces the capability to locate and designate targets for destruction using laser-guided ordnance. *U.S. Air Force*

The horseman reined in, dismounted, and announced, "I am General Dostum. I am glad you have come." Spencer recalled, "He grabbed Mitch and I, went up to this little hill, threw out a map, and said, 'This is what I want to do today.'"

Nelson recalled that the map was incredibly detailed. "It was hand-drawn, of the entire country: the major roads, lines of communication, all the major cities and the known Taliban locations."

The Special Forces team had been told that Dostum was a frail old man suffering from diabetes. Instead they found a robust, energetic commander who "worked 20-hour-plus days, hardly sleeping," according to Nelson. The Northern Alliance commander was six-feet-two and 230 pounds, much bigger than the average Afghan. He had a deep voice, gray, close-cropped hair, and a short beard.

"He was healthy as an ox," Nutsch recalled, "always on the go, always talking to someone, always trying to coordinate actions of the Northern Alliance forces to make it happen." He was impatient and anxious to get the Americans into the fight. "He quickly explained his strategy and campaign plan to us," Nutsch said. "He wanted us to go right away with him to his mountain headquarters, and show us where the Taliban was located. And that was fine with us. We were ready to get up there, and get close to the enemy, and see what we could do." Dostum was convinced that Kabul was the key to controlling Afghanistan . . . and the key to Kabul was Mazar-e Sharif.

Mazar-e Sharif was a critical objective. "Part of the end state for our team," Nutsch pointed out, "was to advise and assist General Dostum . . . [and] specifically to secure the airfield so the U.S. could begin to use it as an air bridge to begin the flow of logistics and troops for a build up to move against the Taliban." Staff Sergeant Stephen Tomat pointed out that, "one airfield is located just south of [the city] and there's another one off to the east." With the city in friendly hands, supply convoys could use Freedom Bridge, the road/rail bridge that spanned the Amu Darya river between Afghanistan and Uzbekistan, "to open up a land bridge to provide a land route for reinforcements," Tomat said.

Mazar-e Sharif was garrisoned by a unit of the Taliban's elite Fifty-Fifth Brigade (the "Arab Brigade"), considered to be the best combat unit in their military. It was comprised mostly of foreign guerrilla fighters from the Middle-East, Central Asia, and South-East Asia, all of whom had some form of combat experience, either fighting the Soviet invasion during the 1980s or elsewhere. Members of the brigade were often deployed in smaller groups to

Northern Afghan warlord Abdul Rashid Dostum sits in his headquarters in Mazar-e-Sharif in February 1997. Dostum, a rough, bearlike figure, went through several metamorphoses: from Soviet-trained general, to regional warlord and power broker, to defeated exile, and finally to resistance commander. *AP photo/B. K. Bangash*

help reinforce regular Afghan members of Taliban. This was often achieved via threats or intimidation designed to enforce discipline and a commitment to Taliban philosophy. Brigade members were fervently committed to bin Laden's cause, and would literally fight to the death. A Defense Intelligence Agency (DIA) representative said, "They give no quarter, and they expect no quarter." The National Security Agency (NSA) targeted the brigade for destruction by signals intelligence, (SIGINT), intercepting its radio communications through the use of Arab linguists aboard air force AC-130H Spectre gunships.

One of the linguists recalled, "Every time one of the brigade's commanders went on the air, we quickly triangulated the location of his radio transmissions and blasted the shit out of his location with our Gatling gun . . . Once our bird was finished chewing up the enemy position, there usually were no more radio transmissions heard coming from that location."

The team found out just how anxious Dostum was to get the team into action. After explaining his strategy, he suddenly rose and announced, "Now we will go and kill the Taliban. We leave in fifteen minutes," leaving the surprised Americans scrambling to gather their gear. One of the team members asked how they were going to travel. "Horses," he was told, "we're riding there."

Mazar-e Sharif

Mazar-e Sharif, Afghanistan's second largest city, is located in the Balkh River Valley, approximately thirty-five miles south of Uzbekistan. The city was named in honor of the son-in-law of the Prophet Mohammed, Hazrat Ali, who was enshrined there in a blue-tiled mosque built during the twelfth century. General Abdul Rashid Dostum had controlled the city for years but was forced to give it up in May 1997 when a subordinate betrayed him and joined the Taliban.

The city had long been a major regional trading center, as well as the cultural, economic, religious, and strategic heart of northern Afghanistan. Its importance to the Northern Alliance lay in the fact that it had two airfields, one of which had the longest runway in Afghanistan. In addition, its proximity to Freedom Bridge, a road/rail bridge that spans the Amu Darya river between Afghanistan and Uzbekistan, provided a land-bridge for vehicles transporting supplies and equipment. The air and road/rail lines made the city a major economic hub. It was said that, "if a man held Mazar, then he could hold the north. And if he held the north, he could capture the capital, Kabul. From there, he could attack the desert wastes in the south, stretching from Kandahar to the border with Pakistan. His army would rule Afghanistan."

There were only enough animals for half the team, including an intelligence specialist, a medic, two communications specialists, a weapons sergeant, and the team leader. The other half stayed behind to establish a base camp and organize their logistics lifeline. Of the men selected to follow Dostum to his headquarters, four hours away, only Nutsch was an experienced horseman.

"A few of them had ridden horses when they were five or six years old that were going around and around in a little carnival or circus," Nutsch said. He studied the "tough little mountain ponies" and noted that "they looked like American mustangs from out West."

Master Sergeant Paul Evans recalled, "I don't remember seeing anything but studs. They were all male horses. And anytime you get that many male horses together, they start to fight, whether you're on their back or not. You'd get out there with a whole group of these male horses with a Type A personality and none of them would want to be last. So they'd start taking off running with you on them. Or they'd start fighting and biting each other. That was a constant hassle with the horses."

Handling the wiry mountain ponies was not the only problem. The stiff wooden saddles that were provided were too small. They were made of three boards hinged together and covered by goatskin. It did not have a pommel, so the rider had to grab the horse's mane in one hand, and the reins in the other in order to mount.

Stanton wrote, "The stirrups were hammered iron rings and they hung down from the saddle on short pieces of leather. There was no way to lengthen them." The big soldiers found them so short that their knees were jammed into their armpits. The stirrups were also too narrow for the Americans' combat boots. Just the toes fitted into the slot.

Nutsch issued a warning to his men. "Keep your feet light in the stirrups," he said. "If anyone is thrown and has a foot caught in the stirrup and the horse doesn't stop, the nearest man has to shoot the horse dead." His team looked on in wonderment. "You'll be killed if you're dragged on this rocky ground," he explained. When his team was all mounted, Nutsch pointed out a narrow, churned-up path heading north. One of the team recalled, "While we were first riding up, you're looking around thinking, 'Here I am riding a horse in the middle of Afghanistan.' It's a little weird. It's kind of a little bit further out than the things you might have thought you'd normally be doing. It was definitely interesting, though."

In *War Made New, Technology, Warfare, and the Course of History 1500 to Today*, Max Boot writes, "Two days after landing, on Sunday, October 21, ODA 595 launched its first attacks in coordination with Dostum using weapons beyond the imagination of any previous generation of cavalrymen. Employing their GPS receivers, the team identified the positions of faraway Taliban bunkers and radioed the coordinates to a B-52 bomber twenty thousand feet overhead. Only a white contrail was visible in the blue sky when satellite-directed bombs began raining down. Those initial munitions missed their targets, because Dostum, fearing for his allies' safety, would not let the Americans get close enough to the front lines to make accurate observations."

Dostum said, "You cannot get closer. I cannot let you get killed. Five hundred of my men can be killed before even one of you is scratched."

But even with the misses, Dostum was happy. The air strikes were good for his men's morale and deadly for the Taliban. Boot wrote, "He picked up a walkie-talkie tuned to the enemy frequency and told the opposing Taliban commander, 'This is General Dostum speaking. I am here, and I have brought the Americans with me . . . if you stay and fight, I will hunt you and kill you.'"

The team finally convinced Dostum to allow them to do their job. "Get me closer to those sons-a-bitches," Nutsch pleaded.

Staff Sergeant Tomat backed up the team leader. "I told General Dostum that we need to get eyes onto the targets to be effective. I would prefer to be within a kilometer of the enemy positions, so I could determine what I was striking."

Nutsch recalled, "We began to push our way down out of the mountains toward Mazar-e Sharif. As the battles went on, we got closer, and everything got better." In quick succession, Dostum's forces captured Bishqab on 21 October; Cobaki on 22 October, Chapchal on the 23rd, and Oimetan on the 25th. His success was due to a combination of precision air strikes and gutsy cavalry charges. "We'd bomb the snot out of them in the morning, right up until the ground forces [Dostum's cavalry] would move into their assault positions about mid-afternoon, and begin to engage the Taliban with direct fire," Nutsch explained. "Then we'd shift our fire onto the rear of their positions to let the Northern Alliance units [close in on] the Taliban front line positions." Dostum would give the signal and his cavalrymen would charge! "Their technique can best be described as the swarm," Nutsch said. "They were at the gallop, firing their assault weapons, not accurately, but it was scaring the hell out of the Taliban. And they would simply ride down any Taliban that attempted to resist against them or refused to surrender."

Staff Sergeant Tomat coordinated the air support. "My main focus was to strike the command and control nodes [because] I knew that once the command structure falls, the grunts [Taliban soldiers] aren't going to have the leadership to carry out the orders." Much of Tomat's success was due to the use of the Joint Direct Attack Munition. "I went after the command bunkers . . . with a B-52 loaded with six JDAMs. The fact that I was using a Vietnam-era airframe in an unconventional warfare scenario with a twenty-first century weapon was absolutely awe inspiring. I had goosebumps." The B-52 dropped its six GPS-guided bombs, and they were all direct hits.

Tomat was ecstatic. "I know the media said, 'Well, they're not accurate.' Bullshit!" he exclaimed. "They will strike the target where you want them to."

Tomat had a heart-stopping moment at a Taliban strongpoint. One of Dostum's officers misunderstood an order to standby for an air strike on the enemy position and launched a wild cavalry charge. ODA 595's men stared in disbelief as the horsemen charged toward the enemy, just seconds before the bombs exploded. One of the Green Berets recalled, "Three or four bombs hit right in the middle of the enemy position. Almost immediately after the bombs exploded, the horses swept across the objective — the enemy was so shell-shocked. I could see the horses blasting out the other side. It was the finest sight I ever saw. The men were thrilled; they were so happy. It wasn't done perfectly, but it will never be forgotten."

Air Force Lt. Col. George L. Bochain stated that "Initially the NA didn't think any of this was going to work. After a couple of successes that's all they wanted to do . . . bomb, bomb, bomb . . . they saw early on that 'we don't have to kill thousands of our guys.' This air power thing is a whole new role for them and they liked it."

As the enemy positions were overrun, the Special Forces team hit their flanks and rear with air strikes to keep them from counterattacking. Nutsch split his team into four three-man elements, and a two-man command and control element, to better support the advance.

"So these teams of three NCOs are spread out over sixty kilometers of rugged mountainous terrain," Nutsch explained. "As we pushed forward with the NA troops and forced the Taliban back, we would reposition elements of my team deeper into their rear." At times, the elements were twelve hours by horseback from him. "They remained out there for almost twelve days, on their own, calling in their own resupply drops and engaging the Taliban," he said. Another element operated on the enemy's flank, while the remaining two elements supported the Northern Alliance's assault

Charge! Dostum's horsemen in the attack. The combination of twentieth-century technology and eighteenth-century light cavalry tactics completely unhinged the Taliban defenses. *Department of Defense*

and breach of the Taliban defenses. Nutsch admitted splitting the team was risky, but, "We felt comfortable with the risk. We saw how protective General Dostum was of us. And we began to have this trust and rapport develop with [his] key commanders."

One three-man team had a close call when they were counterattacked after bombing Taliban positions near the village of Charsu. "The Taliban had established bunkers and basically settled in, prepared to fight and maintain control of the territory," the team's combat controller said. "There were vehicles, armored tanks and personnel carriers stretched across the valley. They were holding their ground and weren't about to relinquish to the Northern Alliance." An F-18 dropped several bombs, one of which exploded right in the front door of a bunker. "It was then the Taliban began a counter-attack," the controller said. "They started firing rocket-propelled grenades at our position and the fire became pretty intense . . . impacting the berm in front of us, and exploding over our heads." A B-52 responded to his call for help. It dropped eight JDAMs, giving the team a chance to break contact and scramble to another position. A navy F-14 came in next and reported that the Taliban were still pursuing the team.

Commander Chip King's section was on station. "I cleared the pilot to come in hot. In seconds the bomber dropped two large bombs on the spot we just left," the combat controller recalled. "We dropped all of our ordnance," King said, "and exited the target area." His bombs were not enough, and the Taliban threatened to overrun the team. "We heard a frantic call for more ordnance and quickly headed back to his location . . . all we had remaining was 600 rounds of 20mm SAFHEI [semi-armor piercing high explosive incendiary ammunition]." Because of the threat from missiles, aircraft were prohibited from descending to an altitude that would allow use of their cannon. King received permission to strafe—"Cleared to prosecute as necessary"—after several requests emphasizing that friendlies were about to be overrun. "We made four full strafing runs, with the guns firing out on the fifth. You could see the SAFHEI rounds exploding on impact, and the flashes of small arms fire shot back in our direction . . . we knew we were out of range, but we never discounted the 'golden bee bee' rule." These strafing runs chewed up the Taliban and gave the team an opportunity to withdraw.

Despite the ODA's success, Rumsfeld was not happy with the results, and pushed Mulholland hard to achieve more results. The colonel in turn sent

Nutsch a message, which in essence said, "When are you guys gonna get off your ass and do something?" The message reached an exhausted Nutsch at the end of a very long day, and he responded in a fit of pique, "that went all the way through the chain of command, through Mr. Rumsfeld, to President Bush."

In regards to your questions about us and the Northern Alliance just sitting around and doing nothing let me explain some of the realities on the ground.

I am advising a man on how best to employ light infantry and horse cavalry in the attack against the Taliban Russian T-55 tanks, Russian armored personnel carriers, BTRs, mortars, artillery, ZSU anti-aircraft guns and machine guns. I can't recall the US fighting like this since the Gatling gun destroyed Pancho Villa's charges in the Mexican Civil War in the early 19th century.

We have done this every day since we hit the ground. The men attack with ten AK-47 bullets per man, with their machine gun (PK) gunners with less than 100 rounds, and with less than 5 rounds per RPG-7 (rocket launchers). They have little water and less food.

I have observed a PK gunner who walked 10 miles to get into the fight who was proud to show his artificial right leg from the knee down, caused by a Talib round years ago.

We have witnessed the horse cavalry use bounding overwatch from spur to spur to carry wounded from Taliban strong points, under heavy mortar, ZSU, artillery, RPG and PK fire.

There is little medical care for the injured, only a donkey-ride to the aid station, which is a mud hut.

We are doing amazingly well with what we have. We have killed over 125 Taliban and captured over 100 while losing 8 KIA. Frankly, I am surprised that we have not been slaughtered.

We will get better at working things out as we go. It is a challenge just to have food and water for a few days. These folks have nothing. I have ridden 15 miles per day since arriving, yet everywhere I go the civilians and the "muj" soldiers are always telling me they are glad the USA has come here with planes to kill the Taliban. They all speak of their hopes for a better Afghanistan once the Taliban are gone. We killed the bastards by the bushel-full today, and we'll get more tomorrow. The team sends its regards.

By the first week in November, Dostum's forces overlooked the strategic Tiangi Gap, the southernmost enemy-controlled entrance to Mazar-e Sharif. The gap had been cut by the Darya Balkh river, creating a mile-long cut through the mountain. It was a natural choke point that was controlled by the ridges on either side. In the early pre-dawn darkness, three of Nutsch's men worked their way toward the summit. As dawn broke, they called in air strike after air strike on the enemy positions on the low ground below them. The Taliban had constructed interlocking bunkers, supported by anti-aircraft guns and a multiple rocket-launcher system.

"Our mission was to be the main push through the pass," Staff Sergeant Tomat explained. "Prior to the push—I mean immediately—a BMP 21 and a ZSU 23-2 laid down fire along the ridgeline, the valley, and back up the other ridgeline. I climbed up the hillside . . . and called in an air strike on the northern side of the pass." In response, the Taliban unleashed almost two dozen rockets that detonated among Dostum's men as they moved through the pass.

"We received the largest number of Northern Alliance casualties throughout our time there," Nutsch recalled, "three separate salvos in and near the pass. Dead and wounded fighters came back draped over a horse, led by their buddies . . . morale started to wane there in the pass." Nutsch and several of his men pushed through the carnage. "It was an incredible sight," he said.

Doug Stanton wrote, "Around them, horses lay kicking in the dirt, riddled with shrapnel. Men walked around holding their eyes, blinded. Arms and legs that had been blown high in the air landed with sickening thuds along the riverbank . . . Ali could see about sixty-five men lying dead on the canyon floor. Their horses were in pieces around them. The blasts had split one horse in half, lengthwise, so the animal was laid out on a pile of its own guts and its feet were spread in all four directions as if staked to the ground."

As Nutsch rode through the pass, "all the fighters were up in the rocks, taking cover from the rockets. And these guys saw us coming. And they just walked down to the road, lining it for a couple hundred meters. It was like something out of a Civil War print. As Pete [team member] and I rode through there on horseback, they just fell in behind us."

As the men made their way through the pass, Nutsch "called in Steve [Tomat] and he called in a couple of more air sorties on the far side of the gap." For this action, Tomat received the Silver Star. The citation noted, in part, "This attack resulted in the death of a key enemy commander, the capture of another and the destruction of 150 enemy troops, the ZSU 23-2, five personnel trucks and a bunker."

Operational Detachment Command (ODC)

An Operational Detachment Command is officially called a Battalion Headquarters Detachment and is commanded by a lieutenant colonel. Included in its organization is a command sergeant major, a personnel section (S-1), intelligence (S-2), operations (S-3), logistics (S-4), civil-military operations (S-5), communications (S-6), and a medical section. The detachment is responsible for the command and control of a Special Forces battalion, including isolating, launching, controlling, sustaining, recovering, and reconstituting ODAs. The detachment plans, coordinates, and directs Special Forces operations separately or as part of a larger force; provides command and staff personnel to establish and operate a forward operation base (FOB); and supplies advice, coordination, and staff assistance on the employment of Special Forces elements to a joint Special Operations Command, Joint Special Operations Task Force, Security Assistance Organizations, or other major headquarters.

Tomat recalled, "Mullah Rezat, the Taliban secretary of defense, was killed, and his aide was captured. The aide was slightly wounded in the arm . . . General Dostum told him to get on the radio and tell his men to give up and go home." The strikes broke the back of the Taliban defense and within a week, Dostum was advancing on Mazar-e Sharif.

Operational Detachment Command 53 (Boxer)

Operational Detachment Command 53, an eight-man element composed of Special Forces soldiers and U.S. Air Force special-tactics personnel under the command of Lt. Col. Max Bowers, was inserted on 2 November along with ODA 534 (Tiger 04). Its mission was to provide high-level liaison with General Dostum, to assist in operational planning, and to provide command and control for additional ODA teams. Ten minutes after dropping off Tiger 04, Bowers's team was on the ground close to Dostum's base camp.

Air Force Master Sgt. Bart Decker recalled, "We ended up living in a cave for the first two nights. The walls were lined with dried-up horse crap as insulation; it served two purposes, as it would be about ten degrees at night when we pulled guard duty, but [when we] got back into the cave, it was fifty to fifty-five degrees in there."

At the first meeting, Bowers asked, "What can we do for you, General?"

Dostum replied, "I want to get out of this valley. I want to take Mazar."

"We can do that," Bowers responded. "We can fight!"

CHAPTER 12

Operational Detachment Alpha 534 Tiger 04

CAPTAIN DEAN NEWMAN'S TEAM, ODA 534, was delayed by bad weather until 4 November, when it was inserted by helicopter into the Dari-a-Balkh Valley to work with Gen. Ustad Atta Mohammed, the head of the Jaamat-e-Islami militia, a predominantly ethnic Tajik political grouping. Newman knew very little about Atta Mohammed except that he was among the Tajik Mujahideen Islamists who fought against Abdul Rashid Dostum in the anti-Soviet struggle in the 1980s. The two had been bitter enemies but had agreed to settle their past differences in order to achieve the shared goal of liberating Mazar-e Sharif.

The planned offensive called for simultaneous attacks through the Darya Balkh valley in the west, and through the Darya Suf river (River of Caves) valley in the east. The advancing forces would meet at the confluence of the two rivers. At the southern edge of the Balkh Valley, where the steep mountain passes give way to fertile plains, Dostum's 2,500 horsemen and Atta's 1,000 fighters would attack on axes parallel to the Tangi Gap. A third commander, Mohaqqeq Mohammed, would conduct supporting attacks in the east to screen Dostum's flank. All three forces would then join for an assault on the heavily mined and well-defended Tangi Gap. Once they passed through the gap, the city of Mazar-e Sharif lay forty kilometers to the north. It was the job of the CIA's Team Alpha and ODA 534 to coordinate the movement of the three forces.

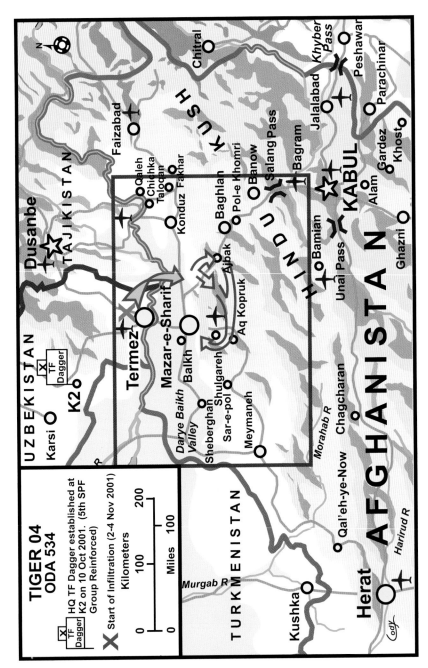

Tiger 04, Operational Detachment Alpha 534, was assigned to support Gen. Ustad Atta Mohammed for a two-pronged attack on Mazar-e Sharif. *Bill Cody*

ODA 534's flight to Afghanistan was anything but comfortable. "We'd been flying about six to six and a half hours," Newman recalled. "Because of the danger of enemy fire, [the helicopter] flew low to the ground, very fast, and it's freezing. All the windows are open, the doors are open. We hit the ground and there's snow everywhere. We're freezing!" Two dozen of Atta's men were waiting to help them off-load supplies and equipment. "We've brought food and medical supplies, [we're trying to] launch all that stuff off the back of the bird and sit it on the ground," Newman said. "Because there's snow, it's just sliding off the mountain." They finally got the supplies loaded on burros. The soldiers mounted horses for the six hour trek over a treacherous, snow-covered mountain trail to Atta Mohammed's headquarters near the village of Ak Kupruk. They arrived early in the morning, battered, bruised, and exhausted. Atta was waiting for them.

Doug Stanton described the Tajik leader as "looking regal, wearing a knee-length blouse, matching cotton pants, a scarf, black leather boots, and beige Pakol hat."

Captain Newman recalled, "He made an excellent first impression on us. He was very concerned about our comfort, our welfare, and our protection." The Americans also wanted to make a good impression. "We wanted

The snow-peaked Hindu Kush mountains posed a significant problem for the helicopters. *defenseimagery.mil*

Tech Sergeant Brian Scott guides the uploading of a 15,000-pound BLU-82 "Daisy Cutter" bomb aboard an MC-130E Talon I. *USAF photo by Captain Patrick Nichols*

A drogue parachute pulls the "Daisy Cutter" from the ramp of an MC-130E Talon I. *USAF photo by Captain Patrick Nichols*

to, first and foremost, to establish a rapport," Newman emphasized, "and to get to know him." After the introduction, the team was led to a walled compound, which contained a low-roofed mud house, their quarters for the night.

Early the next morning the Special Forces officer met with Atta for a planning session. "Right off the bat, we got down to business," Newman said. "There wasn't a lot of time wasted on formality or protocol. We began

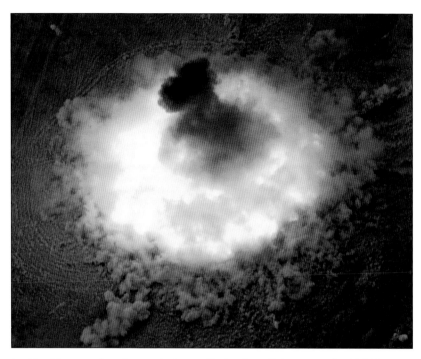

Looking like a small nuclear explosion, a "Daisy Cutter" detonates—the 15,000-pound "Daisy Cutter" is the largest non-nuclear conventional explosive device in the military's arsenal. *Department of Defense*

talking about the battle plan for our first engagement." The first order of business was to capture the village of Ak Kupruk, a Taliban stronghold.

Chief Warrant Officer Stu Mansfield explained that "at the time, General Atta's forces were engaged daily . . . [it] was a full-blown battle with mortars and a lot of gunfire. We started identifying targets and bringing some conventional munitions to the table." The team split into two elements, one to handle supply and logistics and the other to bomb the Taliban positions.

Their first effort was disappointing. The bombs did not hit their intended target, because the sun heated the air in the valley, causing a thick brown haze that literally bent the laser beam. The bomb homed in on the laser and landed off-target. "The planes were pretty high . . . but the [Afghans] definitely saw the impact of the bombs," Mansfield said.

The next day went better. The team ordered a drop of a BLU-82, nicknamed the "Daisy Cutter." Mansfield called it something else. "The Motherfucker of All Bombs!" he exclaimed. The bomb weighed 15,000 pounds, the largest non-nuclear conventional explosive device in the military's arsenal. It was rolled off the ramp of a C-130 at no less than 6,000 feet.

A parachute slowed its fall. A thirty-eight-inch extender fuse allowed it to detonate just above the ground.

Stanton described the effect: "The barrel-shaped container exploded above ground and vaporized any plant or animal within 250 yards from ground zero. The concussion created a flash of over-pressure totaling 2,000 pounds per square inch." In this instance, the bomb was dropped in the vacant desert as a warning to the Taliban that bad things were in store for them. A few minutes later another BLU-85 was dropped in the same area. The Taliban took the hint and evacuated the village.

Newman's team reached the southern end of the Tanghi gap and prepared to spend the night. Dostum's camp was located a half mile further south on the same road. The two commanders "had a big meeting, almost a council of sorts, where we discussed the offensive operations against Mazar," Newman recalled. "We sort of pieced together our battle plan . . . Mazar still had the headquarters of one of the Taliban corps, as well as of one of the Taliban army headquarters. We knew they were well fortified. They had a lot of artillery and a lot of combat power up there. So at that point, we still saw Mazar as our goal, but also as our most formidable battle—at least in our perception at that time." The two agreed that neither would leave for the city before dawn; however Atta did not abide by the agreement. He started moving his force just prior to sunset. Newman claimed that the Taliban were fleeing the city and Atta wanted to "negotiate their surrender or defection."

Doug Stanton wrote, "Hundreds of Taliban vehicles—their headlights bobbing in the dark and visible for miles—were fleeing the city for Konduz, eight hours to the east . . . [and] Atta couldn't wait any longer . . . his prospective power base was slipping away."

Taliban commander Vahid Mojdeh blamed the defeat on their inflexible chain of command. "The leaders would take no orders from anyone except Mullah Omar," he said. "The leaders screamed into the phone that 'we are under aerial bombardment, the lines at Mazar-e Sharif are being attacked from the ground, and inside the city there is an uprising forming. Mullah Omar must tell me what to do.'" Mullah Omar at the time was in hiding because "he was afraid his location would be pinpointed and bombed." Yet he had sent untrained Pakistani volunteers to the city, even though they knew little about it, nor about how to deal with American air power. "These people [Pakistani volunteers] thought they would be engaging American troops in a land war, face to face," Mojdeh said.

With the city within arm's length, Atta "began to mass his forces—vehicles, horses, whatever he could get his hands on, either stolen or taken

A C-130 Hercules transport aircraft seems to thread its way through the peaks on its way to landing at the Bagram, Afghanistan, airfield. *USAF photo by Tech. Sgt. Cecilio M. Ricardo Jr.*

from the Taliban, al-Qaeda, or borrowed from the local population," Newman said. "It was quite a sight. We had mounted troops; we had BMPs and mechanized assets going through the gap."

The sight of the city in the early morning sunlight brought new life to Atta's exhausted fighters. They began a mad dash, according to Stanton. "The men atop their horses sat up and spurred their reluctant animals and began galloping across the plain. The men in trucks raced their engines and shot off in pursuit. Those on foot began running, swinging up to one of the passing trucks if they could."

One team member described his feelings as he approached the city. "We didn't know what to expect. We were locked and loaded and didn't know whether or not there were any Taliban left in the city." However, they were pleasantly surprised: the Taliban had fled.

They tried to put a brave face on the rout: "It is a tactical withdrawal and our forces are grouping," a spokesman in Kabul told Afghan Islamic Press. "There is nothing to worry about. We left these places as part of our strategy."

Sergeant First Class Bobby (pseudonym) said, "It was like a scene out of a World War II movie. . . . The streets, the roadsides, even outside the city, were just lined with people, cheering and clapping their hands and [there were] just celebrations everywhere."

The celebrations turned out to be dangerous because "a lot of what they do was fire weapons into the air," a team member said. "That's one of their biggest party favors."

Atta entered Mazar just prior to sunset on 9 November and established his command post near the center of the city. A group of his men raced to the airport on the western edge of the city and claimed it for him, giving him an advantage over Dostum. Access via air then had to be approved by Atta.

While much of the Taliban and al-Qaeda force had fled the city, the fighting was not quite over. There was still an estimated six hundred hard-core Pakistani Taliban and al-Qaeda fighters holding out in the former Sultan Razzia Girls' School near the heart of Mazar-e Sharif. The school took up an entire city block and was located in a heavily populated residential district, only a few blocks from the Blue Mosque, the Shrine of Hazrat Ali, the cousin and son-in-law of the Prophet Muhammad. Several emissaries who tried to convince the trapped men to surrender were shot and killed.

An Alliance soldier complained, "When the Mujahideen went near, they [the Pakistani Taliban] started shooting." Furious, Dostum ordered the Special Forces to bomb the building. The first JDAM scored a direct hit in the center of the building. Three more followed, wrecking havoc inside the school and killing more than 450 Taliban and al-Qaeda fighters. With their elimination, Mazar-e Sharif was completely liberated.

Reporters from *The Telegraph* wrote that the city's "citizens celebrated their liberation from four years of Taliban rule. Women cast off their burqas and men shaved off beards in gestures of contempt for their former repressive rulers."

CHAPTER 13

Operational Detachment Alpha 585 Tiger 03

*"Our mission is not necessarily to outfight the enemy.
We would rather out think them."*
—Master Sgt. John Bolduc

THREE HEAVILY ARMED MEN CROUCHED in the darkness, listening intently to the unmistakable sound of a helicopter. Suddenly, two blacked-out MH-47E Chinooks appeared out of the night sky and cautiously settled onto the dirt landing zone close to their position. Dirt and debris from the rotor wash blew over them, but none of the men stirred, knowing full well that any sudden movement on their part might trigger a deadly response from the aircraft's gunners. In the moon's dim light they saw several men carefully making their way down the ramp, bent almost double from the weight of the bundles they were carrying. At a whispered signal from their leader, the three men rose upright and cautiously moved forward, their weapons purposely pointing toward the ground in a non-threatening manner. One raised his hand in greeting. "How you doing?" he shouted to the new arrivals over the whine of the bird's turbine engines. "Isn't this an odd place to meet?"

The rendezvous between Master Sgt. Armand J. (John) Bolduc and Breen (Pseudonym), the CIA operative and former U.S. Marine captain,

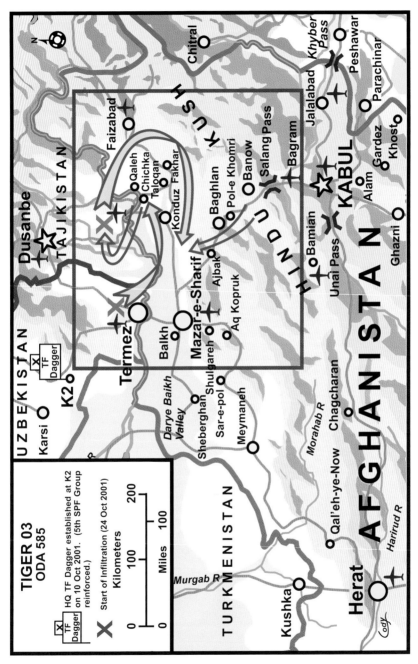

Tiger 03, Operational Detachment Alpha 585, supported Gen. Bariullah Khan for the assault and capture of Konduz, the last Taliban stronghold in the north. *Bill Cody*

took place near the village of Dasht-e-Qaleh in the upper northeast corner of Afghanistan, on the Tajikistan border. Breen had entered the country weeks before to make contact with the local resistance leader, Gen. Bariullah Khan, and smooth the way for Bolduc's ODA 585, code-named Tiger 03. After exchanging brief greetings, Breen introduced Bolduc to his companions, Afghans who spoke very little English. Then, with a shouted "good luck" and a wave goodbye, the officer and one of the Afghans ran aboard one of the remaining helicopters as it lifted off, leaving the team in the care of the remaining Afghan.

Bolduc realized that communicating with the man was going to be difficult because none of the team spoke Dari, the predominant local language—hand signs would have to do until he could find an interpreter. As the helicopter disappeared into the night sky, he shrugged his shoulders and thought to himself, "This is it." He looked at his watch and saw that it was just past 0200 on 24 October. "We're ready," he murmured and motioned the Afghan to lead them away from the zone.

The Afghan guide led the team to a safe house, where they met General Bariullah, a youngish commander with years of combat experience fighting the Taliban. The team found him skeptical of their abilities. "I have been here for three years with hundreds of men and could do nothing," he said. "What are you going to do with just ten men?"

Bariullah kept them cooling their heels until the team was able to convince him to give them a chance to prove their worth. After two days of sitting on their hands, Bariullah suddenly announced that he would take them to the front, a line of observation posts that ran along a rugged piece of high ground about forty miles northeast of the city of Konduz. They set up shop in one of the positions that provided excellent observation of the Taliban positions on the opposite ridge. Bolduc immediately called in an air strike. Unfortunately, the first bombing runs completely missed the target, embarrassing them, and causing Bariullah to be even more skeptical. "The first and second missed," he said. "They landed between the two front lines. No one was hurt, but it was behind our lines. We didn't think much of it, because some of them missed."

A second strike by two Marine Corps F/A-18 Hornets redeemed the situation. They made four passes over the Taliban positions, destroying two enemy command bunkers and several sections of trench line. Bariullah was elated. "The third was an exact hit," he exclaimed, "that's where the Taliban are."

Bolduc was pleased. "We proved to him [Bariullah] that we could be an asset, and this was only our third day in-country."

One team member recalled, "After that, when we got back to the commander's house, people were lining up, clapping and slapping us on the back."

A radio message brought news from Saifullah, a front-line commander. "That's the target, all of them were great. They hit Arab positions." The Alliance reported that the Taliban radio was alive with calls for ambulances and reports of deaths. "We ask the United States to send a hundred planes a day," Saifullah said. "And we ask them to drop their bombs in the right place."

The team continued to pound the Taliban positions for the next month, softening up the enemy for Bariullah's men. The air strikes would last throughout the day, and then an AC-130 Spectre gunship would take over during the hours of darkness. The combination of the two kept the Taliban off-balance and unable to mount a credible defense . . . except on one occasion when Bariullah decided to attack without informing the team. He launched a frontal assault that was bloodily repulsed, which resulted in the loss of several hundred of his men.

"They were like ducks in a barrel with no air cover," Bolduc said. Three journalists were also lost when they tried to escape Taliban fire and fell off the back of a Northern Alliance vehicle. One was shot out of hand and the other two, both females, were captured, raped, and killed.

A Taliban spokesman said, "From today, I want to tell journalists that if in the future they use wrong information from coalition forces or NATO, we will target those journalists and media. We have the Islamic right to kill these journalists and media."

After the failed assault, Bariullah apologized to Bolduc, explaining that he wanted to take credit for the victory without American help. Breen said that "Bariullah was more interested in holding press conferences than managing his area of operations."

Berntsen heard him giving an interview over the radio. "Bariullah told a group of Iranian journalists in Persian that the United States didn't know what it was doing. He stated that if he were given control of the air, he would win the conflict in a week."

Despite the fact that his remarks upset the Americans, they continued to target the Taliban defenses in Taloqan. The air strikes resumed the next day, enabling the Alliance fighters to overrun the enemy defenses, capture the town of Chickha, and continue to push south toward Konduz. In two more days, Bariullah's force was on the outskirts of Konduz, the last Taliban stronghold in the north.

CHAPTER 14

Operational Detachment Alpha 553 Tiger 07

TEAM DELTA, AN EIGHT-MAN CIA team, was inserted into the southern Hindu Kush to support Dr. Mohammad Karim Khalili, the senior Hazara military commander in the Bamiyan region, northwest of Kabul. Khalili, a one-time warlord and Shiite cleric, headed the *Hizb-e-Wahdat Hazara* (Islamic Unity Party of Afghanistan), a primarily Shia Hazara force estimated to consist of between 15,000 and 30,000 men. The *Hizb-e-Wahdat* was the second most powerful military organization that opposed the Taliban. Its Hazara members were closely allied with Iran, who founded the party in 1989 and provided it with economic and military aid after the Soviet defeat. In 1995, Khalili took over the reins of the party and led the resistance against the Taliban after they killed its leader. A year later, the various Hazara groups banded together with the Northern Alliance.

Khalili and his Hazara fighters played a key role in defeating the Taliban assault against Mazar-e Sharif. When the city fell in 1998, the Taliban massacred thousands of Hazaras—any male above thirteen—forcing the survivors to flee to the mountains. Khalili escaped and crossed over the border to Iran, where he remained until February 2001. The Hazaras suffered severe oppression at the hands of the ethnic Pashtun Taliban, who declared them infidels and targeted them for elimination.

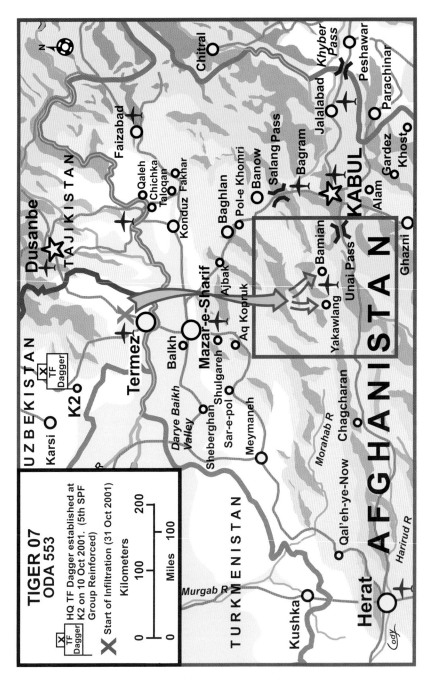

Tiger 07, Operational Detachment Alpha 553, was tasked to support Dr. Mohammad Karim Khalili, the senior Hazara military commander in the Bamiyan region. *Bill Cody*

The world's tallest statue of Buddha, measuring 175 feet from head to toe, as it appeared in 1999 in Bamiyan, ninety miles west of Kabul. Mullah Mohammad Omar ordered the destruction of all statues in Afghanistan, claiming that the Buddha statues violated the Islamic code forbidding idolatry. *AP photo*

Afghan villagers sit near the hole left behind after the Bamiyan Buddha statue was destroyed by the Taliban, 2 January 2002. The statues were part of a large network of smaller temples built right into the side of the mountain around 1,500 years ago, when Bamiyan played a central role in the region's East–West trade route. *AP photo/Brennan Linsley*

"Hazaras are not Muslim, they are Shia," a notorious Taliban commander ranted. "They are *kafir* [infidels] . . . we will kill you . . . wherever you go we will catch you. If you go up, we will pull you down by your feet; if you hide below, we will pull you up by your hair." Team Delta made contact with Khalili and then set out to familiarize themselves with the area.

On the last day of October, a dozen Special Forces soldiers of Tiger 07 (ODA-553) joined Team Delta just west of the city of Bamiyan ("the place of shining light"), the cultural capital of the Hazaras. Bamiyan was the site of the "Buddhas of Bamiyan," the largest examples of standing Buddha statues in the world. In March 2001, the Taliban minister for the propagation of virtue and prevention of vice ordered the destruction of the ancient statues, declaring them "false idols." Despite appeals from governments around the world, the Taliban used RPGs, artillery rounds, and finally a truck load of dynamite to turn them into rubble.

The Taliban ambassador to Pakistan, Abdul Salam Zaeef noted, "The time of the destruction of these monuments was tiresome and particularly hard on me. [However,] the destruction was within the boundaries of Sharia law . . . and a case of bad timing." Zaeef told a Japanese delegation that "the Buddha statues are made out of stone by the hands of men [and] hold no real value for religion." The Japanese delegation included the prime minister, who offered to pay the Taliban for the statues if they could take them apart and reassemble them in Japan. Zaeef contemptuously dismissed their offer.

Tiger 07's mission was to provide air support for Khalili's forces in an attack on Bamiyan. The two-pronged attack called for one Hazara group of about 1,500 men to attack from the southwest, while another group about the same size would attack from the northwest. Team Delta and Tiger 07 split into two sections to support Khalili's forces. On 6 and 7 November, they climbed several thousand feet into the mountains to reach a vantage point overlooking the Taliban positions. Robin Moore wrote that the northern team's observation post was located at 11,000 feet, while the southern team's position was even higher. He noted that "Hazara escorts saved the men from exhaustion in the high altitude by supplying horses to carry their equipment."

The northern team got into action first as American bombers arrived and began striking Taliban positions. Moore wrote that the Taliban used a Russian ZSU-23-4 to shoot at the Special Forces. "As the Soviet antiaircraft system thumped away, putting heavy but ineffective fire on their positions, Tiger 07 called for fire support." An F/A-18 Super Hornet responded to their call for help and "the ZSU was instantly reduced to a smoking ruin." From their position on the peak, the team could plainly see the entire battle-field. They called in flight after flight of aircraft. "The Green Berets of Tiger 07 took advantage of perfect weather and the bonanza of air platforms. They worked over the entire Taliban frontline and its rear positions until nightfall," Moore wrote.

A member of Team Delta described Tiger 07 as "doing outstanding work, hammering the Taliban with airstrikes" during the two-day battle. The Taliban positions were so badly damaged that Khalili decided to launch his attack. By late afternoon on 11 November, Bamiyan was firmly in the hands of the Hazara after the bulk of the Taliban forces withdrew. A handful of die-hard fanatics stayed behind to slow the attack. For the most part, they were ineffective and were quickly overrun. Iranian state radio reported, "Anti-Taliban forces captured the central Afghan town of Bamiyan on Sunday after the provincial governor surrendered to the opposition. Bamiyan Gov. Mowlawi Islam and three hundred of his troops surrendered and joined the (opposition) forces." Iranian radio was silent on the bombing of its embassy. The building had been targeted for destruction because it had been identified as housing a large number of Arab fighters.

The two American teams established a command post and continued to work with Khalili's forces in ferreting out Taliban remnants in the surrounding area. The CIA team (Delta) split into two elements. The team leader remained in Bamiyan with Khalili, while the other worked the southern area. Gary Berntsen described its leader as "a Farsi-speaking SAD paramilitary officer, who was on his first deployment." During a meeting with Berntsen, the officer mentioned that he had contact with a Taliban intelligence officer who might be able to pinpoint Osama bin Laden's location. Berntsen gave him approval to pursue the lead.

"I'd love to have a face-to-face discussion with the contact," Berntsen said. The five-man team proceeded to the city of Ghazni to meet the informer. "If he is willing to help us capture bin Laden, we'll do business with him . . . if he jerks us around, we'll take him prisoner," the SAD officer pledged. The officer was true to his word. When the informant sent two other agents instead of coming himself, the two emissaries were picked up and bundled off to an interrogation center. Team Delta received a congratulatory message from CIA headquarters. "Capturing the number two and three in the Taliban intelligence was a good day's work."

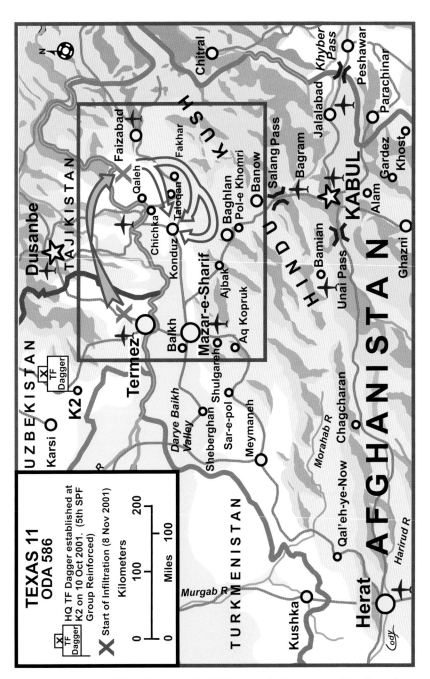

Texas 11, Operational Detachment Alpha 586 was tasked to support Gen. Daoud Khan for the attack on the city of Taloqan. *Bill Cody*

CHAPTER 15

Operational Detachment Alpha 586 Texas 11

A S BARIULLAH'S FORCE PUSHED TOWARD Konduz from the north, Gen. Daoud Khan was advancing from the southeast. ODA 586, code named Texas 11, under the command of Capt. Patrick O'Hara, was inserted on 8 November to support Daoud. Unlike many of the teams, Texas 11 did not fly in a Night Stalkers aircraft. Rather it was inserted by a barely airworthy Russian MI-8 HIP helicopter, which had seen better days. Steve Coll wrote in *Danger Close, The Tactical Air Controllers in Afghanistan and Iraq* that the team dubbed the helicopter "'SGLI Air;' SGLI stood for Serviceman's Group Life Insurance, the life insurance provided to every military member."

Air Force Master Sgt. Tim Stamey took one look at it and despaired. "It was leaking—I mean, not dripping but literally a stream of fuel coming out of the bottom of it." There were unrepaired bullet holes in the fuselage, wires hanging out of the ceiling, and only remnants of paint on the outer aluminum skin. More importantly, regular maintenance was a mere memory to its crew. Robin Moore noted that "it literally took a crew engineer working full time just to keep it from dropping out of the sky."

Despite Texas 11's apprehensions, the old bird delivered them safely, much to their surprise and relief. A security element of Daoud's fighters greeted the team and escorted them to a safe house near the village of

Farkhar where they spent the night. The next day they met Daoud, a tall, strapping man in his mid-thirties. They received a polite reception; Daoud gave them Mujahideen hats and scarves, but gave them a "No thank you, we don't need your help" to their "How can we assist you" question.

Stamey recalled, "He did not want to accept any help from us. So he left, and we're sitting there and we're like, 'Now what the heck are we supposed to do?'" They didn't have to wait long. That afternoon, one of Daoud's commanders asked them if they wanted to see the front lines.

"Oh, yeah, love to!" O'Hara enthusiastically responded. When they got there, they found Daoud launching an attack on the city of Taloqan without bothering to tell them.

"We get up there and one of their tank officers is up on the hill and he's pointing out enemy positions," Stamey said. "We see a ruckus coming up this road . . . there's guys on horses, trucks, and a couple of T-55s [Soviet-made tanks]."

The Americans asked what the heck was going on, and the Afghan responded, "Oh, we're doing our big offensive!" The team immediately requested air support, but before it could arrive, a jubilant Daoud had seized the city, placing his forces only thirty-seven miles from Konduz.

Bay Fang, a *U.S. News* correspondent wrote, "At Taloqan's high school, the commander held a rally before hundreds of men, all dressed in tunics, with an assortment of weaponry and recited the Koran." He ended an emotional speech with, "'At this moment, they [Taliban] are defeated. Congratulations to all the people of Afghanistan!' A cry went up 'Allah Akbar!' . . . and the men head off down the road, a river of fighters surging toward the front." The city's residents were exceedingly grateful to be liberated from the Taliban.

"Taloqan bustled and heaved with returning refugees and Northern Alliance fighters," Jon Lee Anderson, author and staff writer for *The New Yorker*, noted in *The Lion's Grave, Dispatches from Afghanistan*. "Military vehicles, their horns blaring, careened around slow-moving donkey carts, darting children, and porters pulling handcarts located with goods . . . occasionally, a helicopter clattered overhead, and several times a day B-52s added their dull roar to the din."

The capture of Taloqan represented a significant political victory for Daoud. It had once been the headquarters of the esteemed Northern Alliance leader Gen. Ahmad Shah Massoud until the Taliban overran the city in January 2001 after a bloody siege that cost the lives of hundreds of its citizens. After capturing the city, the Taliban conducted a ruthless campaign to cower the remaining population and to instill its brand of Islamic fundamentalism. Anyone who did not respond was dealt with harshly. After Northern Alliance soldiers found a mass grave containing the bodies of seventy women and children, Daoud, who had been Massoud's aide, was not in a forgiving mood.

"For the foreign terrorists . . . there will be no negotiations, we will not deal with them, they are killers," Daoud said, citing their alleged role in the assassination of Northern Alliance leader Ahmed Shah Massoud. "The foreigners are living between life and death. They are desperate and they are trying everything." It came as no surprise that retribution was foremost in the minds of the local citizenry. Newsmen reported that al-Qaeda captives were often killed by the vengeful populace under the watchful eyes of Northern Alliance soldiers, who offered only token resistance.

When Texas 11 reached the city, O'Hara divided the team into a three-element rotation schedule. While one section directed close air support and another rested, the third geared up for the next day. On 13 November, Daoud continued the attack toward Konduz. As his men passed through a mountain pass, they were counterattacked.

"All of a sudden, we started getting shwacked with tank rounds," Stamey recalled. "They're just losing vehicles left and right."

The attack stalled and then was forced to retreat back to Taloqan. The setback was totally unexpected. Daoud anticipated that after capturing the city so easily, the advance to Konduz would be quick and relatively bloodless. A very sober leader approached O'Hara and demanded, "We want air and we want it now!"

Stamey recalled, "We got up there where we could see inside this gap—you could see all the forces massing for a counterattack. I took F-18s and we shwacked them!" Daoud abandoned the ground attack for almost two weeks, while Texas 11 softened up the Taliban positions with air strikes. A refugee eyewitness said, "On one hill there were a lot of Taliban, and after the U.S. bombs hit, there was nothing living there."

The aerial assault spread terror among the Taliban and caused several hundred of them to defect. They brought four tanks and a number of brand new pickup trucks with them. As they crossed the front lines, Northern Alliance soldiers cheered them. According to Afghan custom, when a soldier said he was through, he would be welcomed back into the fold. A CNN correspondent in the area said that at least 300 Taliban fighters had already defected to the Northern Alliance. "It was quite a sight. These Taliban were welcomed as heroes with huge fanfare," he was quoted as saying.

The 509th Bomb Wing at Whiteman Air Force Base, Missouri, took center stage in the war on terrorism when six B-2 Spirits participated in air strikes over Afghanistan during the first three days of Operation Enduring Freedom. All six of the B-2 sorties were longer than forty hours, with the longest lasting more than forty-four hours. *U.S. Air Force photo by Tech. Sgt. John Lasky*

The Taliban vehicles were immediately appropriated and plastered with posters of Ahmed Shah Massoud and became officially the property of the Northern Alliance. Anderson visited Daoud's headquarters in Taloqan the day after the defection. "There was a Toyota pickup truck smeared with mud outside the gate. Daoud's men told me that the truck had been driven across enemy lines and into town during the night by six Taliban field commanders who had defected, along with their three hundred fighters."

Jon Lee Anderson talked with two of them. One said that he had defected "for the good of the country." Anderson was not convinced. "His decision appeared to have more to do with survival."

The mass defections weakened the Taliban defenses, but Daoud wanted the Special Forces to continue hitting the enemy with air strikes. O'Hara described their procedures: "Bomb the mountain, then hit it with artillery, then take the mountain. The next day we are going to the next mountain . . . trying to advance as quickly as possible."

On 15 November, the team reported that air strikes had accounted for an estimated 386 Taliban killed or wounded. Two days later they reported another 300 casualties. At one point the Taliban came up on the Northern

An Air Force weapons loader from the 28th Air Expeditionary Wing preps a 2,000-pound bomb to be loaded into a B-1B Lancer bomber in October 2001. *U.S. Air Force photo by Staff Sgt. Shane Cuomo*

Alliance radio and begged Daoud's men to turn the Americans over to them, promising money in return. The team was surprised to learn that both sides used the same radios, just different channels. "Taliban's channel one, we're channel three," they were told.

Daoud's force continued to drive the Taliban toward Konduz, the only haven of safety for them in northern Afghanistan. At the same time, Bariullah, with Tiger 03, was closing in from the north, and Dostum and Tiger 02 were fast approaching from the west. The Taliban were trapped, their only salvation was to surrender. Daoud did not give them much wiggle-room. "We are ready to enter the city; those that resist will be killed."

Surrender negotiations began immediately, but they were made difficult by the presence of more than two thousand hard-core foreign fighters—Arab mercenaries, Pakistanis, and Chechens—who threatened to kill anyone that surrendered. They preferred martyrdom to surrender. One Northern Alliance commander said that the foreign fighters had killed several local Taliban officials who wanted to give up the city. Of the estimated 7,000 to 10,000 Taliban fighters in the area, more than half were Afghans who were willing to lay down their arms. The talks dragged on, with details constantly changing as the Taliban commanders tried to strike the best bargain. All the while, men were dying under American air power, artillery, and rocket fire.

The talks were further complicated by the presence of dozens of Pakistani intelligence officers, ISI military advisers, and top al-Qaeda officials who had been fighting alongside the Taliban and got caught in the city. Pakistan did not want their involvement with the Taliban exposed. Eyewitnesses reported that starting on 25 November and over a period of three nights Pakistani aircraft evacuated their officers, and much of the al-Qaeda leadership, over a secret air bridge. The Northern Alliance commanders were furious and claimed that the Unites States was involved with assisting the evacuation effort. "How else could these planes have penetrated the American air shield?" Daoud grumbled.

Noted Pakistani journalist Ahmed Rashid claimed that a U.S. intelligence analyst told him that President Pervez Musharraf had personally appealed to President Bush to allow the evacuation. It was reported that Vice President Cheney took charge of handling the details, which included a special air corridor to fly the evacuees to Pakistan. One senior American diplomat alleged that the United States got snookered by the Pakistanis because the evacuation was supposed to be limited; instead, as many as several thousand were airlifted out, according to India's army intelligence service. Frustrated American observers dubbed it "Operation Evil Airlift." Rumsfeld summarily dismissed questions about the airlift. "Well, if we see them, we shoot them down," he declared lamely.

By 23 November, Daoud's forces were fifteen miles west of Konduz, near the tiny village of Bangi. The Taliban positions extended across one end of a small valley, and the Northern Alliance forces held the other end. "Hundreds of Mujahideen armed with rocket propelled grenade launchers and Kalashnikovs began arriving in trucks and pickups at the Bangi front lines," Anderson noted. One of Texas 11's four-man elements worked their way up a mountain overlooking the enemy's positions.

"It was really, really steep—rocks and literally climbing and scratching and pulling on all fours," Stamey explained. "About this time it was starting to be daylight and we could see the whole valley." The Taliban spotted them and started shooting with a machine gun. "He's got us pinned down in a trench," Stamey said. "Our guys are returning fire and I'm trying to get the damn [satellite] antennae set up." There wasn't enough room in the trench, so Stamey had to get out and erect it under fire. "I finally got the thing set up and called the ASOC [Air Support Operations Center]. 'Hey, we're pinned down [and] I need aircraft in here now!'" Stamey was told that a B-52 was about ten minutes out. "I brought him in on the DShK and he obliterated the ridgeline," Stamey recalled.

Anderson observed the airstrike. "A B-52 looped ponderously overhead, dropping bombs on the Taliban positions. B-52s are deceptively unthreatening. They drop their bombs while making banking curves, and there is a strange delay between the curves and the explosions, which appear to occur far from the bombers' flight path. On its third or fourth run, the B-52 dropped a tremendous bomb on the summit of the ridge . . . sending a giant brown-gray cloud of dust and dirt cascading down the mountainside."

Daoud's men advanced under the protective umbrella of American air power. In eight days, according to Texas 11's bomb damage assessment reports, 51 Taliban trucks, 44 bunkers, 12 tanks, and 4 ammunition dumps were destroyed. In addition, they reported more than 2,000 enemy soldiers were killed or wounded. On one day, Stamey reported that a B-52 checked in to drop its ordnance. A woman's voice, "sounding like an angel," filled the

airwaves. The Afghan interpreters "just stopped dead in their tracks," Stamey recalled. They could not believe that a woman was not only flying the aircraft but was going to drop bombs on the Taliban.

At one point, Stamey called in an aircraft armed with CBU-100 cluster bombs [each bomb filled with multiple smaller bomblets] on a large mass of Taliban in the open. The bombs completely demoralized the survivors and sent them fleeing toward Konduz. With this defeat, the pace of negotiations picked up. After four more days of sporadic fighting, several hundred Taliban surrendered. "The men [Daoud's fighters] were screaming 'Talib! Talib!'" Anderson recalled. "And some of

An Air Force B-52 bomber from the 28th Air Expeditionary Wing takes off from Diego Garcia for a combat mission on 22 October 2001. Note the row of B-1 Lancers parked in the foreground. *U.S. Air Force photo by Staff Sgt. Shane Cuomo* them were pointing down the right side of the valley, where billowing dust clouds followed several pickup trucks headed in our direction."

Jon Lee Anderson had a difficult time telling the difference between the Taliban and Daoud's fighters. "There seemed to me to be precious little to distinguish them. Usually, the Taliban came across the front in vehicles covered in mud, to avoid detection from the air, but they wore virtually the same clothes as the Mujahideen: pocketed vests, patou blankets, tunic, and pantaloon outfits, a motley assortment of winter blankets, turbans, and scarves. They also carried the same weapons: Russian-made Kalashnikovs and anti-tank weapons." Anderson thought the Taliban had fuller, longer beards than the Northern Alliance and "wore black turbans, sometimes wrapped Tuareg style over their faces and necks, against the wind and cold. Their commanders usually wear white turbans. The trademark headgear of the Mujahideen is a flat-brimmed felt cap (brown, gray, beige, or white) called the pakul." Anderson thought the Taliban had more discipline than the Northern Alliance soldiers, who seemed to be "an unruly, noisy rabble most of the time."

While Daoud advanced on Konduz from the east, Dostum on the northwest side of the city was conducting his own negotiations. Mullah Mohammed

Arriving in theater only days before, F-15E Strike Eagles prepare to fly their first bombing missions into Afghanistan from a base in Southwest Asia on 17 October 2001. Here, the weapon system operator on the flight lead for the mission, call sign "Pugs," pre-flights his F-15E. *U.S. Air Force photo by Master Sgt. Dave Nolan*

Fazel, the senior remaining Taliban commander, continued to stall until Dostum finally demanded, "Put your guns down, take your jackets off, and march in here or we'll turn the Americans on to you with their death ray." Fazel caved in, but not before receiving a "gift" of $500,000 and safe passage to Herat. The agreement stipulated that the Afghan Taliban would be allowed to either join the Northern Alliance or go home. The foreign fighters were left out in the cold; their fate was to be decided by Dostum. Fazel told them to give up their weapons, but failed to tell them that they would be taken into custody.

Amir Jan, a former Taliban commander said, "The foreigners thought that after surrendering to the Northern Alliance they would be free. They didn't think they would be put in jail." Following the surrender, Texas 11 and Daoud's men quickly moved into the city.

"There was a lot of activity on the street," Anderson recalled. "Many ordinary people, men and youths, were walking around, smiling, and giving the thumbs-up sign."

Hundreds of Taliban and foreign fighters were rounded up and disarmed. However, their captors did a poor job of searching them. The

Northern Alliance troops under General Dostum's command in Mazar-e Sharif take a break on a wall in the median of the town's busiest street in December 2001. It was difficult to tell the anti-Taliban apart from their enemies. They wore the same clothes and carried identical weapons. One American thought the Taliban had fuller beards and "wore black turbans." *Department of Defense photo by Staff Sgt. Cecilio Ricardo, USAF*

CHAPTER 16

Uprising in the House of War

"The Castle of Death"
—Justin Huggler, *The Independent* (UK)

QALA-I-JANGI LOOKED LIKE SOMETHING OUT of the Middle Ages. It was constructed of adobe-style mud bricks and was almost three quarters of a mile in diameter. It was complete with moats, ramparts, and parapets atop massive sloped walls that were sixty feet high and forty-five feet thick. The thick walls contained a labyrinth of barracks, store rooms, and passages. Inside there were two large compounds with open spaces, trees, and one-story buildings that were separated by a dividing wall. The northern quadrant held Dostum's headquarters, while the southern half contained the armory. The main entrance to the fort was located on the eastern side. The fort had seen a number of occupants come and go—the Royal Afghan Army, the Soviets, anti-Taliban Mujahideen, and the Taliban. In November 2001, Dostum chased the Taliban out and claimed it for his headquarters. When the Taliban pulled out, they abandoned huge stocks of weapons and ammunition that remained in the fort after Dostum took over.

24 November

Tensions were high among the foreign fighters as they arrived at Qala-I-Jangi. Most of them believed they had not surrendered and resented being held inside the prisonlike fortress. Eyewitnesses said that, while they were dirty and disheveled, their eyes and facial expressions registered pure hatred. The Uzbeks among them were ecstatic. Qala-I-Jangi was where they had trained under the Taliban. They knew the storage rooms were literally overflowing with weapons and ammunition that had been confiscated and stored in the southern compound. They wasted little time in causing trouble. One die-hard beckoned to Nadir Ali, one of Dostum's senior commanders. As Ali came close, the man armed a hand grenade, locked his arms around the commander, and held him until the explosive went off. The blast killed both men. The dramatic scene was caught on video tape—the sound of a muffled explosion, a puff of smoke, and men running from the scene. Another clip showed several men carrying the body away, while another body lay on the ground with blood covering its head. Later that day, another al-Qaeda fanatic killed Saeed Asad, a Hazara leader. Despite the two deadly incidents, the guard was not reinforced, nor were the prisoners searched again. The Northern Alliance guards had violated every basic procedure for handling enemy prisoners of war.

The killings put the guards on edge; there were several hundred prisoners and only a hundred of them. Gen. Majid Rozi, the fortress commander, ordered his men to herd the entire mob of al-Qaeda prisoners into the underground basement of a sturdy, pink Soviet-built schoolhouse for the night, thinking they would be easier to guard. A thorough search would have to wait until morning. The basement's stacked brick entranceway was located about fifty feet from the side of the building. Mud steps led down to the lower level. Its walls and ceilings were several feet thick, reinforced with rebar, making it a virtually bomb-proof shelter. After the prisoners were crammed into the basement, one of the guards, in a fit of anger, tossed a hand grenade through an opening. According to witnesses, several prisoners were injured and another killed.

That night the fanatical al-Qaeda fighters argued about what to do. The Saudis and Uzbeks planned an attack. All they needed was a diversion to get to the weapons that were stored only a few yards away. Their goal was to escape Qala-I-Jangi and rejoin the Taliban forces on the outskirts of Mazar. The Pakistanis however, just wanted to surrender and go home, but few expressed an opinion, fearing that the unrepentant al-Qaeda would kill them.

25 November

The next morning two SAD operatives, Johnny Micheal "Mike" Spann, a former U.S. Marine Corps officer, and David "Dave" Tyson, an Uzbek speaker and area expert, arrived to start interrogating the prisoners. They hoped to identify senior members of al-Qaeda for further questioning. The two entered the prison through the northern compound and passed through the gate into the southwestern half of the fortress, where over a hundred prisoners were seated on the ground with their hands bound behind their backs by their turbans. "They are evil," a guard stated. "If you untie them, they have the habit of killing people."

Other prisoners wandered freely within the compound, having been untied by the guards so they could wash and pray. Two television crews, from the German station ARD and Reuters, filmed the two Americans interviewing the prisoners. Spann was shown wearing blue jeans and a black sweater with an AK-47 slung across his back. From a distance, the bearded Tyson looked Afghan; he wore a black shalwar kameez, the traditional Afghan pants and long shirt, but his square-cropped haircut gave him away.

A short segment of the film showed Spann squatting on the edge of a blanket talking to a wild-haired, heavily bearded man sitting cross-legged with his elbows tied behind his back. The prisoner's head was bowed, long hair obscuring his face. He was wearing loose black trousers and a black tunic that reached to his calves. Spann had picked him out because of his Caucasian features and the British Army sweater he was wearing.

"What's your name?" Spann asked in English. "Who brought you to Afghanistan?" The prisoner stared at the ground, silent, refusing to look Spann in the eye. "Where are you from?" Spann continued with a series of questions. "You believe in what you're doing here that much [that] you're willing to be killed here? How were you recruited to come here? Who brought you here?" The prisoner remained unresponsive. Exasperated, Spann shouted, "Hey!" and snapped his fingers in the man's face in an effort to get some sort of reaction. "You got to talk to me. All I want to do is talk to you and find out what your story is. I know you speak English."

When the man did not respond, Spann took out a digital camera and tried to take his picture. "Put your head up," he ordered. "Don't make me have to get them to hold your head up. Push your hair back. Push your hair back so I can see your face." When the man did not comply, an Afghan soldier pulled his hair back and held his head for the photograph. At that moment, Tyson walked over. "He won't talk to me," Spann said to him. "I was explaining to the guy we just want to talk to him, find out what his story is."

Tyson responded, "The problem is he's got to decide if he wants to live or die and die here. We're just going to leave him, and he's going to fucking sit in prison the rest of his fucking short life. It's his decision, man. We can only help the guys who want to talk to us. We can only get the Red Cross to help so many guys."

Spann turned back to the prisoner. "Do you know the people here you're working with are terrorists and killed other Muslims?" he said. "There were several hundred Muslims killed in the bombing in New York City. Is that what the Koran teaches? I don't think so. Are you going to talk to us?" After getting no response, the two Americans walked away toward the line of prisoners. The individual was later identified as John Walker Lindh, coined the "American Taliban" by the media.

Suddenly there was an explosion and shouts of "*Allahu Akbar.*" A wave of prisoners rushed toward the two Americans. Accounts differ about what happened to the two men on that Sunday morning, but it appears that Mike Spann was simply overwhelmed by a crush of bodies and died in hand to hand fighting. One Afghan witness was within thirty feet of Spann when the fight broke out. He said he heard an explosion, saw prisoners rush out and kill an officer and four of his guards at the entrance to the pink house, then immediately rush Spann. He said Spann fired his AK-47 and pistol until he was out of ammunition and then he fought them hand to hand until he was overcome by the prisoners. Two Northern Alliance doctors were treating injured prisoners nearby when the revolt broke out. Their account was the same as that of the first witness. They said the only reason that they, and several others, were able to live was because Spann stood his ground and fought off the prisoners, which enabled them to run to safety.

The prisoner revolt happened so quickly that Spann's partner was only able to get off a few shots, which may have killed two or three rioters, before Spann was overwhelmed. Tyson was forced to run for his life because there were just too many assailants for one man. The German ARD crew filmed him sprinting to the main building in the northern compound, directly toward them. The next segment showed him inside their building, talking excitedly to a member of the Red Cross who had arrived at the prison sometime that morning.

"He burst in and told us to get out of there," Simon Brooks, one of the Red Cross members, said. "He was really shaken up." The camera caught

American Taliban

John Walker Lindh, a.k.a "Suleyman al-Faris" or "Abdul Hamid," was born in Washington, D.C. in 1981. Ten years later he moved to California. After dropping out of high school, he converted to Islam in 1997. The next year, and again in early 2000, Walker traveled to Yemen and Pakistan to study Arabic and Islam. In May 2001 he joined a paramilitary training camp run by the *Harakat ul-Mujahideen*, a Pakistan-based Islamic militant group operating primarily in Kashmir. He attended a seven-week al-Qaeda training camp north of Islamabad, where he personally met Osama bin Laden. The paramilitary training included courses in weapons, orienteering, navigation, explosives, and battlefield combat. Upon conclusion of the course, he volunteered to fight with the Taliban. He was issued an AKM rifle and sent to Kabul with approximately thirty other fighters. From Kabul he went to the front lines in Takhar to defend against Northern Alliance attacks. After being pounded by U.S. air strikes, Walker and his unit retreated to Kunduz, then to Mazar-e Sharif, and surrendered.

After being recaptured, Lindh was given basic first-aid for a bullet wound and then questioned for a week at Mazar-e Sharif, before being taken to FOB Camp Rhino on 7 December 2001, the bullet still within his thigh. When Lindh arrived, he was stripped, restrained to a stretcher, blindfolded, and placed in a metal shipping container, which was the procedure for dealing with a potentially dangerous detainee. On 8 and 9 December he was interviewed by the FBI and transferred to the USS *Peleliu* on 14 December 2001, where his wound was operated on, and he received further care. While on *Peleliu*, he signed confession documents admitting that he was not merely Taliban but al-Qaeda. On 22 January 2002, he was flown back to the United States to face criminal charges. Six months later, on 15 July 2002, he was offered a plea agreement for serving in the Taliban army and carrying weapons, which he accepted. "I plead guilty," Walker said. "I provided my services as a soldier to the Taliban last year from about August to December. In the course of doing so, I carried a rifle and two grenades. I did so knowingly and willingly, knowing that it was illegal." On 4 October 2002, Judge T. S. Ellis III formally imposed the sentence: twenty years without parole.

Tyson fumbling with his pistol, trying to holster it. "He said there were twenty dead Northern Alliance guys, and the Taliban were taking control of the fort." Tyson spotted a satellite phone that one of the TV crew was carrying and used it to place an urgent call for help to the American defense attaché in Tashkent. It was the only phone number he had. He quickly gave the officer a rundown of the situation as he knew it, emphasizing that his partner was missing. The information was immediately relayed to Special Forces Lt. Col. Max Bowers in Mazar-e Sharif, who scrambled to put together a rescue force. All of the ODAs were at Konduz, at least a day away, so he had to put together a scratch force of headquarters staff, bolstered by a team of British Special Boat Service operatives who just happened to be in the city.

While Tyson radioed for help, the two Red Cross members climbed up on the fort's parapet and slid down the mud walls to safety. Inside the fortress, the prisoners had broken out of the underground basement, smashed through the armory doors, and retrieved a large stock of weapons and ammunition. The surviving Northern Alliance soldiers took them under fire from positions on the southeast corner of the southern compound and from the north wall and roof of Dostum's headquarters building. Gunfire exploded as the two sides exchanged a heavy volume of small arms fire. Casualties mounted. Tyson and the TV crews were pinned down, expecting to be overrun and killed at any moment.

At 1400, Bowers's rescue force reached the prison in two minivans and a pair of white Land Rovers. There were nine Special Forces soldiers and six to eight British SBS operatives, with an attached U.S. Navy SEAL, Chief Petty Officer Stephen Bass, under the overall command of Maj. Mark E. Mitchell, The American part of the ad-hoc outfit consisted of two air force intelligence officers, a Special Forces battalion surgeon, two Special Forces enlisted men, an Afghan interpreter, and a CIA operative.

As the rescuers dismounted, they clearly heard the crackle of automatic weapons fire and RPG explosions within the fortress. The SBS men climbed up the cement stairs to the entranceway tower and took up firing positions along the northeast corner of the wall. In addition to their personal weapons, they also had two 7.62mm L7A1 General Purpose Machine Guns (GPMG), which they had dismounted from their vehicles. The vantage point allowed them to pour automatic weapons fire into the southern compound, which kept the Taliban from overrunning the fortress. Major Mitchell deployed his men in positions along the southwest wall and then proceeded to bring in close air support. During the remaining hours of daylight, seven 1,000-pound JDAMs were dropped on Taliban positions in the southern compound. While the airstrikes reduced the enemy's small arms and RPG fire, they did not eliminate it. Under cover of the airstrikes, Tyson and the TV crews escaped by sliding down the inclined walls of the fortress. "He just climbed over and hitched a ride into town," a rescuer explained.

Mitchell didn't know that Tyson had escaped and organized a search team to find both of the CIA operatives. The team stripped off all equipment

Johnny Michael Spann

Johnny Michael Spann was born in March 1969 in the small town in Winfield, Alabama. He graduated from high school in 1987 and then attended Auburn University, graduating with a bachelor of science degree in criminal justice/law enforcement in 1992. While in college, he joined the Marine Corps and, upon graduation, attended Officer Candidate School at Quantico, Virginia. After being commissioned, he served as an infantry officer for six years, including a tour with an Air Naval Gunfire Liaison Officer unit, specializing in directing artillery, air, and naval gunfire. He was stationed in Okinawa, Japan, and Camp Lejeune, North Carolina. In June 1999 he joined the CIA and went on to serve in the Special Activities Division as a paramilitary officer. He was the first American killed in combat during Operation Enduring Freedom.

In a break with tradition, the CIA published Spann's name and connection to the organization. He is memorialized with a star on the CIA Memorial Wall at CIA headquarters in Langley, Virginia, that commemorates individuals who died in the line of duty. He was posthumously awarded the Intelligence Star (equivalent to the Silver Star) and the Exceptional Service Medallion. On 10 December 2001 he was buried with full military honors in section 34 at Arlington National Cemetery. A small memorial to him exists at Qala-i-Jangi Fortress outside of Mazar-e Sharif, Afghanistan.

U.S. Marine honor guard preparing to receive CIA paramilitary officer Johnny Michael Spann's remains. He was killed during the prison revolt at the Qala-i-Jangi revolt. *defenseimagery.mil*

bar their weapons and ammunition, climbed over the wall, and into the interior of the fortress. They searched several hallways, eventually ending up on the exposed roof of Dostum's headquarters building, where they could see into the southern compound. From this position they called in several air strikes.

Maj. Mark Mitchell, Distinguished Service Cross citation

"As the Ground Force Commander of a rescue operation during the Battle of Qala-I-Jangi Fortress, Mazar-e Sharif. Afghanistan, Maj. Mitchell ensured the freedom of one American and the posthumous repatriation of another. His unparalleled courage under fire, decisive leadership and personal sacrifice were directly responsible for the success of the rescue operation and were further instrumental in ensuring the city of Mazar-e Sharif did not fall back in the hands of the Taliban. His personal example has added yet another laurel to the proud military history of this nation and serves as the standard for all others to emulate. Maj. Mitchell's gallant deed was truly above and beyond the call of duty and is in keeping with the finest traditions of the military service and reflects great credit upon himself, the 5th Special Forces Group (Airborne), the United States Army, and the United States of America."

Maj. Mark Mitchell received the Distinguished Service Cross for leading the rescue force at Qala-I-Jangi prison. His heroic action was above and beyond the call of duty. *U.S. Army*

During the night, an AC-130 Spectre gunship pounded the southern compound, preventing the Taliban from escaping. The 28 November 2001 London *Times* reported, "The nighttime raids left many bodies half-buried in the ground. Limbs and torsos rose out of the disturbed earth like tree trunks after a forest fire." The next morning, several hundred Northern Alliance fighters and a Soviet-era T-55 tank arrived to put down the rebellion. They established a command post near the northern gate.

26 November

By mid-morning the reinforcements were joined by additional Special Forces. They formed two Close Air Support (CAS) teams and a Quick Reaction Force (QRF) consisting of four Special Forces soldiers, a navy surgeon, and eight men from the 10th Mountain Division. One CAS team cautiously made its way inside the fortress, along the bottom of the northeast tower, and the second positioned itself near the main gate. The team's combat controller made contact with a section of Marine F-16 Hornets from VMFA-251.

After receiving the coordinates, the pilot cautioned him, "Be advised, you're dangerously close . . . about a hundred yards from the target."

The combat controller replied, "We have to be, to get the laser on target. We are about ready to pull back."

Friendly Fire

A navy F-14 pilot was monitoring the radio conversation between the combat controller and the Marine pilot. "We could hear that there was some confusion between the Special Forces on the ground and the guys in the air." The navy pilot checked the target and friendly coordinates that the Marine was given and noted that "they were too close . . . less than 300 meters separation between the two."

The Marine gave the controller a warning, "We're ready to release," and a two-minute mark. It would take the bomb that long to fall from 10,000 feet. At 1053, a 2,000-pound JDAM exploded about ten yards from the combined US/British/Northern Alliance command post, sending dust and debris hundreds of feet into the air. The navy pilot thought that in the confusion the two sets of coordinates were reversed—friendly became the enemy—and that "the 2,000 pound GBU-31 JDAM went precisely where it was directed."

Chief Petty Officer Stephen Bass
Navy Cross Citation

"For extraordinary heroism while serving with the British Special Boat Service during combat operations in Northern Afghanistan on 25 and 26 November 2001. Chief Petty Officer Stephen Bass deployed to the area as a member of a Joint American and British Special Forces Rescue Team to locate and recover two missing American citizens, one presumed to be seriously injured or dead, after hard-line Al Qaeda and Taliban prisoners at the Qala-I-Jangi fortress in Mazar-e-Sharif over powered them and gained access to large quantities of arms and ammunition stored at the fortress. Once inside, Chief Petty Officer Bass was engaged continuously by direct small arms fire, indirect mortar fire and rocket propelled grenade fire. He was forced to walk through an active anti-personnel minefield in order to gain entry to the fortress. After establishing the possible location of both American citizens, under heavy fire and without concern for his own personal safety, he made two attempts to rescue the uninjured citizen by crawling toward the fortress interior to reach him. Forced to withdraw due to large volumes of fire falling on his position, he was undeterred. After reporting his efforts to the remaining members of the rescue team, they left and attempted to locate the missing citizen on the outside of the fortress. As darkness began to fall, no attempt was going to be made to locate the other injured American citizen. Chief Petty Officer Bass then took matters into his own hands. Without regard for his own personal safety, he moved forward another 300–400 meters into the heart of the fortress by himself under constant enemy fire in an attempt to locate the injured citizen. Running low on ammunition, he utilized weapons from deceased Afghans to continue his rescue attempt. Upon verifying the condition and location of the American citizen, he withdrew from the fortress. By his outstanding display of decisive leadership, unlimited courage in the face of enemy fire, and utmost devotion to duty, Chief Petty Officer Bass reflected great credit upon himself and upheld the highest traditions of the United States Naval Service."

About ninety seconds after the explosion, a voice came over the radio shouting, "Check fire, Check fire, Check fire!" It was then that the pilots realized that something had gone dreadfully wrong. The force of the explosion flipped a thirty-five ton T-55 tank completely over, killing its crew. Several Northern Alliance soldiers were pinned underneath it. Debris buried several men, while others staggered from the site with blood streaming from their bloodshot eyes and ruptured ear drums. The bomb left a hole the size of a swimming pool in the north wall. Rescuers rushed forward through Taliban fire to evacuate the wounded and the dead. At least six Northern Alliance soldiers were killed and eighty seriously injured. Five

Americans and four British SBS soldiers were also injured and evacuated. By this time the fortress was taking on the sights and smells of a charnel house. The southern compound was littered with the mangled remains of over 200 al-Qaeda fighters. The bodies were beginning to decompose, polluting the air with the smell of death. The Northern Alliance commander estimated that he had lost 50 men killed and 250 wounded.

At a little after 2200, a Lockheed AC-130, call sign Grim 12, arrived to rake the southern compound with its 30mm and 105mm cannon. After an hour, it ran out of ammunition and its sister ship, Grim 11, took over. The aircraft was directed to hit a long building just inside the wall that separated the two compounds. As it pounded the building with 105mm rounds, its third round caused a massive fireball. Thunderous explosions shook the entire fortress. Debris showered down, threatening to injure anyone not in a covered position. Secondary explosions lasted throughout the night. "Fireworks you'll never forget," one Special Forces soldier exclaimed. The fireball could be seen eleven miles away. As the shock waves rumbled through the building, it was thought that no one could have survived. However, much to everyone's surprise, sporadic shooting continued throughout the night.

27 November

Early the next morning, General Dostum arrived with an additional two hundred fighters, including a second T-55 tank. By this time, dozens of news reporters and TV camera men were on hand to capture the action. Their on-scene reports and video feeds made for sensational news and were immediately shown throughout the world. They filmed Dostum's men taking up positions along the southwestern wall, where they laid down a heavy volume of machine gun and cannon fire.

The 28 November London *Times* reported, "To clear the last pockets of Taliban resistance in the afternoon, Alliance soldiers approached the houses in the middle of the compound and fired at random into basement windows. Some twenty-liter petrol canisters were thrown in, then grenades." A BBC reporter asked Dostum if he was shocked by the violence. He shrugged his shoulders and said, "*Jang*," the Dari word for "war."

Near dark, a line of Northern Alliance soldiers crept down into the courtyard, intent on finishing off the remaining al-Qaeda fighters. They ran into heavy resistance near one of the horse stables when dozens of the fighters suddenly jumped up from hiding and launched an attack. In the shootout that followed, it was estimated that over a hundred al-Qaeda

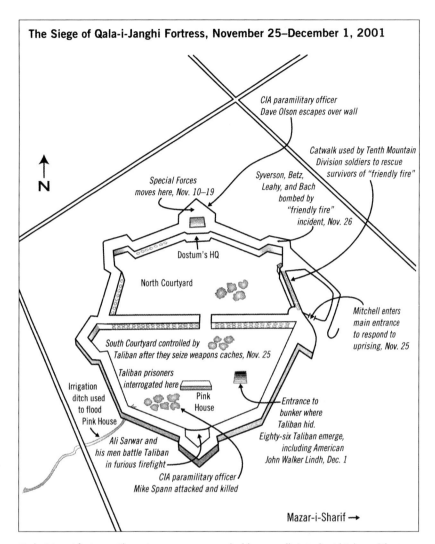

The Siege of Qala-i-Janghi Fortress, November 25–December 1, 2001

N

CIA paramilitary officer Dave Olson escapes over wall

Catwalk used by Tenth Mountain Division soldiers to rescue survivors of "friendly fire"

Special Forces moves here, Nov. 10–19

Syverson, Betz, Leahy, and Bach bombed by "friendly fire" incident, Nov. 26

Dostum's HQ

North Courtyard

Mitchell enters main entrance to respond to uprising, Nov. 25

South Courtyard controlled by Taliban after they seize weapons caches, Nov. 25

Taliban prisoners interrogated here

Irrigation ditch used to flood Pink House

Pink House

Entrance to bunker where Taliban hid. Eighty-six Taliban emerge, including American John Walker Lindh, Dec. 1

Ali Sarwar and his men battle Taliban in furious firefight

CIA paramilitary officer Mike Spann attacked and killed

Mazar-i-Sharif →

Qala-I-Jangi fortress. The prison was surrounded by a wall sixty feet high and forty-five feet thick. Inside there were two compounds separated by a dividing wall. The northern quadrant housed Dostum's headquarters, while the southern half contained the armory, which the prisoners seized during the revolt. *Robin Moore*

and Northern Alliance fighters were killed. Clearing the compound was proving to be a brutal up-close and personal brawl.

28 November–1 December

Pockets of die-hard al-Qaeda fighters still held out and had to be cleared from the compound and buildings. One ragged looking fighter stepped out of a doorway, appearing to surrender. As he was approached, the fanatic detonated a hand grenade, killing himself and wounding five Northern Alliance soldiers. A search party found Spann's remains among the many bodies in the southern compound. His body had been booby-trapped with a hand grenade. A squad of Northern Alliance soldiers carried it to the northern compound, from where the rescue force transported the body to the airfield at Mazar-e Sharif. A flag was draped over the body bag. "I had the only American flag there," Company Sgt. Maj. Mario Vigil said, "so we used it to cover his remains." Vigil had carried the flag in the Gulf War. 5th Special Forces Group chaplain Lt. Col. Mark Bojune conducted a brief yet solemn ceremony before Spann's remains were flown to K-2.

Everything in the southern compound was under Northern Alliance control except for the basement of the pink house. An unknown number of al-Qaeda fighters still held out. Muhammad Karim led a group of workers into the basement to recover bodies. "It was dark," he recalled. "We could not see anything, and suddenly they fired on us. I saw a flash when they started firing. We got down by the wall and then came back out. They fired three times, from about ten yards away. We were just the people sent in to pick up the bodies. We could not know they were still alive."

Dostum's men threw hand grenades through holes they had hacked in the brick foundation, but the fanatics still refused to surrender. They also tried burning the fanatics out with oil that was poured through the holes and then set on fire. When that didn't work, they dug a trench that diverted water from a stream into the basement, flooding it to within inches of the ceiling. That did the trick.

On the morning of 30 November, eighty-six emaciated survivors emerged, John Walker Lindh among them. He had minor shrapnel wounds in his leg and back and a gunshot wound in his foot. A reporter from *Newsweek*, Colin Soloway, found Lindh in the back of a truck and asked him if he was an American. Lindh said, "Yeah."

French photographer Damien Degueldre filmed the interview. "Lindh wasn't too keen to be filmed," he said. "[He] looked completely in shock. The visual of this young American with his long hair and beard, and his face covered in dirt, was really amazing."

A Northern Alliance fighter said, "It's been said he should be given to an international court, but personally, if I catch him, I'll kill him. I won't forgive him." United Nations records later showed that 514 al-Qaeda fanatics died at Qala-i-Jangi and only 86 injured survived. Sixty Uzbek guards also died.

CHAPTER 17

Operational Detachment Command and Control Element Shark 85

"The fight has now begun, it is the best opportunity
to achieve martyrdom."
—Mullah Omar

IN EARLY NOVEMBER, LT. COL. Chris Haas, call sign Shark 85, and his command element were inserted into the Panjshir Valley to plan and coordinate the attack on Kabul. His plan called for a two-pronged approach. "Basically, one assault would be on the desert floor tracking along the new highway from Bagram airfield straight into Kabul," Robin Moore described, "while another would be along an old highway along the western wall of cliffs that bordered the rolling plain south of Bagram."

The attack was supposed to kick off on 8 November; however, the promised air support did not show up. The Northern Alliance's Marshal Fahim was furious. "Where are the big bombers [B-52s]? " he shouted in Dari. The planes had been diverted, without informing either Haas or Team Jawbreaker's Gary Berntsen.

"My guys on the front have had their relationships with the Afghan commanders strained to the limit because of this," Berntsen told CentCom. "The loss of credibility is huge!"

Markham recalled, "I was starting to doubt the amount of close-air support we were going to get. It almost became comical that we would show up there and somebody sitting thousands of miles away was deciding whether or not I needed air support."

Two days later, the promised air support showed up in the form of B-52s and even a B-1. "Now we were dropping some serious ordnance," Markham recalled. "Not only were we breaking the enemy's back, we were totally annihilating them and their war-making effort." Beginning on 10 November, Markham called in twenty-five airstrikes, which accounted for over 2,000 enemy soldiers killed, and twenty-nine tanks and six command posts destroyed. Markham said, "We set up an observation post in a mountain ridge overlooking the Taliban. The valley was literally filled with enemy tanks, personnel carriers and military compounds. Working with

Master Sgt. William "Calvin" Markham
Silver Star Citation

"The President of the United States takes pleasure in presenting the Silver Star Medal to William "Calvin" Markham, Master Sergeant, U.S. Air Force, for conspicuous gallantry and intrepidity in action while serving with the 23d Special Tactics Squadron in support of Operation ENDURING FREEDOM, near Kabul, Afghanistan, from 14 October to 30 November 2001.

On 21 October 2001, within forty-eight hours of the detachment's arrival in Afghanistan, Sergeant Markham planned, organized,

U.S. Air Force Master Sergeant William C. Markham receiving the Silver Star for conspicuous gallantry. Attached to Operational Detachment Command 85, Markham was responsible for directing close air support, which greatly assisted the Northern Alliance in capturing Kabul. U.S. Air Force the Northern Alliance leadership, the target was selected—a command and control building. I called in the first CAS and a U.S. military fighter arrived over the area and dropped his ordnance and hit the building."

From that point onward, Fahim advanced rapidly. "We tried to stay ahead of them with the bombings," a Team Jawbreaker member recalled, "but at some point we did have to stop, because they were moving faster than we could calculate their location. We knew their objective was Kabul, and they weren't going to be slowed down by our bombing." When the Taliban offered resistance, the Special Forces team hit them with an airstrike, and everyone would press on. Whenever possible, Fahim tried to convince the Taliban to switch sides.

"There was a lot of handshaking involved, especially between Afghani and Afghani," a team member recalled. "We absorbed the native Afghanis." However, it was a different story for the foreign fighters. "The Pakis and other foreigners, they [the anti-Taliban] couldn't care less about; they were going to kill them," he said.

and led a close air support reconnaissance mission to within two kilometers of the Taliban front line in order to identify potential observation posts from which his team could execute missions. Almost immediately upon arrival, Sergeant Markham's team came under direct enemy fire from tanks, mortars and artillery.

Despite heavy incoming fire, in which numerous rounds impacted within fifty to seventy-five meters of his position, Sergeant Markham instinctively and successfully directed multiple close air support sorties against key Taliban leadership positions, command and control elements, fortified positions, and numerous anti-aircraft artillery sites.

Throughout this highly successful mission, Sergeant Markham skillfully directed multiple air strikes involving over one hundred seventy-five sorties of both strategic and attack aircraft resulting in the elimination of approximately four hundred and fifty enemy vehicles and over three thousand five hundred enemy troops. The resulting close air support operations were decisive in supporting the Northern Alliance ground offensive, which resulted in the successful liberation of the capital city of Kabul and led to the eventual surrender of hundreds of al Qaeda and Taliban ground forces.

Master Sergeant Markham's valor and calmness under enemy fire were a constant source of inspiration to his detachment and General Fahim Khan's Northern Alliance forces. By his gallantry and devotion to duty, Sergeant Markham has reflected great credit upon himself and the United States Air Force."

David Diaz pointed out, "In a lot of cases, the native Afghanis in the Taliban units were killing them [foreign fighters] themselves."

The combination of air strikes and mass defections broke the back of the Taliban resistance. Reports indicated that hundreds of members of the Taliban militia were leaving Kabul and heading for Kandahar, the regime's stronghold in the south. "Everybody was running to save his own skin," a captured Pakistani fighter said. Anthony Davis of *Time* reported, "Some headed toward Maidanshahr, Ghazni and the southwest; others, south toward Logar province; and still others, east toward Jalalabad and the al-Qaeda stronghold of Tora Bora in Nangarhar province."

Reporter Alan Philps of *The Telegraph* wrote, "Dozens of pick-up trucks loaded with Taliban families and their possessions were seen leaving the city. Lights went out at key ministries and Taliban institutions in Kabul, which has been ruled by the militia since 1996."

His report was disputed by Mullah Abdul Salam Zaeef, the Taliban ambassador to Pakistan. "This news is false and baseless that the Taliban are leaving Kabul. We have decided to defend Kabul." Alliance forces halted their advance just north of the village of Karabagh, about fifteen miles from the capital. The rapid Northern Alliance advance caused consternation in Washington because there was no government to take charge.

George Tenet noted that "the worry now was that the Northern Alliance was getting ahead of the nascent resistance . . . and if they took Kabul too quickly, intertribal fighting and score-setting would break out and chaos would reign."

Early the next morning, 13 November, Fahim's troops entered Kabul in spite of the agreement. The Special Forces team was ordered to stay out of the city. "Everybody was so afraid about us going into Kabul, but there was nothing we could do," Markham recalled. "We were in their [Fahim's] trucks."

Another team member recalled. "It was a mad rush. Something that we thought would take a couple of weeks happened in a matter of hours." The outskirts of city was blocked by an enormous traffic jam, and the army was ordered to halt. Soldiers who had clambered on top of every tank and armored vehicle, hoping for the traditional ride into a liberated city, had to get down and walk. Welcoming crowds showered them with plastic flowers and chanted "Down with the Taliban."

"It was surreal," according to one team member. "I mean, heck, we'd gone into Afghanistan about a month after the towers fell, and, a month after that, we were in the capital city of what had been an enemy country. People lined the streets. There we were in the convoy. They didn't know we were Americans, but we were in the convoy with the Northern Alliance, and people were just standing at the side of the road, cheering and laughing."

Five hours later, Bismullah Khan, the Northern Alliance's deputy minister of defense, drove toward the city center with other senior commanders and the Special Forces team in a convoy of pickup trucks and jeeps packed with cheering fighters. ODA 555 officially entered the city at 0800, their twenty-sixth day in-country and the thirty-eighth day of American combat operations. The residents of the city lined the streets, cheering and laughing. It was the first time in five years that they were not under the Taliban's harsh Sharia laws. "It was just like an immense weight had been lifted off them," a team member said. "I'll always remember the children playing with kites because the whole time, the Taliban didn't allow that." Cabdriver Mohammed Zahir said, "I never thought I'd see the Taliban leave without a fight."

There were reports of widespread looting of abandoned Taliban stores and homes, but by afternoon the Alliance had stationed troops and police all over the city to enforce the law. The Red Cross reported that twenty bodies had been found, apparently Taliban stragglers, but it was not clear whether

General Bismullah Khan, the Northern Alliance deputy minister of defense, shown with Gen. Peter Pace, chairman of the Joint Chiefs of Staff, during a visit to an Afghan military training facility in Kabul. *Department of Defense*

they had been killed in gun battles or murdered in revenge attacks. Most of the victims appeared to be Pakistani volunteers who were abandoned to their fate. Northern Alliance soldiers brandished Pakistani identity cards taken from the bodies as proof.

The Telegraph's David Rennie wrote, "One soldier flourished a student identity card from a young Pakistani fighter named Abdul Jabbah. The photograph showed a painfully young face, with only the faintest traces of a moustache." The soldiers eagerly showed off a letter of introduction stolen from one dead Taliban, bearing the logo of the Pakistani-based Jaishi Mohamed group, which an officer said was "part of the al-Qaeda network." Six bodies were displayed in a public park, one of them with a wire twisted around his neck. A crowd of men on bicycles gathered to gawp and spit on the bodies. The Alliance denied that they had been summarily executed.

On the day the city fell, an NSA radio intercept picked up a message that Mullah Omar broadcast to his troops. "I order you to obey your commanders completely and not to go hither and thither. Any person who does is like a slaughtered chicken which falls and dies. Regroup yourselves. Resist . . . This fight is for Islam."

Radio intercepts also picked up cellphone conversations between the Taliban and al-Qaeda after an airstrike had leveled a building thought to be their headquarters. "[There were] some excited or angry exchanges indicating that one or more al-Qaeda leaders had been killed in the building," an official said. It was later discovered that the building housed the Kabul offices of the al-Jazeera television network. Abdul Salam Zaeef, the Taliban ambassador to Pakistan, confirmed the death of Mohammed Atef, the number three man in bin Laden's al-Qaeda organization. Zaeef was quoted as saying the former Egyptian policeman was "martyred in the U.S. bombing of Kabul", but gave no other details.

Haas and Berntsen drove to the former U.S. embassy, which had been closed and boarded up for the past twelve years. They cut the locks on the front door and cautiously entered, keeping a sharp eye out for booby traps. "I climbed the concrete steps past the United States seal," Berntsen said. "Entering the lobby was like entering a time warp. Our flashlights illuminated President Ronald Reagan's official photo with Vice President George H. W. Bush. On a reception desk off the main lobby I spotted the first rotary-style telephone I'd seen in years."

Robin Moore reported that the team found a CONEX box [Container Express—a shipping container] "holding thousands of unopened bottles of Johnnie Walker Label scotch" a treasure trove that eventually found its way into "the secret UN bar, various hotels, and a host of diplomatic offices . . . at a price, of course!"

On 17 December, the U.S. embassy was reopened. A Marine color guard in camouflage uniforms ran the American flag to the top of the flagpole in the center of the embassy compound. It was the same flag that was taken down in 1989 and had been discovered in a desk drawer. The flag came with a handwritten note from the former commander of the Marine detachment, Gunnery Sgt. James M. Blake. "For those of us that were here it means a lot, for those of you yet to enter Kabul, it could mean a lot to you."

Colonel Andrew P. Frick, 26th Marine Expeditionary Unit (Special Operations Capable)'s commanding officer, spoke at the ceremony. "Unfortunately, when an embassy shuts down, the Marine security guards and the U.S. ambassador are always among the last to leave because they have the responsibility to lower the American flag from sovereign U.S. soil . . . I think that it's only fitting that the Marines, 'America's 9-1-1 force' . . . be the ones to stand with the new U.S. ambassador as he raises the flag over sovereign American soil. It is a fitting and poignant moment and we're happy to be a part of it."

Sergeant David J. Wood, an infantryman with Battalion Landing Team 3/6 told a newsman. "I am very proud to be here, to represent my country, and to represent the people in New York who paid so very much. We all share their pain, and we're here for them."

Days after the flag raising ceremony, several members of Triple Nickel happened to be outside the embassy. "There was a large crowd on the main street in front of the embassy," one of the team recalled, "when General Sharif [one of Fahim's commanders] stops by to say hello to his troops . . . [he] made eye contact with us and raises his hand, big smile. So, right in the middle of the road . . . we end up hugging . . . Afghani kisses on the cheek . . . [He] whisks us away and we end up having chai [tea] and talking about old times . . . it was kind of funny."

CHAPTER 18

Tora Bora

"We will retreat to the mountains and begin a long guerrilla war . . ."
—Taliban military commander

Jawbreaker

GARY BERNTSEN WAS AT HIS headquarters in Astana when he received word that the Taliban were evacuating Kabul. "The city is in a state of confusion," he told his men. "We need to move quickly in order to receive maximum benefit from our enemy's retreat." On 13 November, the command group quickly packed up and made its way to Kabul. They set up headquarters in a former government guest house in the northwest sector of the city, near the former Taliban intelligence center. The building had previously housed President Najibullah before his assassination in 1996. Berntsen was soon joined by an eight-man team Special Forces team, all of Triple Nickel, and several CIA augmentees, including the legendary SAD operative Billy Waugh; at seventy-two years old, he was the oldest member of the team by far. Waugh was a highly decorated American Special Forces soldier, who had retired as a sergeant major before joining the Central Intelligence Agency. Berntsen's team wasted little time in combing the city for evidence pointing to where Osama bin Laden might have fled. "I want to start killing him and his people immediately," he emphasized.

There were reports that bin Laden had been seen heading east toward Jalalabad in a heavily guarded convoy of white Toyota trucks. Bin Laden's

Gary Berntsen, CIA paramilitary leader of Team Jawbreaker. Under Berntsen's leadership, the CIA teams successfully molded with the U.S. Army's Operational Detachment Alphas to produce a winning combination that helped bring down the Taliban. *U.S. Government*

Arab fighters had used the city as a base and as a command center for a number of years. It had always been a traditional meeting place for Pashtun tribesmen from the area bordering Pakistan. In early November, witnesses placed bin Laden in the city. Malik Habib Gul, an Afghan tribal leader, was in the basement of the Taliban's intelligence headquarters when bin Laden arrived with fifteen of his elite Arab commandos. Gul said that "the crowd of Pakistani and Afghan tribesmen rose to their feet, threw flowers, and shouted: '*Zindabad Osama*!' (Long Live Osama!)"

Bin Laden spoke to the assembly: "If we are united and believe in Allah, we'll teach the Americans [a lesson], the same one we taught to the Russians," Gul reported. Like the other tribal elders in attendance, Gul received a white envelope full of Pakistani rupees, which he thought was a down payment for their help in the future.

Within days, forces loyal to the Northern Alliance forced bin Laden and his disorganized Taliban and al-Qaeda remnants to flee Jalalabad under cover of darkness. A villager reported that a large convoy of four-wheel-drive vehicles passed through his village, two hours south of the city. "There were many nationalities in the convoy," he bragged. "Some were

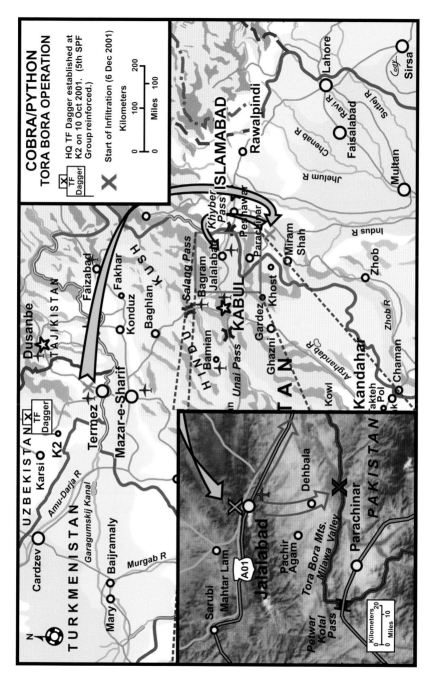

COBRA/PYTHON
TORA BORA OPERATION

[X] TF Dagger   HQ TF Dagger established at
K2 on 10 Oct 2001. (5th SPF
Group reinforced.)

X   Start of Infiltration (6 Dec 2001)

Kilometers
0   100   200
0   100
Miles

CIA team Jawbreaker coordinated the attack on al-Qaeda forces in the Tora Bora
Mountains in an attempt to keep them from escaping into Pakistan. *Bill Cody*

Tora Bora, the fortress-like section of the Spin Ghar Mountains, where bin Laden and several hundred of his al-Qaeda fled after the fall of Kabul. The mountain fastness stretched across a collection of narrow valleys, snow-covered ridges, and jagged peaks. *defenseimagery.mil*

black-skinned, some white. Most were Arabs. They were well-armed and good Muslims carrying the Koran in one hand and their Kalashnikovs in the other."

The information was verified by Northern Alliance spies. Their reports indicated that the convoy, which included a custom-designed white Toyota Corolla, was moving south and east toward Tora Bora, a fortress-like section of the Spin Ghar, or "White Mountains," so named because their peaks were covered with snow all year. The 1.5 square mile section was approximately six miles long and six miles wide and stretched across a collection of narrow valleys, snow-covered ridgelines and jagged peaks that reached over 14,000 feet. Tora Bora was close to the Pakistani border and the autonomous tribal regions, where the mainly Pashtun population sympathized with al-Qaeda and would give them sanctuary.

Mulholland recalled that "Tora Bora emerged very quickly on the radar screen, at least from my headquarters, as there was the potential that al-Qaeda and possibly other personnel could be hiding there."

Berntsen thought that bin Laden's flight to the southeastern mountains made sense. "We knew that he had a training camp at the base of the Tora Bora Mountains and maintained a complex of as many as two hundred highly defensible caves at higher elevations that had been developed during the anti-Soviet jihad." Berntsen was correct, bin Laden was no stranger to the Tora Bora. In 1987 he fought a pitched battle with the Soviets at Jaji, an Afghan village a few miles west of the Pakistani border and close to Tora Bora. That same year, he spent six months overseeing the building of a road through the mountains to allow the Mujahideen to move from the Pakistani border to Jalalabad. He flew in dozens of bulldozers and other pieces of heavy equipment from his father's construction company to build the road. According to some accounts, bin Laden himself drove one of the bulldozers. In 1996, bin Laden began expanding the fortress at Tora Bora. He built base camps at higher elevations for himself, his wives, and numerous children, and other senior Al Qaeda figures. Some rooms were reported to be concealed 350 feet inside the granite peaks. The mountain-sides leading to those upper reaches were steep and pitted with well-built bunkers cloaked in camouflage.

Berntsen believed strongly that bin Laden and anywhere from 500 to 3,000 of his men were in the mountains and decided to go after them. He requested additional men from Mulholland, but the Special Forces officer turned him down.

"I'm just not prepared to send my men into a place where we don't know the [Afghan] commander," Mulholland said. "[And] we lack significant

Members of Team Juliet at their headquarters close to Tora Bora. The team was dispatched to kill bin Laden and his al-Qaeda followers before they could escape over the mountain passes to Pakistan. *Department of Defense*

intelligence . . . what we do know indicates a high probability that a small force could run into an extremely large force and be overwhelmed."

Berntsen agreed that the risk was high, but felt that an attempt had to be taken. "I assembled a team [Team Juliet] and sent them down to Nangarhar province immediately," Berntsen explained. "I knew that if I didn't deploy my teams immediately, critical opportunities would be missed." Berntsen's eight-man team—four CIA, three Joint Special Operations Command officers and a Special Forces medic—was under the command of his assistant, George (pseudonym). Ten Afghans were assigned to them as escorts. On 18 November, the joint force traveled to Jalalabad in eight heavily armed vehicles, a six-hour trip along a torturous road that included negotiating deep gullies, steep ascents, and narrow roadways. Berntsen heaved a sigh of relief when he received word that they had arrived without incident at midnight.

Team Juliet relied heavily on three relatively minor warlords: Haji Hazarat Ali, a forty-five-year-old Sunni Muslim from the Pashai tribe; Haji Zaman Ghamsharik, a wealthy drug smuggler who had been lured back to Afghanistan from exile in France; and Hajji Zahir, a twenty-seven-year-old

The bombing of Tora Bora continued unabated for days at a time in an effort to destroy the al-Qaeda positions and to kill as many as possible before they escaped. This May 2002 photo of Royal Canadian Army soldiers—as they prepare to blow an opening into what was believed to have been an al-Qaeda-occupied cave at one time—shows how difficult the terrain of Tora Bora is. *Department of Defense photo by Staff Sgt. Jeremy T. Lock , USAF*

who was widely regarded as the most trustworthy commander of the three. Ali, a small, wiry, hard-eyed man had a fourth-grade education, was barely literate and had a reputation as a bully. He had fought the Soviets as a teenager in the 1980s, and later he had joined the Taliban for a time. Ghamsharik was fluent in English and French, and was known as a polished raconteur. He also had fought the Soviets, but when the Taliban came to power he decided to go into exile. Both men were schemers and were intent on feathering their own nests. Their loyalty to the United States was based more on CIA money than on a love for American values.

Dalton Fury (pseudonym) wrote in *Kill bin Laden: A Delta Force Commander's Account of the Hunt for the World's Most Wanted Man*, "To secure the friendship [of Ali], George brought along millions of U.S. dollars, conveniently packaged in $250,000 bundles." Ali told the CIA officer that "to muster enough fighters to pursue bin Laden into the Tora Bora Mountains it would cost, oh, say about $250,000." George handed over a bundle that was described as "a brick of hundred-dollar bills about the size of a small microwave oven." Ali emerged as the primary commander at Tora Bora because of his connections to the Northern Alliance.

The three warlords fielded a force of small local militias numbering approximately 2,500 men. However, there were questions from the outset about the competence and loyalties of the fighters, because their leaders distrusted each other. Fury did not conceal his feelings. "Our nation was relying on a fractious bunch of AK-47-toting lawless bandits and tribal thugs who were not bound by any recognized rules of warfare or subject to any code of military justice, short of random executions or firing squads."

At times, the Ali and Ghamsharik factions were at each others' throats rather than at their Taliban and al-Qaeda foes. Having secured the dubious "loyalty" of the Eastern Alliance, George co-located his headquarters with Ali in a schoolhouse at the base of the mountains. He then sent a four-man team to set up an observation post, which became known as OP25-A. The team had to climb to an altitude of 10,000 feet. After an exhausting two-day ascent, they finally reached a crest overlooking an al-Qaeda base camp. The position gave them a bird's eye view of vehicles, barracks, and hundreds of men in the open. It was a dream target. They quickly set up their SOFLAM and began calling in strike after strike—B-1 and B-52 bombers, F-14s—one after the other for fifty-six straight hours. Their spot-reports and battle damage assessments convinced Mulholland to commit an A-team.

On 6 December, the twelve-man ODA 572, codename "Cobra 25" arrived at the school house. Its mission was "to go in and assist Gen. Hazrat

A Special Forces A-team deployed in the Tora Bora Mountains in an effort to destroy the al-Qaeda forces. *U.S. Government*

Ali with his offensive plan against the Taliban and al-Qaeda fighters in the Tora Bora region," a team leader recalled. "We were just there to help call in the air support," and not to engage in direct combat. The operation was already underway by the time they arrived. Their commander deployed them along the high ground of the Milawa Valley. Half the team established an OP (Cobra 25A) on the valley's eastern ridgeline and immediately began directing air support.

The next day, the other half relieved a Team Jawbreaker element that had been in position calling air strikes for five days, and established a second OP (Cobra 25B) on the northwestern side of the valley. Small Afghan security elements provided protection while they called air strikes. The split teams coordinated their air strikes in an attempt to prevent the al-Qaeda fighters from escaping and to support the attack of the Eastern Alliance forces. "We would pretty much soften up [the al-Qaeda positions with airstrikes], while General Ali's troops would push forward," a team member explained. "We would engage targets . . . and General Ali's troops would move ahead."

On the first day, the teams rained fire on the al-Qaeda positions for over seventeen hours, well into the night. When the sun went down, weather conditions on the mountain turned brutal, temperatures dropped like a stone. "It was quite cold at night," one team member said wryly. "You welcomed the daylight, because you could get some warmth from the sun."

The enemy lit fires to keep warm, but the team showed them no mercy. They used thermal imagers to bring in more airstrikes, including a number of deadly attacks by AC-130 Spectre gunships. "As each day went by, you could see the snow line just creeping down," the soldier recalled. Because the men had to "hump" their gear, carrying it on their backs, much of their "snivel" (comfort) items had to be left behind.

"The icy weather was about ten degrees with a steady wind, and an inch or two of snow falling every day," Fury noted. One of his teams "huddled

Signals Intelligence

Signals intelligence (SIGINT) is intelligence-gathering by interception of signals, whether between people (COMINT, or communications intelligence), whether involving electronic signals not directly used in communication (ELINT, or electronic intelligence), or combinations of the two. As sensitive information is often encrypted, signals intelligence often involves the use of cryptanalysis. Also, traffic analysis—the study of who is signaling whom and in what quantity—can often produce valuable information, even when the messages themselves cannot be decrypted.

In the United States and other nations involved with NATO, signals intelligence is defined as:

- A category of intelligence comprising either individually or in combination all communications intelligence (COMINT), electronic intelligence (ELINT), and Foreign instrumentation signals intelligence, however transmitted.

- Intelligence derived from communications, electronic, and foreign instrumentation signals.

The National Security Agency (NSA) is responsible for providing foreign Signals Intelligence (SIGINT) to the United States' political policymakers and military forces. NSA's SIGINT mission is specifically limited to gathering information about international terrorists, as well as about foreign powers, organizations, or persons. Its principal listening post covering the Mid-East and Near East is the Gordon Regional Security Operations Center located at Fort Gordon, Georgia.

For the operation in Tora Bora, a half-dozen SIGINT collection teams systematically searched the airways looking for any sign of bin Laden and his al-Qaeda forces. A squadron of highly skilled SIGINT specialists from the five-hundred-man U.S. Army Security Coordination Detachment (formally known as the Intelligence Support Activity) worked with the operators from the U.S. Army Delta Force. Based at Fort Belvoir, Virginia, the unit's unclassified nickname was Grey Fox.

close together in the freezing temperatures. There were seven of them, each with a thin local blanket, but there were only two sleeping bags. They took shelter from the knife-sharp wind inside an old al-Qaeda trench and spent that whole miserable night rotating through security and restless sleep."

A few days after the offensive started, a radio was scavenged from a dead al-Qaeda fighter. The lucky break allowed the Americans to monitor al-Qaeda's communications on the mountain. "We're listening to bin Laden speak to his men," Berntsen reported. "We're listening to him pray with them. We're listening to them talk about him." Highly trained signals intelligence specialists monitoring the radio net placed bin Laden somewhere in the mountains. They thought that he was personally leading the fighters.

Fury explained that "Al-Qaeda fighters used unsecure radios, which were easily intercepted by his team and a sophisticated listening post a few miles from the mountain. Our special intelligence interceptors . . . eavesdropped around the clock on all al-Qaeda's transmissions." The interceptions gave the American real-time intelligence, allowing them to track enemy movements, effectiveness of the bombing, and morale. "The enemy was overheard repeatedly calling out in anguish, crying, obviously hurting bad and requesting help from others located a valley or two away," Fury recalled. He indicated that bin Laden's voice was often picked up by one of the "foremost" SIGINT specialists, who worked on bin Laden's voice for seven years and so knew him better than anyone else in the West.

CHAPTER 19

Operational Detachment Delta Delta Force

W ITH CLEAR EVIDENCE THAT BIN LADEN was in Tora Bora, CentCom committed the 1st Special Forces Operational Detachment-Delta (Airborne), better known as "Delta Force" to the fight. Code-named "Task Force 11" (TF-11), it consisted of fifty Delta Force soldiers, twelve British Special Boat Service commandos, and one British Royal Signals Specialist from 63 (SAS) Signal Squadron (Volunteers). Jane Corbin wrote in *Al-Qaeda: In Search of the Terror Network that Threatens the World*, "Acting on information procured by British intelligence, two squadrons of the SBS, around sixty men, were sent into the area in what was described as a 'parallel' mission involving killing known al-Qaeda targets."

In August 2008, the German newspaper *Frankfurter Allgemeine Zeitung* reported that special forces operators of the German KSK ("*Kommando SpezialKräfte*," Special Forces Command) took part in the battle as well. They were purportedly responsible for the protection of the flanks in the Tora Bora Mountains, as well as conducting reconnaissance missions. TF 11, whose mission was to support the Eastern Alliance offensive and to capture or kill enemy leaders, assumed command and control of the battle from JSOTF-N.

Dalton Fury, the Delta Force leader, and his command group rolled into Ali's headquarters by mid-afternoon on 7 December. They were welcomed

1st Special Forces Operational Detachment-Delta (Airborne)

The 1st Special Forces Operational Detachment-Delta (Airborne), better known as "Delta Force" is the U.S. Army's primary counter-terrorism unit. It was created by Col. Charles Beckwith in 1977 following the lines of the British Special Air Service. The unit is usually referred to by the government as the "1st Special Operations Detachment" or the "1st Combat Applications Group." Its missions include direct action, strategic reconnaissance, unconventional warfare, foreign internal defense, counterterrorism, theater search and rescue, and other activities as specified by the U.S. government. Delta Force is small, with estimates of its size ranging from less than 800 to more than 2,500 men. It's organized into five squadrons—three operating squadrons, a command and control squadron, and a Communications, Intelligence, and Administrative Support Squadron—along with a medical detachment, aviation platoon, and an intelligence platoon. Its headquarters in located at Fort Bragg, North Carolina.

by George, Team Juliet's leader, who introduced them to the warlord. Ali expressed the same reservations that other special forces had experienced. "It is too dangerous for you Americans. It will be very bad if one of you is killed . . . I will be blamed."

Fury responded that his commandos were "ready to fight, not drink tea." His men were itching to get in the fight.

The initial meeting ended inconclusively. Ali simply responded in Pashto, "Momkin," meaning "maybe." The response did not come as a surprise. George warned that Ali was a master of doublespeak.

"He would promise the world," Fury remarked, "but rarely deliver if he did not see the promise as being useful or helpful to his own agenda."

On 8 December, TF 11 formally assumed command and control of the battle space. The task force established its command post in a small U-shaped compound, a short distance from Ali's headquarters in the school house. The next day, Fury accompanied the Eastern Alliance commander on a trip to the front lines. He learned firsthand that al-Qaeda were well dug in and ready to fight.

"Six or seven mortar rounds landed and detonated simultaneously to our front . . . about fifty meters away," Fury recalled. "The barrage lasted at least two minutes and flung rock, shrapnel, and soil in all directions at blistering speed. The sound was deafening and all too personal." The Special Forces officer noted that there were no front lines, only clusters of troops that were scattered haphazardly along a narrow front.

On the afternoon of the 9th, the rest of TF 11 reached the compound. With the additional men, Fury decided to reinforce the two Cobra OPs and establish three additional posts. Ali decided to take advantage of Fury's request for action on the 10th, and he asked for men to direct airstrikes in support of a planned frontal assault.

Fury sent two operators and a translator to the front lines with Ali. Despite being under heavy enemy fire for several hours, they managed to call in flight after flight of aircraft. "Not a second would pass without a fighter plane passing over our heads, night and day," bin Laden recounted on an audiotape. "American forces were bombing us by smart bombs that weigh thousands of pounds, and bombs that penetrate caves, and other kinds of bombs that enter into caves." Bin Laden's cave was surrounded by a series of trenches, "to protect the Mujahideen from the insane American strikes." One night in early December, the area was bombed. An intercepted radio message from one of bin Laden's men said, "We were awakened to the sound of massive and terrorizing explosions . . . we received horrifying news, the trench of Sheikh Osama had been destroyed."

A contingent of the 1st Special Forces Operational Detachment-Delta (Airborne), known as Delta Force, and British Special Boat Service commandos were committed to Tora Bora. They were assigned to kill bin Laden and his al-Qaeda fighters. *Department of Defense*

Late in the afternoon of the tenth, Fury received information from signals intelligence that pinpointed bin Laden's location. He quickly gathered a reaction force, and drove into the foothills as dusk fell. As he reached a position about two kilometers from bin Laden's reported position, he learned that three of his men with Ali were in a ferocious firefight, and that the warlord was pulling out, leaving the Americans stranded and potentially surrounded. Fury felt he had to pull back to help his team. He agonized over the decision. "It was both the hardest call I ever had to make and the easiest."

His cut-off team had no recourse but to escape and evade. "Warpath, Warpath, Warpath," they broadcast over the radio, the code word to alert the task force of their plight. For more than two hours they worked their way back some two thousand meters to friendly lines, under fire most of the time. A disturbing footnote to their adventure was that they had to bribe their way through several "friendly" checkpoints. Fury was overjoyed to see them. "I honestly thought we wouldn't see them alive," he exclaimed.

The withdrawal of Ali's men at sundown turned out to be their modus operandi. A Special Forces soldier explained that "They don't have a well-developed logistics system like we have . . . all their meals have to be cooked right there for them. They'll battle all day . . . and then pull back because it's dinner time. Then the enemy reoccupies the position that had been taken from them." It was also the religious holiday of Ramadan. "They're not eating or drinking all day." When the sun goes down, they can break the daily fast. "When it's their time to eat and drink, they want to eat and drink!"

Task Force 11 changed the rules by refusing to pull back, and by continuing to hit the al-Qaeda positions with airstrikes. On the eleventh, Ali's rival Ghamsharik suddenly announced that he was negotiating with al-Qaeda for a conditional surrender. "One of our interpreters came in and said 'Stop, no more bombs,'" a Special Forces soldier said. As the ceasefire fire dragged on, the Americans grew impatient: "Why are we stopping for so long?"

The interpreter stalled. "No, no. Don't drop any more." The Americans were furious. They smelled a rat and set a deadline for an unconditional surrender, or they would resume bombing.

"We attack in one hour," Fury told Zaman.

As expected, the surrender did not occur. "That night al-Qaeda and the Taliban all escaped to Pakistan," Mohammed Musa, Ali's brother-in-law said. "We only captured thirteen people . . . we did not want the cease-fire, it was Haji Zaman [Ghamsharik] who agreed to it."

Ali later admitted that it was "just a tactic to enable them to escape." The bombing resumed. From 11 to 14 December, TF 11 continually rained fire on the enemy positions. At one point, one of Fury's teams radioed they had bin Laden in sight. "The Operation Jackal team observed fifty men moving into a cave that they hadn't seen before . . . they saw an individual, a taller fellow, wearing a camouflage jacket. Everybody put two and two together, 'Okay, that's got to be Osama Bin Laden egressing from the battlefield.'"

The team dropped several tons of bombs on the cave. However, they were disappointed when, on 13 December, SIGINT specialists intercepted a message from bin Laden. "I'm sorry for getting you involved in this battle, if you can no longer resist, you may surrender with my blessing." Fury interpreted the message as bin Laden's acknowledgement of defeat and signifying that he was going to flee Tora Bora. A Yemeni doctor who was treating al-Qaeda casualties in the mountains said that bin Laden seemed preoccupied with his own

Mujahideen mountain fighters. At Tora Bora, the anti-Taliban forces did not aggressively pursue bin Laden and his al-Qaeda soldiers. They attacked during the day and then fell back at night, allowing the enemy to regain lost ground. *militaryphoto.com*

escape, "and, to be frank, he didn't care about anyone but himself."

Bin Laden's escape was facilitated by Pashtun tribesmen. Fury believed "a gentleman brought him in . . . he and his family were supporting al-Qaeda during the battle . . . providing food, ammo, water. We think he [bin Laden] went to that house, and received medical attention for a few days." Schroen was convinced that "bin Laden was wounded in some way . . . something to his left side."

Gary Berntsen received information on how he escaped. "It's my understanding he got into a vehicle [and] moved as far as he could and then got out and walked across or was carried across into Pakistan, free and clear." He learned some time later that a "group of two hundred Saudis and Yemenis . . . was guided by members of the Pushtun Ghilzai tribe, who were paid handsomely in money and rifles." Ahmed Rashid wrote in *Decent into Chaos: The U.S. and the Disaster in Pakistan, Afghanistan, and Central Asia*, that "bin Laden and a few bodyguards on horseback escaped into Parachinar, one of the tribal areas in Federally Administered Tribal Areas (FATA) in Pakistan."

On 14 December, Ali finally agreed to continue the attack and to keep his men in the mountains overnight. His men slowly advanced under cover of American firepower. They found that the rush of al-Qaeda fighters out of Tora Bora, which had been a trickle and then a stream, now became a mad dash for freedom. The fighters had lost their will to fight. As panic overtook them, Afghan villagers on the outskirts of Tora Bora were waiting in the wings to reap the harvest. They collected an average of $1,200 per person for taking the injured, the elderly, and women and children into Pakistan's tribal areas.

An Afghan elder said, "This was the golden opportunity our village had been waiting for." The villagers were glad to guide the survivors for money. "The only problem for the Arabs was the first five to ten kilometers from Tora Bora to our village," he said. "The bombing was very heavy. But, after they arrived in our village, there were no problems. You could ride a mule or drive a car into Pakistan." Some fighters were picked up by Pakistan's Frontier Corps before they could blend in with the locals. They were turned over to the ISI, and many were then handed over to the United States and housed in secret locations before being transferred to Guantanamo, Cuba.

The failure to kill bin Laden and the escape of hundreds of his fighters led to a round of finger pointing. Donald Rumsfeld, in *Donald Rumsfeld: Known and Unknown, a Memoir,* wrote, "I was prepared to authorize the deployment of more American troops into the region if the commanders requested them." Berntsen and several other officers requested Gen. Tommy Franks to deploy U.S. Rangers along the Pakistani border to keep the Saudi from escaping. Berntsen recalled his frustration. "Day and night I kept thinking, we need U.S. soldiers on the ground. We need to make sure that not one single member of al-Qaeda gets out of there alive!" Franks refused, even though there were several thousand troops available.

General Franks claimed that "bin Laden was never within our grasp," despite hard intelligence to the contrary. Democratic presidential contender John Kerry claimed that Franks had let bin Laden escape . . . a claim that Franks vehemently denied. CentCom was relying on the Afghans themselves to block the border. Ali paid one of his lieutenants to do the job. "I paid him 300,000 Pakistani rupees ($5,000) and gave him a satellite phone to keep us informed," he said. "Our problem was that the Arabs had paid him more . . ." Berntsen summed up his opinion. "The biggest and most important failure of CentCom leadership came at Tora Bora when they turned down my request for a battalion of U.S. Rangers to block bin Laden's escape."

Operational Detachment Alpha 561 was sent into the mountains on 20 December to search for any remaining al-Qaeda who might have stayed behind. After several days of combing the area, they did not find evidence that any of the key al-Qaeda or Taliban leaders had been killed or wounded, despite the claim of an estimated 250 killed. Jane Corbin wrote, "In May 2002, the SBS would return to the valley leading Canadian [Joint Task Force 2] coalition troops investigating what had happened to bin Laden and his bodyguards after Tora Bora." The Canadians located a grave site, "where villagers revealed that the Taliban had told them to bury Arabs killed in the U.S. bombing." The bodies were disinterred and DNA samples were taken in an attempt to identify the dead—bin Laden was not among the remains. Sometime in late December al-Qaeda released a video of bin Laden. The CIA confirmed it had been made post-Tora Bora.

An ordnance-filled cave in the Tora Bora Mountains discovered by SEALS and other Special Forces after al-Qaeda and the Taliban had fled the area. *defenseimagery.mil*

CHAPTER 20

Operational Detachment Alpha 554 Texas 08

"You can't buy an Afghan, but you can rent one."
—Pakistani ISI Afghan Bureau motto

ON 11 NOVEMBER, ODA 554 (Texas 08) was inserted by helicopter into western Afghanistan near the city of Herat, just fifty miles from the Iranian border. Their mission was to support Ismail Khan, the "Lion of Herat," who was perhaps the single most important military and political figure in the vast region along the Iranian border. Khan was a Persian-speaking Sunni Tajik who, in March 1979, as a major in the Afghan army, led an insurrection against the Taraki regime. Khan's revolt resulted in the slaughter of Soviet Afghan advisors and their families. This insurrection was met by a brutal Afghan and Soviet response that killed an estimated 24,000 Heratis in a single week and destroyed much of the famous Central Asian crossroad city. For the next decade Khan waged a bitter guerrilla war against Soviet occupation as a Mujahideen commander. In 1992, two years after the Soviets left Afghanistan, Khan's militia took back Herat and Khan declared himself Emir of the West. However, three years later, he was forced to flee the city after the Taliban captured it. In May 1997, while organizing opposition to the Taliban, he was betrayed and captured by two

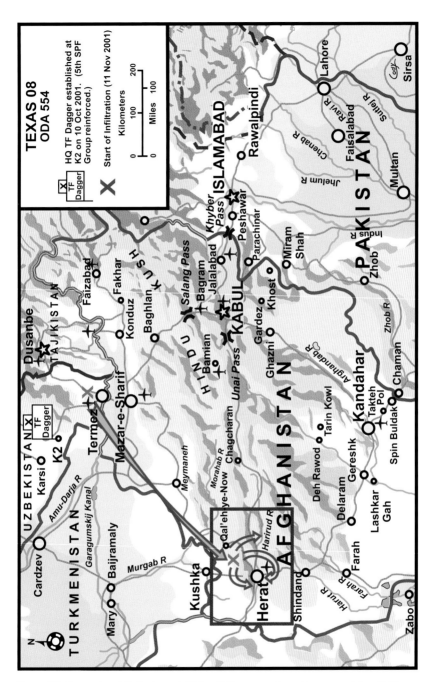

Texas 08, Operational Detachment Alpha 554, was assigned to support Ismail Khan for the attack on the city of Herat in western Afghanistan. The city was located on the main commercial corridor from Iran to Afghanistan's interior cities. Customs tolls earned millions for whoever controlled the city. *Bill Cody*

of Dostum's deputies, who had defected to the Taliban. Khan was thrown into a Kandahar prison but managed to escape to Iran with the help of two former Mujahideen guards.

Texas 08 was well aware that their mission was going to be difficult. Ismail Khan was thought to be an Islamic fundamentalist with strong economic and military ties to Iran. Khan played down the relationship, claiming that "the Iranians are good neighbors, nothing else," which belies the fact that Herat Province and Iran share a common four-hundred-mile border and have a brisk commercial goods trade. The money collected at customs houses in Herat is Afghanistan's largest source of revenue, bringing in $1 million a day in duties on goods imported from Turkmenistan and Iran. Herat has long been considered to be under Persian influence. "Iran supported the struggle of the Mujahideen, as did other countries," Khan freely admitted.

A senior Afghan official agreed. "Without Iran, most Northern Alliance commanders could not have operated in Afghanistan at a time when they had no other source of international support." There was evidence that Iran continued its support of Khan even after Texas 08 was inserted. However, according to Thomas H. Johnson in *Ismail Khan, Herat, and Iranian Influence*, "Ismail Khan has demonstrated that he is a pragmatic Afghan nationalist who abhors foreign influence. Khan himself downplays his relationship with Iran and states it is a 'disgrace to be dependent on outside help . . . after the experiences the Russians and the Pakistanis had with us, every neighbor should know that it does not pay to meddle in our affairs.'"

The Special Forces team was briefed that Khan did not particularly like Americans but would tolerate them because they brought him badly needed supplies, equipment, and, most important of all, access to American air support. Within a short time after arriving, Texas 08 had the opportunity to showcase their capability by destroying several key Taliban positions. Khan was clearly impressed with the results and allowed them to accompany his front-line units as they approached the outskirts of Herat. The constant air bombardment seriously weakened Taliban morale, and when the news of Kabul's fall reached the city's defenders, resistance collapsed. The disorganized survivors fled westward to Iran, where they were welcomed with open arms. Khan's men quickly brushed aside the few die-hard fanatics that tried to delay his approach and entered the city on 12 November. The rapidity of the advance surprised Texas 08. It turned them from warriors to humanitarians in short order.

"We directly negotiate with local commanders for the placement of multinational humanitarian assistance teams to be stationed at the Herat airfield," the team reported. "We are instrumental in assessing the population and the situation inside the city and in surrounding towns to the south and east. Without our presence and perseverance, Ismail Khan and his followers would not be as supportive of the interim government as they currently are."

The overwhelming Iranian influence kept the team from working in their advisory capacity, but it did not stop them from gathering intelligence on Iranian activity in the region. They found that the Quds Force, a special unit of the Iranian Revolutionary Guards, was actively funding various Afghan leaders throughout Afghanistan in an attempt to buy their loyalty and destabilize the Kabul government. Khan was given large sums of money for infrastructure repair, as well as military supplies and equipment that were flown in by Iranian aircraft. They learned that the entire police force was being supplied with new Iranian assault rifles. Khan also received revenue from Iranian imports, which brought in over a $1,000,000 a month from across the border, that he did not share with the central government. The team also learned that Hasan Kazemi Qomi, a Revolutionary Guards commander who served as the Iranian regime's chief liaison to Hezbollah in Lebanon, was now its chief "diplomat" in Herat. Qomi oversaw distribution of aid and projects ranging from road construction to power generation in the province. Iran also infiltrated Revolutionary Guardsmen and intelligence operatives posing as construction workers and teachers. On 8 March 2002, Afghan commanders intercepted twelve Iranian agents and proxies who were organizing armed resistance among Afghan commanders.

The team also reported that Khan had appointed a number of Islamic fundamentalists to important positions in his administration and was being advised by as many as ten Iranian generals posing as Afghans. Khan was reported to have released several high ranking al-Qaeda and Taliban leaders, which was particularly galling, since many of them could have provided important information. It was also reported that Iran was paying for the release of enemy leaders and providing them sanctuary. According to intelligence sources, Tehran was involved in trying to destabilize Kabul's currency exchange by circulating counterfeit money, as well as introducing an anti-American propaganda and a disinformation campaign through its news agency. After performing yeoman service for several months, Texas 08 was relieved by another ODA from the 19th Special Forces Group.

PART III

Boots on the Ground, Southern Afghanistan

CHAPTER 21

Operational Detachment Alpha 574 Texas 12

SOUTHERN AFGHANISTAN, THE BIRTH PLACE of the Taliban, represented a difficult challenge for the United States. The area's Pashtun majority overwhelmingly supported Mullah Omar's movement. Those who stood in opposition had been ruthlessly eliminated, leaving few anti-Taliban leaders to carry on the fight. The CIA was able to identify only three possible candidates—Abdul Haq, Hamid Karzai, and Gul Agha Sherzia. In late October 2001, the list was shortened to two when Haq was captured and executed by the Taliban after entering the country in an effort to raise a resistance movement. According to most sources, Haq jumped the gun by entering Afghanistan without adequate security. He and a small band of supporters were only a few miles inside the country when they were trapped by a large force of Taliban. In the ensuing gunfight, Haq's men were wiped out and he was captured. Vince Cannistraro, a former CIA director of counterterrorism, said that there was "credible information" that the ISI tipped off an Afghan tribal leader about Abdul Haq's whereabouts, and he passed the information to the Taliban. A senior Afghan politician said, "Losing him [Haq] was like losing the best leader Afghanistan never had." The CIA was severely criticized for not supporting Haq, so it went to great lengths to assist Karzai and Sherzai.

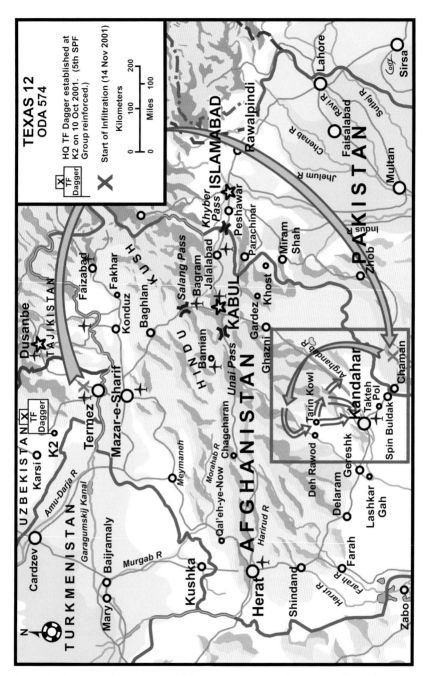

Texas 12, Operational Detachment Alpha 574, was assigned to support the Pashtun
leader Hamid Karzai in southern Afghanistan, the heart of the Taliban movement.
Bill Cody

In mid-November, two ODAs and a Special Operations Command and Control Element (SOCCE) were placed on alert for an operation into southern Afghanistan. Major Donald Bolduc, SOCCE 52 explained their mission: "We were to provide command and control and conduct unconventional warfare to assist Hamid Karzai and Gul Sherzai in organizing anti-Taliban forces, and to conduct combat operations against the Taliban and al-Qaeda forces." ODA 574 (Texas 12) was tasked to support Karzai. "Our mission was to work with Hamid Karzai, who at the time was sort of a wild card," Capt. Jason Amerine said. "He was our biggest hope for a good Pashtun leader that could really rally the people and bring legitimacy and change to the government."

Hamid Karzai

Hamid Karzai was a relatively unknown figure before 9/11 but as the United States searched for an anti-Taliban leader in southern Afghanistan, his

Hamid Karzai was from a highly respected Pashtun family that had opposed the Taliban and al-Qaeda from the very beginning. In 2001, Karzai was almost killed when he entered Afghanistan to start a resistance movement. Only the timely arrival of an American rescue helicopter prevented his capture. *U.S. Army*

name quickly surfaced. "We think we have a Pashtun leader . . . a man of character and great reputation," Mulholland was told. The CIA thought that Karzai was the linchpin between north and south.

"The Uzbeks, the Tajiks, the Hazara, they all respected Karzai," Lt. Col. Martin Compton, Central Command spokesman, said. "They knew he understood the concept of nation-state." Lieutenant Colonel Warren Richards from Mulholland's staff, two ODA commanders, and a CIA operative named "Craig" flew to Jacobabad, Pakistan, to meet secretly with Karzai and several of his lieutenants. The team was tasked to find out whether the Afghan could assemble a force that was willing to fight the Taliban.

At the first meeting, the Americans asked Karzai what they could do to support him. "That," he replied after a long moment, "is something I have waited a long time to hear." The Karzai family, highly respected Pashtun tribal leaders, had fiercely opposed the Taliban and al-Qaeda from the very beginning. Because of their intense and very public opposition, they were forced to leave Afghanistan, but continued their anti-Taliban resistance. In 1999, Hamid assumed the role as the Popalzai tribal chief after his father was assassinated by the Taliban, as many people believed.

Richards recommended supporting Karzai with one ODA team, which was approved by Mulholland. "It was clear to us that the Taliban recognized him [Karzai] as a different kind of threat," Richards said. "Here's one of their own, a Pashtun coming right into the heart of the Taliban homeland."

On the night of 14 November, a six-man CIA team (Team Echo), the twelve-man Texas 12 team, and a three-man Delta Force element were inserted near the village of Tarin Kowt, seventy miles north of Kandahar, by Black Hawk helicopters. The insertion went awry when the first aircraft created a brownout of powdery sand that obscured the plateau's small landing zone. One of the aircraft aborted the landing and dropped off its four passengers two miles away. The two groups could not communicate, but fortunately a patrol of Karzai's men found the missing members and led them back to the main body. The reunited group worked its way off the plateau with a great deal of difficulty—a two-hour descent down a narrow trail covered with patches of gritty sand that was extremely slippery. Upon reaching the bottom, the men were crammed into a truck and a minivan. Any thought of tactical integrity went out the window as the last man slid himself on to the shoulders of those who were already stuffed inside.

Despite their safety concerns, they safely reached a small village of sixty to eighty families, dubbed "Haji Babur's Cove," where they spent the night in one of the clay buildings, sleeping on carpets. The following day, Texas 12's leader, Captain Amerine, met with Karzai, who spoke English with a slight British accent. "I had to find out whether or not if I trusted him, and he had to figure out whether he could trust me and my men," Amerine said. "When you speak to him, you feel like you are speaking to a statesman or at least a scholar of some kind." He found the Afghan leader to be insightful and intelligent. "I felt like I got to know him to the point where I trusted him," Amerine explained. "That I trusted the insights and the intel that he was providing us in terms of what we would be doing in Southern Afghanistan. And I think he likewise trusted us that we were going to do our best with him." The two discussed how they were going to defeat the Taliban. "The goal of the campaign was to start in Oruzgan [Province], the birthplace of the Taliban movement," Amerine recalled, "and then make our way down to Kandahar and force the Taliban to surrender. Taking Kandahar, as I saw it, was probably going to be the end of the war."

The first step in taking Oruzgan Province was to seize its capital, Tarin Kowt, right in the heart of the Taliban movement where Mullah Omar and several key leaders lived. Author Jon Lee Anderson described the town as a "bucolic-seeming place, a market town of flat-topped adobe houses and little shops on a low bluff on the eastern shore of the Tirinrud River, in a long valley bounded by open desert and jagged, treeless mountains. Almost everything around Tarin Kowt is some shade of brown. The river is a khaki-colored wash of silt and snowmelt that flows out of the mountain range to the north, past mud-walled family compounds. About ten thousand people live in the town." Its capture would represent a great psychological victory and bring the area's Pashtuns over to Karzai's forces.

"That was where Karzai and I had a bit of a disagreement in terms of what it would take [to win the campaign]," Amerine said. "He didn't believe we actually needed to raise an army, or believe that there would be any kind of combat. He really saw it more as a matter of negotiating with the tribal belt to get them to roll over and surrender." The Special Forces officer did not see it that way. "I just had to make it clear to him that the Taliban were not going to just roll over and die," he said. "This was going to get bloody." Amerine proved to be correct. The residents of Tarin Kowt revolted, killed the Taliban governor and his bodyguard, and forced his supporters to flee. Amerine knew it would only be a matter of time until the Taliban mounted a counterattack to retake the city and punish its residents. "We had to go in there and try to do what we could," he told Karzai.

Karzai rounded up a couple of dozen men and, together with Texas 12 and Team Echo, piled into a collection of beat-up trucks, ancient station wagons, minivans, and one small shuttle bus for the drive to Tarin Kowt. The forty-five-mile narrow, rutted track followed the Helmand river to Mullah Omar's home town of Deh Rawood and then east across a small range of mountains to the capital. They arrived close to midnight to find the streets empty and eerily quiet, almost like a ghost town; not what they expected in a city that had experienced a violent revolt. The convoy proceeded to a compound where the Americans off-loaded their gear, while Karzai went off to meet with the city's leaders.

A short time after he left, Amerine and Casper (pseudonym), the CIA Team Echo chief, got word to meet Karzai at the deceased governor's house. The two were shown into a room to meet the city's tribal and religious leaders. Karzai introduced them and offered tea. Then, in a matter of fact way, he said, "A large convoy of one hundred trucks carrying 500 Pakistani Taliban is on its way from Kandahar to retake Tarin Kowt and punish the inhabitants."

The news was electrifying, and it took Amerine a moment for the information to sink in. "I won't say it was panic," he related, "but on our side we had twelve Special Forces soldiers and a bunch of highly motivated but untrained guerrillas numbering between thirty and sixty, opposed by a lot of men that were very angry and really wanted to retake the town."

Amerine's first thought was to excuse himself, but the Afghans would not hear of it. They insisted he join them for something to eat. It was the first

Capt. Jason Amerine (right) and an unidentified Special Forces soldier in the streets of Tarin Kowt, where Texas 17 stopped a major Taliban offensive to kill or capture Hamid Karzai. U.S. Army

day of Ramadan and they had fasted all day. Trying not to offend, Amerine gulped down some of the beef stew, stayed just long enough to satisfy civility, and then hurried back to the safe house. He quickly briefed the team, who wasted little time in preparing to meet the threat. Air Force Sergeant Yoshi Yoshita, the combat controller, radioed "Boss Man," the Airborne Warning and Control System (AWACS) aircraft that coordinated aircraft support, and requested immediate assistance. Boss Man vectored two Marine Corps Harrier pilots from VMFA 251 toward Tarin Kowt. While the combat controller worked the air nets, Amerine's communicators sent priority messages to Task Force Dagger, alerting them to the threat and asking them for help in pressuring headquarters for continued air support. Other team members did a map study to identify the best terrain to set up an observation post (OP). They located a ridge south of the city that overlooked the main road from Kandahar. The road ran through a mountain pass at the southern end of a valley, forming a natural choke point, the most logical place for the OP. "You could not have asked for better terrain," Amerine exclaimed.

Sometime after 0130 the Marine Harriers checked in with Texas 12's combat controller. They reported forty plus vehicles headed toward Tarin Kowt and asked for instructions. There was a moment of silence as the controller looked to Amerine for a response. "Smoke'em," Amerine replied emphatically, knowing that anything headed their way was Taliban. The Harriers made several passes and managed to destroy two pickups near the bridge at the entrance to the valley before low fuel forced them to leave the area. The plume of smoke from the burning trucks provided a great marker for the next flight of bombers that arrived just after first light. Two navy F-14 Tomcats from VF-102 had just finished tanking when they overheard the Marine pilots briefing the AWACS. "We quickly realized that the convoy was only forty miles away from us," one Tomcat pilot said, "so our section headed south . . . we knew there was a lot going on down there."

At first light, the team piled into two trucks, while thirty of Karzai's guerrillas followed in another pair. They reached the ridge and hurriedly placed the guerrillas in fighting positions, while the team set up an observation post on a rocky outcrop overlooking the valley. They spotted a large dust cloud and within minutes dozens of Taliban vehicles streamed out of it. "It was like the beginning of a race," Amerine recalled. One of the navy Tomcats released a 500-pound bomb. Two seconds later it exploded, missing the lead vehicle, much to the team's disappointment. But a second bomb followed, making a direct hit . . . and then a third and a fourth. The valley floor was soon littered with burning vehicles, but the Taliban kept coming.

"This was the first time that I had seen this kind of determination," the navy pilot recalled. "I started panicking, because I knew that as soon as the Taliban got into the town, we would not be able to attack them due to their proximity to friendly forces and civilians."

The surviving Taliban vehicles sped toward Karzai's men, who panicked. One, then another, and finally a flood of the scared Afghans piled onto the vehicles and started to pull out. Amerine's men tried to stop them but could not; they were hell bent on getting away. One of the team exclaimed in frustration, "The guerrillas just pulled defeat from the jaws of victory." Amerine was extremely upset. He had been warned to keep the vehicle keys to prevent something like this happening but had forgotten the advice. There was nothing for the team to do but join the rush back to the village. All was not lost however, as one of the navy pilots was a qualified airborne forward air controller (FAC [A]) who took over control—"the ground controller was happy to let us handle the air assets," he recalled. "the first thing [I] did was detach my wingman and direct him to the northernmost truck," he explained. "He got a direct hit and I got another. The convoy ground to a halt, at which point the Taliban started to spread out into the valley on foot."

Amerine's vehicle braked to a stop in front of Karzai's headquarters. The officer jumped out and ran up to the puzzled leader, who was standing in the street wondering what had happened. "The Taliban are coming and there are a lot of them," Amerine hurriedly explained. "The fighters who were with us don't understand our capabilities and they ran." He asked Karzai to gather up everybody who would fight and send them back to support the team.

Karzai nodded and exclaimed, "Go, go."

Amerine ran back to the trucks and they roared off. One of the team yelled, "Drive' em like you stole 'em!" They reached a knoll just outside the town; set up again—the Taliban had already reached their first position— and called in flight after flight of fighter-bombers. "By now Boss Man had figured out that more assets were needed to stop the Taliban, and additional jets were vectored in," the VF-102 pilot said. Soon dozens of smoldering wrecks littered the valley floor. The punch of a 500-pound bomb hurtling from thousands of feet in the air turned trucks into scrap metal, and their passengers into fragmented body parts.

"They were just pouring in the birds," Staff Sgt. Wes McGirr recalled, "because we had the hottest situation going right at that time. We were in immediate contact and in immediate danger, so they just started throwing in the birds, so they were just raking them up."

Despite the pounding, the Taliban continued to close in on the village. Enemy troops kept on remounting the vehicles and taking to the scrub in

Texas 17 team photo with Hamid Karzai. *U.S. Government*

an effort to get around the destroyed trucks. Bombs would then destroy a vehicle or two, but as the jet noise decreased, the Taliban would emerge from the scrub, board the surviving trucks, and drive another quarter mile until the next bombing pass. They were determined to get to Tarin Kowt. In the midst of the fight, the team suddenly became aware that the townspeople had returned—oldsters with antiquated weapons, young men with AK-47s, women, and even children—and were meandering through the position, giving the hilltop a circus-like atmosphere. The team corralled the men and put them in defensive positions, while pleading with the women to take the children out of harm's way.

Suddenly, small arms fire broke out on the western side of Tarin Kowt. Several Taliban had managed to force their way to the edge of town. "That is where things got pretty dicey again," Amerine said. "It was the second time that morning that I wasn't sure if we were going to hold, but in the end the townspeople fought them off."

The aircraft continued to pound the Taliban, first hitting the lead vehicles and then taking on those further on the flanks and in the rear. "We ended up handling six sections of Hornets [F/A-18s] and Tomcats," the FAC (A) said. At one point, several Taliban vehicles, including a tank, made a dash for town. "We went for a classic forward quarter attack," he explained. "We made two passes and it stopped . . . ." After more than two hours of continuous bombing, the surviving vehicles slowed and then turned around, heading back toward Kandahar.

"That was the point at which we knew we had won," Amerine explained. "The decisive point of the battle had been reached." Aircraft continued to pound the fleeing vehicles. One pilot was quoted by Robin Moore as saying, "Let's go, boys, I've got six JDAMs on this bird and I'm itching to drop 'em."

Yoshita replied, "We're running out of targets here, dude, I'm having to sort through the wreckage." The Taliban retreat was marked by a line of destroyed vehicles and charred human remains.

Tarin Kowt was a turning point in the liberation of southern Afghanistan. "When we took Tarin Kowt, it was like taking Richmond during the Civil War," Amerine said. "Hamid turned to me and said, 'We have broken the back of the Taliban.'" Vahid Mojdeh, the Taliban foreign minister, said that "Mullah Omar decided to abandon Kandahar after American planes destroyed all the forces he had sent to retake Oruzgan Province." Karzai correctly assessed that it was the enemy's center of gravity and, with its loss, the Taliban rapidly lost their grip on the population. "For the next few weeks," Amerine pointed out, "everybody was just giving up loyalty to the Taliban and surrendering to us." Karzai's ability to win the support of the population was critical in building a force to challenge the Taliban's hold on Kandahar. "Tarin Kowt solidified Karzai as more than just an expatriate," Amerine stated, "he was a leader and recognized as a major force in southern Afghanistan."

CHAPTER 22

Special Operations Command and Control Element 52 Rambo 52

O N THE EVENING OF 27 NOVEMBER, Lt. Col. David Fox and three members of Special Operations Command and Control Element 52 (SOCCE 52), call sign "Rambo," boarded two Sikorsky MH-53J Pave Low helicopters in Pakistan for the six hour flight to Tarin Kowt. Fox, a battalion commander, was sent in because Donald Rumsfeld wanted higher-ranking officers working with the anti-Taliban leaders. His mission was to advise Karzai in seizing Kandahar and to help him gain support for an interim government. After a midair refueling, the helicopters dropped low for the final approach to the landing zone. On the way in, they received sporadic and inaccurate ground-fire, but what worried Fox the most was whether the link-up party was going to meet them. "I was very concerned that night if there would be someone in the landing zone, because I only had three guys [with me]." As the helicopter came into the zone, it created a brownout. "The rotor wash of the helicopters about 10 to 15 feet off the ground raises such a cloud of dust that you can't see your hand in front of your face," Fox explained.

For the last several feet, the pilots could not see the ground. They just maintained a steady rate of descent until the helicopter's landing gear hit the ground—hard. "It was a controlled crash," one of the men joked. The crew chief pointed out the ramp and yelled, "Go."

"We went out into this cloud of dust where you can see absolutely nothing—not a thing," Fox recalled.

The men moved away from the helicopter in an attempt to get out of the dust cloud. "We stopped and waited for that cloud to dissipate," Fox said. "We put on our night vision goggles which allowed us to see a beam of light where the anti-Taliban soldiers were who were supposed to meet us. I looked over my right shoulder and saw a beat-up pick-up truck. There were four men, obviously Americans, sitting in the back of it. My breathing relaxed and my heartbeat slowed down, because I knew we'd made link-up."

Jason Amerine appeared out of the darkness and welcomed his new boss to Tarin Kowt. After an early morning brief to bring him up to speed on recent events, Fox was taken to Karzai's compound, where he met the Afghan chieftain. "The thing I remember is I immediately took a liking to him," Fox said. "He was very easy to talk to, very friendly." Karzai offered tea and, after exchanging pleasantries, the two began a discussion about goals and objectives. Fox found Karzai to be "very serious, very well educated and a very well-informed man, as far as what he believed the problems facing his country."

The discussions went on for three days, while Karzai tried to negotiate with the Taliban in Kandahar. The Taliban were making surrender overtures but the al-Qaeda forces in the city were dead set on fighting to the last man. Fox thought they were just stalling and told Karzai, "Unless we move south to prove that you have a credible force . . . the surrender negotiations are not going anywhere." Karzai finally agreed and scheduled the move for the 30th. Karzai was all set to go when his satellite phone rang. "It was someone from Bonn [Germany]," Fox said.

The United Nations had brought together representatives of the various anti-Taliban factions to work out the details for a representative government that would satisfy all the ethnic groups. Karzai was invited to speak to the attendees. "I spoke to them on satellite telephone from a very, very cold room," Karzai said. "I had a bad, bad cold and I had no speech written . . . I just spoke from my heart." At the time, Karzai was exhausted but determined to continue with the advance on Kandahar.

The convoy's two elements left Tarin Kowt in an odd assortment of beaten-up vehicles that someone described as "leftover props from a Mad Max movie." Amerine and half his team traveled with the main body, which he portrayed as an "enormous mob."

Major Donald Bolduc described the pandemonium as the vehicles raced hither, thither, and yon. "It was crazy because the Afghans didn't understand convoy operations. They were turning around and driving back and forth, passing each other. So, on our first stop, I said, 'Hey, sir. We have to get control of this.' We got the ODA . . . and Karzai together and we told Karzai to tell everybody that they could not pass a certain vehicle." Between Karzai and the Special Forces, a degree of organization was established, and the convoy was able to proceed to the village of Shawali Kowt, where it encountered the first organized Taliban resistance. Up to this point, the Taliban had retreated before Karzai's force reached them.

"We had air cover overhead," Fox explained. "We used it to keep them [the Taliban] away from us." The main convoy stopped while Amerine, half of his team, and a couple dozen Afghans made their way to a hill that overlooked the town and the Arghendab Bridge, which spanned a dry riverbed. Suddenly, the Taliban started shooting from the town. "It was pretty withering fire," the officer said. The Afghans started to withdraw but stopped when the Americans reached them.

"We got up there . . . and started shooting," Amerine explained. "The Taliban ran away because we could outshoot them."

Amerine determined that the hill—twenty-five feet above the surrounding terrain—was a good defensive position and, as it was getting

An AC-130H Spectre gunship using its mini-guns to fire on Taliban positions.
U.S. Government

late in the day, decided to spend the night there. The hill, dubbed the "Alamo," was quickly outposted and security established for the night. Shortly after dark, machine gun tracer rounds lit the night sky. A company-sized force of Taliban was counterattacking. Most of Karzai's men fled, leaving Texas 17 surrounded. "A lot of my guerrillas got cut off in their retreat," Amerine recalled, "so we . . . marked their positions with strobe lights. Then we brought in an AC-130 gunship that pounded the Taliban all night until they retreated." By dawn on 4 December, there was no sign of the enemy. A few hours later, the guerrilla's that had hastily retreated began to show up, bravely waving their weapons as if they had won the battle. Amerine's men were too tired to be angry.

Late in the afternoon, Karzai's advance force—Amerine and half his team with about a hundred Afghans—moved through Shawali Kowt to a hilltop close to the Arghendab Bridge. The hill was the dominant piece of terrain, and, from its height, defenders could easily control access to the bridge. The Taliban contested the move from positions on the south side of the bridge. The advance force scrambled up the hill under fire, and established a command post in an old ruin. While firing on the Taliban, one of Amerine's men, Wes McGirr, was shot through the throat and severely wounded. He was evacuated, and the team pulled back to the Alamo for the night. At 0345, four Pave Low helicopters inserted the remaining members of SOCCE 52. "I was able to get the remainder of my headquarters element in," Fox said. "That was another eight individuals . . . I needed additional help in organizing logistical support." The newcomers were "put to bed immediately" and roused the next morning "about 0630, so they got about two to three hours sleep," Fox commented.

After rousing his men, Fox directed one of the combat controllers to bomb a cave that the Taliban were using to fire on them. The first 500-pound laser-guided bomb hit just short of the entrance, sending a pillar of brown dust and black smoke into the air. Over the next few minutes, three more bombs were dropped, none of which hit the cave. In the meantime, another controller, Rambo 85, established contact with a B-52, Aetna Seven Nine, carrying a full load of 2,000-pound JDAMs, and gave the navigator the grid coordinates of the target. The controller used a handheld laser target designator to transmit the target's GPS coordinates. The B-52 was carrying two types of bombs: a delayed action bomb that burrowed into the ground before detonating and another that detonated upon impact. The controller selected the delayed option. In the process of transmitting the coordinates, he got a low battery warning. He replaced the batteries, which unknown to him automatically zeroed out all the data and transmitted its own GPS coordinates as a self-test operation.

Fox described the next sequence of events. "The navigator asked the controller to confirm the grid coordinates and he read them off [from the designator], but when you are only talking 1,000 meters from the target and you are using geo[graphic] coordinates you are talking one second off. The navigator asked him to confirm, which the controller does, but they are the coordinates to the designator, which is only 30 feet from my position." The aircraft launched the bomb from 25,000 feet, and it homed in on the designator. "I was down on one knee and I bent over to pick up my binoculars out of my rucksack," Fox recalled, "and I was knocked to the ground."

Amerine was sitting twenty yards northeast of the command post when the bomb hit. "Out of the blue, our position exploded," he said. "I was thrown over the side of the hill." The explosion burst Amerine's eardrums and bomb fragments hit him in the upper thigh. At the time of the explosion, Karzai was in a meeting with several tribal chiefs. He recalled a big bang, the doors and windows blowing in, and being thrown to the floor, bleeding from minor facial cuts. Casper, the CIA team chief, instinctively covered Karzai with his own body, to shield him from further injury. Captain Jeff Leopold remembered, "There was a lot of people yelling and screaming. We weren't sure if we were under attack from the Taliban or whether it was friendly fire or what."

The shock wave had barely subsided before soldiers rushed to the blast site to care for the injured. Fox thought that many of the wounded survived because their comrades provided immediate battlefield treatment. "We went into a kind of a trauma mode at that point," Amerine said. "We pulled guys off the hill and went to work. It was hard for me to estimate, because there were just so many people wounded." At that point, the estimate of casualties included two Americans dead, one missing and nineteen wounded, six were in critical condition, and one expectant (not expected to survive). Afghan casualties ran as high as twenty dead and at least fifty wounded, nine of whom were critical, and three expectant. The exact number of casualties was difficult to tell in the confusion of the moment.

"In the first few minutes there was a tremendous amount of confusion," Fox said. There had been a large group of men standing near where the bomb hit who simply disappeared in the explosion. Within minutes, situation reports were on the way to Task Force Dagger, who requested immediate medical support. The priority message reached the 16th Special Operations Wing at Jalalabad, who scrambled a rescue mission.

Within forty-five minutes of receiving the alert order, a cobbled-together force of twenty-four men in two MH-53J Pave Low helicopters (Knife 03 and 04) launched from Jacobabad (J-Bad), Pakistan, with an expected flight time of two and one-half hours to reach the wounded. The alert order said three injured by mortar fire, and then it quickly jumped to seven. Air Force Paramedic Senior Master Sgt. Patrick Malone said, "I had a funny feeling. I'd been on enough missions where one [casualty] is twenty, or one is fifty, and it's not seven. I wanted to beef up the crews."

At the same time that Malone got the alert, two Air Force Special Operations MC-130 Combat Talon aircraft, configured as Joint Medical Augmentation Units (JMAU), were ordered to land at Camp Rhino, a U.S. Marine base located in the desert just west of Kandahar, and transport the wounded to Oman, the closest military hospital equipped to handle serious casualties. Major Chris Miller's ODB 570, ODA 524, and a forward surgical team were tasked to be a quick reaction force. They launched from K2 and headed to Camp Rhino. They were to transfer to Marine Corps helicopters and fly to Shawali Kowt to provide additional security and medical assistance. SOCCE 540 was to accompany them from Rhino aboard the Marine CH-53s.

At the blast site, the wounded were gathered together at a casualty collection point (CCP). "The northeast wall of the medical clinic had become the forty-foot-long backstop of the CCP," Eric Blehm wrote, "where the wounded lay on blankets, litters, sleeping bags, and doors that had been ripped off their hinges. Casualties fanned out from the clinic, covering a space roughly the size of a basketball court." Everyone was pressed into service treating the seriously wounded and recovering the dead. Despite being wounded, Amerine searched for the missing members of his team. He found one man, Sgt. 1st Class Daniel Petithory, lying dead beneath a truck. Master Sergeant Jefferson Donald Davis, his team sergeant, was nowhere to be found. He was last seen at the western end of the Alamo, near where the bomb exploded. "This slope of the Alamo had been blasted clean: there were no body parts, not even rocks," Blehm noted, "nothing but the smooth surface of the sandy soil." The bomb landed approximately thirty meters from the chest-high wall.

"The Americans and Afghans that died that day were outside the wall, in two manned positions around that hilltop," Fox related. "They just didn't have the protection of that wall. They were down in low dugout positions."

In the midst of the rescue efforts, Karzai received an unexpected satellite call. "It was Lyse Doucet of the BBC with news from Bonn [Germany]," he recalled in an interview with the writer Jon Lee Anderson. "She said, 'You have been selected to lead the government.'" The United Nations had sponsored a meeting of prominent Afghans to plan for governing the country. They selected Karzai to be the chairman of the Afghan Interim Authority. A short time later, he received another call. "Nurses were cleaning my face of the debris and the blood," Karzai said. "A call came, and when I answered, it was the Taliban calling to surrender." Karzai exclaimed, "Nine, nine-twenty, the call about Bonn, ten o'clock, ten-fifteen, the Taliban were coming to surrender. One hour!"

Karzai had developed a good relationship with several of the Taliban's key leaders, and now it was paying off. As they approached Karzai's security, "we would allow one vehicle to come across with four folks," Fox recalled. "That's when Karzai and those four individuals negotiated for the surrender of Kandahar."

The rescue helicopters arrived. "The minute we stepped off that plane and the dust started to settle, you got the vision of the chaos of war," Sergeant Malone recalled. "It was so evident. The first guy that approached us was completely shell-shocked, almost to the point of incoherency." Bomb-damaged trucks appeared. "As the trucks roll up, now we start to see every type of blast injury you can imagine. Some guys were on litters; some weren't. Some were on blankets, bed pads, whatever they could find to put them on. And we started carrying to get them on the helicopter." Many of the men were dazed. "I wouldn't quite call everybody zombies, but they were kind of in a catatonic state."

The wounded were quickly re-triaged and loaded aboard, the critically injured going to Knife 04, the less-injured to Knife 03. Technical Sergeant Ryan Schultz said that "we just kept loading, and we crammed [until] we couldn't put anybody else in the aircraft. There was one person that they wanted to load, but we couldn't. He would've been on top of somebody. And we already had people on top of each other."

Knife 04 was loaded, and the mission commander authorized it to fly single-ship. "Get all the criticals out of here!" he emphasized. At 1245, it lifted off for the forty-minute flight to Camp Rhino, followed by Knife 03 with eighteen wounded and the remains of Sergeant 1st Class Petithory.

"When we looked down, he was in a bivvy sack, zipped up, with an American flag pinned on it," Malone recalled solemnly. One of the CIA field officers had carefully pinned the flag to it and then saluted as the remains were carried away. The medics struggled to treat the injured.

"Guys were throwing up all over the back of the helicopter," Schultz explained. "The two guys on the ramp were bleeding out. One guy had half

U.S. Air Force medical evacuation crew members carrying a Texas 17 team member off the aircraft in Germany. *U.S. Government*

his hand blown off . . . [and] the other guy was bleeding out his leg. And I'm just going back and forth between these two guys, treating the injuries as I find them. . . . The first guy I bandaged up was bleeding out his hand . . . I rolled him over and find that most of his arm's blown off . . . there's not much left. He had basically mid-forearm down, and then a lot of mush, and then from about mid-humerus up was viable. I just went ahead and amputated the arm with a scissors."

Knife 04 reached Camp Rhino just minutes after the two JMAUs. Malone recalled, "When we landed, the place went black with fine dust . . . and the patients are lying in this mess. There's nothing you can do but try and get 'em out of the environment as quickly as you can." Fortunately the 15th Marine Expeditionary Unit (MEU) Shock Trauma Platoon (STP) had arrived the previous evening and was on hand to assist with the stabilization of the wounded, nineteen of which were quickly transferred to specially configured MC-130s where surgeons performed damage-control surgery in the forward portion of the aircraft. Special curtains closed off the space to keep it as sterile as possible. Unfortunately, before the surgeons could work their miracle, Staff Sgt. Brian Cody Prosser passed away.

Malone and Schultz were emotionally and physically drained. They sat down for awhile and then began the unpleasant job of cleaning up the helicopters. "We cleaned up as best we could," Schultz said. "[I] grabbed a big body bag and threw all the stuff in there, the bloody blankets and as I picked one up, an arm fell out."

Twenty Afghan casualties, including one dead, were flown by Marine CH-53 helicopters to the USS *Peleliu* and USS *Bataan* for treatment. The surgeons aboard the *Peleliu* logged over one hundred hours in ship's four operating rooms, treating thirty-six life and limb saving procedures. Aboard the *Bataan*, two surgeons conducted twenty-nine surgical procedures in a twenty-nine hour period.

The deceased Afghani was returned to Forward Operations Base Rhino and was buried with full military honors. The body lay in a white shroud next to the open grave. Corporal Anis Trabelsi, a Muslim from Baltimore with the 15th MEU, performed the graveside service in Arabic. The body was placed in the grave according to Islamic custom, with his head facing Mecca. Seven U.S. Marines wearing helmets and flak jackets fired three crisp volleys from their M-16s into the cold morning air. Brigadier General James N. Mattis and more than a dozen other Marines stood at attention while others watched from atop a mound of sand. At Trabelsi's request, journalists covering the event were not allowed to watch the body being lowered into the ground. Eventually the body was exhumed and returned to the family in Kandahar.

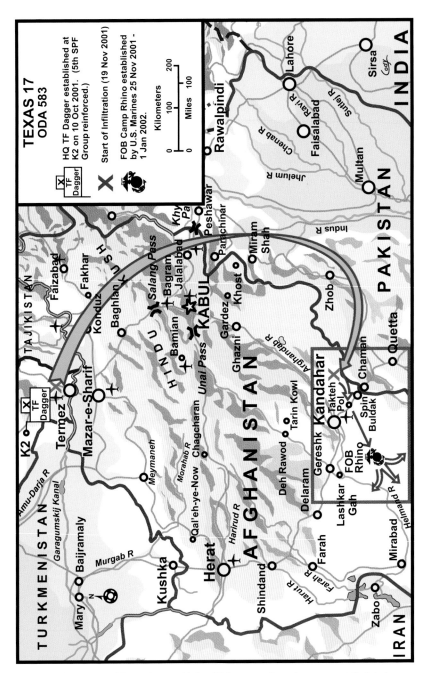

TEXAS 17
ODA 583

HQ TF Dagger established at K2 on 10 Oct 2001. (5th SPF Group reinforced.)

⊠ TF Dagger

✕ Start of Infiltration (19 Nov 2001)

FOB Camp Rhino established by U.S. Marines 25 Nov 2001 - 1 Jan 2002.

Kilometers
0   100   200
0   100
Miles

Texas 17, Operational Detachment Alpha 583 was assigned to support Gul Agha Sherzai, an anti-Taliban Pashtun commander. Their area of operations included Kandahar, the spiritual capital of the Taliban movement. *Bill Cody*

CHAPTER 23

Operational Detachment Alpha 583 Texas 17

*"I will respect the Koran, and kiss it,
and put it in my pocket, and then shoot them."*
—Northern Alliance fighter

ONE DAY AFTER THE BATTLE of Tarin Kowt, Capt. Harry Sims (pseudonym), two other members of ODA 583, and a six-man CIA team were helolifted into the Shin Naray Valley, southeast of Kandahar. They were to meet a potential anti-Taliban Pashtun leader, Gul Agha Sherzai, nicknamed the "bulldozer" because of his rough-hewn tactics. Sims was told that he might be on the ground for only "two or three days, just to keep an eye on Sherzai and determine if he had 500 men under arms." The rest of his team would wait in Jacobabad until they were called in. Sims went in cold. He knew little about Sherzai, except that he was the son of a famous Mujahideen fighter and a former governor of Kandahar in the 1990s. A newspaper article described Sherzia as: "a large man of large appetites, not just for food, but for battle and laughter and power. He speaks in a rough growl, as if his mouth is full, which it often is, but even when it isn't, his words are slurred, like Marlon Brando. The absence of a front tooth or two only partly explains matters." Sims explained that Sherzai looked like a typical warlord, but "he was our warlord and seemed to fit our purposes as to getting after the Taliban and [al-Qaeda]."

As Sims stepped off the ramp of the Pave Low helicopter, he was met by Sherzai, who warmly welcomed him but seemed somewhat surprised and dismayed to see only a few Americans disembark. He quickly recovered and led them to his base camp, where they were shown to a small mud-walled hut, which became their headquarters. After dropping his gear, Sims joined Sherzai for a strategy session. During the course of the conversation, Sherzai requested weapons, ammunition, food, and medicine for his band. Sims politely delayed answering until he had an opportunity to see Sherzai's band for himself.

At first light on 19 November, Sims was pleasantly surprised to see hundreds of men gathered in small groups in and around the base camp. He estimated there were at least 600 and possibly as many as 800 men. Sherzai told him that he had several hundred more in other locations that he could call upon. Sims recalled that the men looked more like an armed band than a military organization: "Sherzai's forces were lightly armed with a mix of small arms. Ammo was generally scarce. There were some light mortars and heavy machine guns that were inoperable. Uniforms were nonexistent and were a mix of local Pashtun garb. Vehicles were four-door Toyota pick-up trucks, tractors, a few sedans and motorcycles, and several large trucks. The force was organized with numerous commanders of varying loyalty and men under their command."

Despite the appearance of Sherzai's men, Sims felt they could take on the Taliban with his team's help. He immediately requested the rest of the team. Master Sergeant Nick S. Nowatney recalled, "The detachment cross-loaded onto two MH-53 helicopters for the flight into Afghanistan. After crossing the border we dropped down to one hundred feet off the deck." However, five minutes after entering Afghan airspace, one of the pilots on his aircraft shouted out "SAM!" and executed a series of gut-wrenching evasive maneuvers to avoid the missile. The men in the back grabbed whatever they could to keep from bouncing around. Fortunately all were strapped in, or there could have been injuries. If that was not exciting enough, "a second pilot reported a master caution light had come on." The pilots quickly determined that the aircraft was still flyable and decided to go back to Quetta, Pakistan. Upon reaching the friendly airfield, the men hastily transferred their gear and piled into the good aircraft to continue the mission.

"Twenty minutes out from the LZ," Nowatney said, "the advance party relayed word that they were in a firefight!" After several minutes of orbiting, the helicopter landed safely. The firing was determined to be several of Sherzai's men, who were spooked by what they thought were Taliban infiltrators.

With the entire detachment reunited, Texas 17 was ready to fight. On the afternoon of 20 November, Sherzai held a council of war attended by a dozen of his sub-commanders and the Americans. At one point Sims addressed the Afghans through an interpreter. At the end of his speech, he challenged Sherzai. "Do you want to sit here in the Shin Naray, or do you want to be in Kandahar where you were once governor?" Sherzai reacted as Sims expected . . . impassioned, excited, and anxious to get under way. They planned to advance west through the Shin Naray Valley to the town of Takteh-pol and block Highway 4 (one of only two highways in the country) that ran from Pakistan to Kandahar. After taking Takteh-pol, the force would move north to the Arghastan Wadi, seize the bridge over a mile-wide dry riverbed, and continue on to take the Kandahar airport, the key to the city. Kandahar was the most important political center of gravity in the south.

The following day, the entire force moved out in a 100 vehicle convoy— Toyota pickups, large multi-axle Ginga transport trucks, and farm tractors pulling trailers—carrying over 800 Pashtun fighters, the CIA operatives, and Texas 17's twelve-man team. Master Sergeant Nowatney explained that, while there was only a dozen Special Forces, they had over thirty weapons systems: "ten rifles, thirteen pistols, three M203 grenade launchers, one M79 grenade launcher, two SPR rifles, two Mossburg shotguns, two M24 sniper rifles, one Barrett sniper rifle, and one .300 Winchester Mag.

Nangarhar Provincial Governor Gul Agha Sherzai conducts a press conference at Bagram Air Field on 20 February 2009, following a ceremony recognizing the twentieth anniversary of the Soviet Union's withdrawal from Afghanistan. Nicknamed the "bulldozer," he was an aggressive warlord with an appetite for power. According to an intelligence report, he received up to $1 million a week from his share of import duties and from the opium trade. *Department of Defense*

sniper rifle." The radios and GPS systems that connected them to air support gave them overwhelming firepower. After two and a half days, the convoy reached a bowl-shaped depression five miles east of the Taliban garrison at Takteh-pol without incident. Nowatney said that Sherzai wanted to try to negotiate with the Taliban before launching an attack. "The majority of the Taliban were just locals that had been forced to join. They were his people and if he was to ever be the governor again, he [Sherzai] would need their support." Before the negotiators left, Sherzai sent half his force to a low ridgeline two miles east of the town to provide them support in case there was trouble. Sims tagged along with half the team, which he split into two four-man CAS teams.

With the covering force in position, the negotiators made their way into town. As darkness fell, the men on the ridge noticed several pickup trucks leaving the town and maneuvering to surround their position. At the same time Sherzai reported the same thing was happening to his position in the depression. Sensing that the Taliban were planning an attack, Sims told his combat controller to request air support. At 2000, the negotiators reported Sherzai's "suggestion" to surrender had been rejected, and that they were on the way out of the town. As they started back, the Taliban suddenly launched an attack from the high ground north and south of the ridge, as well as straight out of Takteh-pol. Sherzai's men immediately returned fire, while Staff Sgt. Andrew D. Kubik, the combat controller, called in an AC-130 (Spectre) that had just reached the area.

"The Air Force combat controller was the team's ace in the hole," Nowatney explained. "He quickly called in CAS and directed priority to the hilltops, which quickly gave us fire superiority and allowed us to withdrawal back to the main body." The aircraft's advanced optics allowed it to place accurate fire on the Taliban positions as well as on several vehicles they were using. Within minutes, the Spectre had destroyed six trucks, one of which was filled with ammunition that exploded and burned for almost an hour. The airstrike not only stopped the attack, but caused the Taliban to flee the town. In their panic, they left abandoned trucks and equipment littering the desert.

Sherzai followed up the victory by establishing two roadblocks to cut Highway 4; one five miles north at the Arghasten wadi, just short of the bridge and the other five miles south toward Spin Boldak. The following day, the Taliban hit the northern roadblock with rockets from positions located at Kandahar airport. Sims thought the shelling might be a prelude to a counterattack, so he hastily established an observation post on a ridge south of Arghastan Wadi Bridge, ten miles from the Kandahar airport. From here, his team called in devastating airstrikes on the Taliban, many of whom took shelter under the concrete bridge because they thought the Americans would not bomb it. And they were correct: however, they were not safe from the effects of the AC-130s 105mm and 40mm cannons. Shrapnel from the high-explosive shells sprayed the Taliban hiding underneath with lethal results but did not significantly damage the bridge structure.

Master Sergeant Nowatney recalled that "for the next ten days straight, 24 hours a day, the team to the north (four NCOs) called airstrikes onto the Kandahar airfield and surrounding area." They were unable to use some of the laser equipment they brought in because of its limited range, so the NCOs identified the target through their optics and walked the aircraft onto the target. They dropped so many bombs that the pilots nicknamed them, "Cleared Hot!" Intelligence reports indicated that Mullah Omar was hiding in an underground water tunnel in Kandahar. Airstrikes by navy planes dropped several 2,000-pound bombs against the target but missed. A later strike by an air force fighter-bomber carrying a GBU-28 "bunker buster," with a 4,400-pound penetrating warhead collapsed the tunnel but did not kill Omar.

Staff Sergeant Andrew D. Kubik
Silver Star Citation

"Staff Sergeant Andrew D. Kubik distinguished himself by gallantry in connection with military operations against an armed enemy of the United States near Tactaplo, Afghanistan, on November 23, 2001. Kubik was attached to Operational Detachment Alpha [583], which was attacking north through a valley toward Kandahar, Afghanistan, with a 500-man anti-Taliban force when they became decisively engaged by a well-planned and executed three-way ambush. A withering barrage of anti-aircraft gunfire as well as rocket propelled grenades and small arms fire pinned down the entire team. As a massive volume of fire rained down on them, stunning the coalition force, Kubik stayed in an exposed position and calmly coordinated emergency close air support. With devastating effectiveness, Kubik controlled numerous bombing runs that set the conditions for a counterattack by the Special Forces team and anti-Taliban force, which led to the battlefield being swept of enemy forces. Kubik's decisive actions were overwhelmingly responsive for breaking the back of Taliban resistance and cleared the way for the final offensive on Kandahar and subsequent victory in southern Afghanistan."

On 2 December, a large detachment of Sherzai's men crossed the bridge and established defensive positions on the opposite bank. After dark, the Taliban counterattacked through a maze of dry canals but were spotted by surveillance aircraft and destroyed. The following morning, Sherzai's men continued the attack toward Kandahar. Throughout the day, they were heavily engaged with al-Qaeda fighters. At one point they suffered several casualties from heavy machine gun and cannon fire, and were forced to withdraw. It was only the actions of the Special Forces air controllers that kept them from being surrounded and overwhelmed. With Sherzai knocking on the door at Kandahar, the Taliban attacked the southern roadblock, hoping to take some of the pressure off their forces in the city. On 5 December, the Taliban shelled the outpost in preparation for a ground attack. Sims sent one of his four-man CAS elements to help repel the Taliban. They went into action as soon as they arrived. The first air strikes knocked out several mortar positions and an anti-aircraft gun. The Special Forces team spotted the Taliban using the bridge as cover, similar to the Arghastan Bridge incident. This time, however, it was decided to drop the bridge spans to block the Taliban advance. A fast moving fighter-bomber dropped two 500-pound laser-guided bombs, which brought down the spans and destroyed a mobile rocket launcher as well as a truck loaded with ammunition. A Taliban fighter admitted that after the pounding he received, "Thoughts of 'run today to fight another day' were creeping into his thoughts."

Vahid Mojdeh reported that "Mullah Omar was forced to spend his nights in open spaces or places where he would not be seen. Even though Mullah Omar was officially in charge of the military, in fact he had no contact with the front because he was afraid his location would be pinpointed and bombed."

Jalaluddin Haqqani, Omar's right hand man, was quoted in *The News*, a Pakistani newspaper: "Mullah Omar, Osama bin Laden and all other commanders are safe and sound and carrying out their duties," he bellicosely declared. "We are eagerly awaiting the American troops . . . they are creatures of comfort. We have so far held to our defenses. There is no retreat anywhere." Haqqani gave the interview as Sherzai's main body came within striking distance of Kandahar.

"Our forces are five kilometers east of Kandahar airport," Mohamed Jalal Khan, a local commander said, "We hope to capture Kandahar soon."

A large number of Taliban were still in position near the airport and had to be eliminated before Khan's men could advance. Sims' team called in an

AC-130H gunship. The aircraft identified the targets and started firing on the Taliban positions. Almost immediately, a crewman spotted a missile launch, the first indication that the Taliban had infrared missiles. The pilot immediately jettisoned flares to confuse the missiles' guidance system and executed a series of evasive maneuvers. The missiles exploded harmlessly and the pilot repositioned the aircraft to continue the firing mission. At one point a secondary explosion illuminated the aircraft, and the Taliban launched another missile, which was also defeated, enabling the aircraft to finish the mission.

On the morning of 7 December, Sherzai received an excited call on a satellite phone from his son. The young man was standing in the governor's arched sandstone headquarters in the center of the city. He had driven there without meeting any resistance. The Taliban had seemingly slipped out of the city with their arms and equipment.

Owis Tohid of the *Daily Times* reported that in the confusion of the surrender, Mullah Omar was able to escape. "It was Mullah Abdul Ghani Baradar who came up with the idea to make an escape on motorbikes," he wrote. "Mullah Baradar gave a burqa to Mullah Omar, who—after initially refusing but later putting it on—mounted a [Honda] motorbike like an Afghan woman. Baradar himself rode the bike and dodged the Americans."

The remains of a Soviet surface-to-air missile launcher at Kandahar after an air strike. The damage made it difficult to determine exactly what the wreckage was. *USMC*

President Musharraf quipped, "The best advertisement for Honda would be an advertising campaign showing Mullah Omar fleeing on one of its motorcycles with his robes and beard flowing in the wind." Omar was able to cross the Pakistani border with the help of the ISI and establish a new headquarters in Quetta, Baluchistan Province, Pakistan, which became known as the Quetta Shura.

Sherzai was overjoyed with the news from Kandahar and immediately left to join his son. Sims hesitated; JSOTF-N had ordered him to stay out of the city. Mulholland had personally told him, "We have reports that Sherzai's troops are looting the city, and the various factions are fighting each other. It's not safe." Sims was caught in the middle because, a short time later, Sherzai's translator arrived with a message. "Sherzai invites you to his palace," the Afghan related. "He asks why you're not there with him."

Sims thought it over and decided that he knew the situation better than his boss several hundred miles away. "I determined that first, I had

Captain Nathan C. Green
Silver Star Citation

"Captain Nathan C. Green distinguished himself by gallantry in action in connection with military operations against an opposing armed force near Kandahar Airport, Afghanistan, on 5 December 2001. On that date as an AC-130H aircraft commander, Green's mission was to provide close-air support and armed reconnaissance to a combined team consisting of U.S. Special Forces and anti-Taliban forces. Surveying the area between the friendly position and the heavily defended airport, Green realized the required attack orbit would take them directly over the heavily defended airport, so he led the crew through a unique partial orbit attack. While destroying targets, the crew detected the launch of two infrared missiles coming from an area near the airport. Green directed the aircraft and crew through defensive maneuvers and procedures to perfection, defeating the missiles. He displayed great leadership ability and bravery as he directed the crew of 13 officers and non-commissioned officers back into the extremely hostile environment. Green repositioned the aircraft to precisely engage an enemy compound containing multiple targets that threatened air and ground forces. As the crew scored numerous direct hits, the enemy weapons ignited and engulfed the entire compound in flames. As the intense fire from this explosion illuminated the gunship, another infrared missile was launched at the aircraft from a much closer range than the previous missiles. He flawlessly handled this threat as he had the other two, defeating the missile. Intelligence credited the crew with destroying six SA-3 missiles, one truck, three towed artillery pieces and two towed rocket launchers."

to maintain rapport with Sherzai and accept the invitation; second that he had made it to the palace . . . so maybe things were somewhat safe; third, that if there was an implied intent to prevent forces of Sherzai and Karzai from conflicting I could do it better in the city than outside the city; fourth, making ballsy unexpected moves had served me well so far; fifth, Colonel Mulholland couldn't blame me if I made an on the ground assessment that going in would do more good than not going in if a positive advantage presented itself; and sixth, the whole team was itching to get into the city and the fighting was quickly dying out around the airport." He turned to the translator and said, "Hell, yeah, we're coming!"

As the team rode into town with the anti-Taliban soldiers, thousands of enthusiastic residents lined the streets cheering them for ousting the Taliban. Occasionally someone yelled "Welcome" and "Thank you" in broken English. The team saw evidence of the power shift as they watched the Taliban's white flags being torn down from buildings along the street. They passed several luxurious houses, which were said to belong to senior Taliban and al-Qaeda officials. When the team reached the blue arched governor's house, Sherzai's men were already celebrating. They'd captured one of Mullah Omar's cars, a sinister black Lexus 4x4, and were parading it around the driveway of the governor's house. Others were smoking hashish in the garden. Inside the mansion, several the Afghans were horsing around with a bunch of leather straps that the Taliban's dreaded religious police used to whack men whose beards were too short or women who dared to wear white socks.

The team heard reports that a large number of Taliban fighters had refused to surrender and were holed up on the outskirts of the city. Looting and gunfire were reported in some parts, but by nightfall a commander overseeing the handover said peace had returned. "The process of surrender has been completed and now the city is calm and peaceful," Haji Bashar said.

A spokesman for Sherzai said that a former Taliban commander who had switched sides and had switched back was now leading the fighters again. The spokesman said that "he is actually protecting the Taliban." Other sources attributed the sporadic fighting to a power grab among the newly arrived anti-Taliban commanders, some of whom had formerly ruled the region as warlords. A senior Pakistani intelligence officer said that "Kandahar was divided into fiefdoms. Naturally, they are now going to hold the area they occupy." The three biggest competitors were Karzai, Sherzai, and Mullah Naqeebullah, the former Taliban commander who had surrendered the city and switched sides. The Mullah had been promised the governorship of the city, but Sherzai's occupation of the palace nullified the deal.

Sherzai's occupation of the city infuriated Karzai, who seriously considered launching an attack to evict the interloper. Lieutenant Colonel David Fox, the senior Special Forces advisor to Karzai said, "It was everything I could do to calm Karzai down because he was prepared to conduct a military action to force Sherzai out of the mansion and out of Kandahar. So I looked at him and I said, 'Listen, because the fall of Kandahar and the surrender was really the final state. Do you want to start a civil war?' The country at that point was pretty secure. The Taliban had fallen apart and had either gone back into the mountains or had dispersed into Pakistan or wherever. Karzai thought it over and did not attack." A few days later, the three contenders sat down and worked out their differences. Naqueebullah was allowed to keep his religious title and his home in the city, but he gave up all other claims. Sherzai became Kandahar's governor, while Karzai went on to national office.

Karzai and Triple Nickel moved into Mullah Omar's large walled compound, which bin Laden had built for him on the edge of the city. The compound was nestled in a grove of pine trees on a rise beneath a sharp rock mountain. The property resembled an American ranch, with a large open-air compound and ample stabling for horses and camels. There was an outdoor pool, a fountain, and spacious living quarters. Omar even had his own private mosque, which was painted a lurid shade of green and blue. Its minarets had bits of mirror stuck to them to catch the light. The complex had been heavily bombed and strafed. About half of it lay in ruins, with entire buildings reduced to rubble.

"Untidy piles of bricks and masonry lay everywhere," Jon Lee Anderson reported. "The section where Omar lived was mostly intact, thanks to twelve-foot-thick bombproof roofs, reinforced with steel rods. The outer walls of the house are covered with murals depicting lakes and ornamental gardens and flowers." Omar's private apartment was painted pink and green. The floor was covered with plastic terrazzo tiles. His small bedroom had a ceiling fan, a double bed, and two white and faux gilt mini-chandeliers. The walls were decorated with molded Formica painted brown to look like wood.

Omar's bomb-proof bunker was located two hundred yards from the edge of the compound, at the base of a large hill. From a distance it appeared to be just another of the hillsides, at the foot of the mountain range overlooking Kandahar. Three large craters—the result of 2,000-pound

Mullah Omar's walled compound outside the city of Kandahar. The compound featured an outdoor pool, private mosque, and spacious living quarters. *U.S. Government*

Mullah Omar's house suffered major bomb damage. Unfortunately he was not at home when the bomb came knocking. *U.S. Government*

bombs—marked each of the cave's steel door entrances. A placard stated in Arabic that the bunker was the work of one of Osama bin Laden's construction companies. The metal framework holding the cement roof in place was bent in half from the bombs' force. A seven-foot-high concrete-lined, gently sloping tunnel ran some forty feet below ground. Fifty yards from the entrance it split into a "T"-shaped junction that led to cavernous rooms that had modern air-conditioning—powered by the cave's own electricity supply—that served as sleeping quarters, bathrooms with squat toilets, and two rooms for weapons and ammo storage. An intricate plumbing system piped in fresh water from a nearby well. The bunker was a substantial piece of civil engineering.

The Special Forces teams set up their antennae on the roof and tried to be as inconspicuous as possible however, one reporter noted, "The commandos are here to protect the other new tenant of Omar's house: Hamid Karzai, Afghanistan's new prime minister. With wrap-around shades, M-16 rifles, lap-tops, and their MREs full of peanut butter, the commandos are a curiosity for Karzai's many visitors and well-wishers. These are turbaned tribal elders who gather in the old Taliban's war council room, sitting cross-legged and fingering their prayer beads in a gas lantern's blue light. Some of them greet Karzai with a good Pashtun hug; others kiss his hand. 'Is my turban all right?' laughs Karzai when photographers appear. 'And I haven't touched my beard in months now.'"

Reporters questioned Karzai about Mullah Omar. "I want to arrest him," he said. "I have given him every chance to denounce terrorism and now the time has run out. He is an absconder, a fugitive from justice." He vowed to bring Omar to justice. "The Taliban rule is finished. As of today they are no longer a part of Afghanistan." Karzai said he believed Omar, and that what was left of the Taliban and al-Qaeda had headed for mountain hide-outs in Zabul province, northeast of Kandahar.

With the surrender of Kandahar, Texas 17's mission was complete. The detachment was one of the most heavily decorated teams, being awarded one Silver Star, three Bronze Stars with "V" device, and eight Bronze Stars. During its ten days in the field, the team called in 185 air missions, which dropped 471 tons of ordnance.

CHAPTER 24

Rangers Lead the Way

"Sua Sponte (Of Their Own Accord)*"*
—75th Ranger Regiment motto

IN THE EARLY MORNING HOURS of 20 October 2001, four air force MC-130 Combat Talon II transports from the 1st Special Operations Wing, carrying one hundred and ninety-nine men from the 3rd Battalion, 75th Ranger Regiment, and four members of Tactical PSYOP Detachment (TPD) 940, B Company, 9th Psychological Operations Battalion, staged a low-level parachute assault to seize a remote desert hunting camp and landing strip, code named "Rhino," sixty miles southwest of Kandahar.

Major Robert Whelan, Ranger battalion S-2, described the facility as "a frontier outpost, with a 2.5 meter high wall and 9 meter high towers. It was a self-contained compound attached to a 6,000 foot runway right in the middle of Afghanistan." The Rangers' mission was fivefold: seize the landing strip, destroy any Taliban forces, gather intelligence, assess the suitability of the landing strip for future operations, and establish a forward aerial refuel/rearm point (FARP) for helicopters. Rhino was divided into four separate objectives: Tin, Iron, Copper, and Cobalt, a suspected Taliban billeting area. Objectives Tin and Iron were assigned to Alpha Company, while Objective Cobalt was given to two platoons of Charlie Company.

Prior to the assault, B-1 bombers dropped 2,000-pound bombs on various targets around the objective, concentrating on Objective Tin. AC-130s gunships followed the initial strike, accounting for eleven Taliban

Ranger tab.
U.S. Government

killed and forcing nine to flee the target area. The gunships also fired on Objective Cobalt's buildings and guard towers in support of Charlie Company's assault. According to reports, an air force special operations weather team (SOWT) from the 10th Combat Weather Squadron, 720th Special Tactics Group, was on the ground prior to the operation to provide last minute weather conditions. An hour before the scheduled drop, they reported heavy ground fog on the target. The Ranger commander considered aborting the operation. Before he could give the order, however, the SOWT team radioed that it would clear up in about fifteen minutes. The weather cleared, and the operation continued.

Twenty minutes from the drop zone, the jumpers conducted a last minute inspection of their equipment and signaled the jumpmaster that all was a go. At the ten-minute mark they hooked up their static line to the anchor cable that ran the length of the aircraft's interior. As the aircraft neared the drop zone, code named "Vengeance," they assumed an in-trail formation, with 2,200 feet between each transport, and a lateral dispersion of 130 feet to keep them out of the turbulence of the aircraft in front of them. At three minutes out, the transports slowed their airspeed to 130 knots, while maintaining an altitude of 800 feet above ground level. The aircraft's crewmen opened the jump door. One Ranger said that he knew they were close to the ground when dust blew into the plane.

A combat cameraman caught the action over the drop zone with the aid of a night-vision lens. The grainy phosphorescent greenish video showed the closely packed jumpers guiding their static line snap hooks into the waiting hand of the jumpmaster and then leaping from the door, feet together, knees slightly bent, arms folded over their reserve parachute, rapidly falling through space. The jumpers were able to orient themselves on their objective because it was burning from the airstrikes.

Once on the ground, Alpha Company secured the landing zone, cleared the two objectives, and established their blocking positions without incident. "The assaulting element that was responsible for seizing a complex at the end of the runway took fire as they breached the complex and entered," Maj. David Doyle recalled, "but the resistance was quickly overwhelmed." Charlie Company attacked Objective Cobalt, killing one enemy soldier in the process. They were able to get into the interior of the compound through a hole in the wall that one of the AC-130s had blasted. Once inside, they found that the buildings' concrete walls and reinforced roofs had sustained little damage.

75th Ranger Regiment coat of arms. *U.S. Government*

The process of clearing the buildings took more time than anticipated, because many of the steel room doors were locked and had to be breached with multiple shotgun blasts or demolition charges. As Charlie Company worked its way through the buildings, the PSYOP specialists broadcast messages on loud speakers in Urdu, Pashto, and Arabic in an attempt to coax any defenders into surrendering. The four PSYOP specialists split up into two teams, TPT 941 and TPT 943. One team began broadcasting from a loudspeaker. "It told anyone in the area that U.S. forces were present and that they needed to exit the buildings, stay away from the airfield, drop any weapons, and get down on the ground if they wanted to survive," one member explained. "We played the message for about 5 minutes [and then] we bounded forward to join the rest of the Ranger element at building #1, secured a room, and awaited orders."

Charlie Company soon discovered that, although the Taliban had fled from the compound, there was still the possibility of danger. "We were told to assist in searching the buildings for any intelligence and weapons, and to be watchful for booby traps," a TPT member recalled. "We found a Soviet RPK machine gun with a belt of ammo in the feed tray, expended shell casings, belt links on the ground, a [rocket-propelled grenade] launcher with 10 to 12 rounds nearby, and two AK-47 assault rifles. The rooms had articles of clothing strewn about, mattresses and bedding, and other personal effects. After collecting the weapons, we distributed about 400 leaflets in and around the building."

The Rangers also left a "calling card," an image of the firemen at the ruins of the Twin Towers. One Ranger explained, "The Fireman leaflets were

Rangers performing an equipment check prior to "suiting up" for a parachute jump.
Department of Defense

actually attached to the kit bags that we left behind on the drop zone for the locals to police up. To the best of my knowledge every Ranger that was on that jump had one. The size was approximately 5 x 8 inches. According to the battle damage assessment after the operation the locals did pick up the bags and clean up the area."

While the Rangers secured their objectives, air force combat controllers were busy surveying the landing strip, assessing it for landing larger aircraft. Within minutes, an MC-130 landed with medical personnel onboard. They treated two Rangers who had been injured on the jump. This MC-130 was soon followed by several others, which contained fuel and ammunition that were used to establish the FARP. Six minutes later, several MH-60 and MH-47 helicopters arrived to refuel and rearm. While they were being serviced, orbiting gunships spotted several enemy vehicles headed toward the objective. The enemy was quickly taken under fire and destroyed. Upon completion of the refueling, the helicopters departed, which was the signal for the Rangers to withdraw aboard the MC-130s. The last MC-130 departed five hours and twenty-four minutes after the assault started.

Objective Gecko

While the Rangers attacked Objective Rhino, a helicopter-borne force consisting of a reinforced Delta Force squadron based on the USS *Kitty*

Eyewitness Jump Account

Staff Sergeant Jack Thomas, a member of the PSYOP detachment, described the low-level parachute drop. "It was completely black outside. . . . I could see one of the secondary objectives burning furiously from a bomb hit. . . . I hear sporadic fire coming from Rhino. . . . As I was descending, the last of the aircraft flew overhead, dropping its load of Rangers. Just as it passed over, flares started popping out of it, illuminating the night sky and the airfield blow just in time to orient myself on the horizon and prepare to land. I hit the ground like a rock and promptly found myself entangled in parachute suspension lines and ¼-inch cotton webbing. I cut myself free, chambered a round in my weapon, activated my [night vision goggles] NVG, and scanned the immediate area for the enemy. Convinced that I was in no immediate danger, I gathered my chute and stuffed in into my kit bag, found a Ranger buddy, and moved to the assembly area."

Jump master performing a last minute equipment check prior to reaching the drop zone. *Department of Defense*

Hawk assaulted Objective Gecko, a large walled compound on the outskirts of Kandahar that belonged to Mullah Omar. Delta's objective was to raid the compound, kill its Taliban defenders, and collect any intelligence found there. "Be kinetic. Kill or capture any enemy found there," General Franks told the Delta commander.

Prior to the assault, MC-130 and HF-60L DAP gunships pounded the area around the compound. The gunfire caused several fires, the light of which played havoc with the pilots' night vision goggles (NVGs). In addition, the explosion raised clouds of dust obscuring the landing zones. One helicopter had to abort the landing. As it exited the area, the aircraft struck the side of a hill, shearing off three of its landing gear and jamming the rear ramp. The pilot brought the ship around and, in a remarkable feat of airmanship, held it in a hover a foot off the ground, while his crew chief crawled through a gap at the top of the ramp and pulled the Delta members out. The damaged aircraft made it back to Pakistan, where the pilot carefully landed it on a jury-rigged cradle of pallets. The Taliban later displayed the landing gear as a trophy, claiming, falsely, that a helicopter had been shot down.

The raiders quickly stormed the compound and secured it without casualties. They thoroughly searched Omar's house, but did not find anything that might provide useful intelligence. Unfortunately, as the force withdrew, it came under heavy fire by a considerable number of Taliban, who were armed with a seemingly unending supply of rocket-propelled grenades. "The shit hit the fan," one senior army officer exclaimed. "It was an ambush . . . Delta found itself in a tactical firefight and the Taliban had the advantage."

An Afghani informer said, "The Taliban expected an attack, [and] they were ready and waiting." In *The New Yorker*, Seymour M. Hersh reported "twelve Delta members were wounded, three of them seriously." The Taliban said they retrieved an American boot, containing a foot. Hersh also said, "The soldiers broke into separate units—one or more groups of four to six men each and a main force that retreated to the waiting helicopters. According to established procedure, the smaller groups were to stay behind to provide fire cover."

The operation was subject to criticism. One unnamed Delta member said that it was a "total goatfuck," slang meaning that everything that could go wrong did go wrong. Hersh wrote a critical article titled "Escape and Evasion: What happened when the Special Forces landed in Afghanistan?" in which he quoted various unnamed sources criticizing the operation. In one paragraph he said that senior officers in Delta Force were "still outraged that the Pentagon could not tell the American people the details of what really happened at Kandahar . . . because it doesn't want to appear that it doesn't know what it's doing."

General Franks angrily dismissed the quotes as coming from "one of those ill-informed, disgruntled leakers finishing a dead-end career in some Pentagon cubicle." General Richard Myers said on *Meet the Press,* "My belief is that every soldier that came back from that particular raid is back on duty today; none of them seriously injured, certainly none of them injured by the Taliban." Franks added, "We had a bunch of these young people who, you know, had scratches and bumps and knocks from rocks and all this sort of stuff. And so, it's–it's probably–it's probably accurate to say that maybe–maybe five or maybe 25 people were, quote, 'wounded.' We had no one wounded by enemy fire."

Another tragedy occurred when a Black Hawk helicopter belonging to the Quick Reaction Force crashed in Pakistan. Two Rangers from Bravo Company, 3rd Battalion, 75th Rangers, Specialist Jonn Joseph Edmunds and Private First Class Kristofor T. Stonesifer, were killed. Major Robert Bowers said that the helicopter "came in at an oblique angle. That made their rotor wash blow up all the [talcum powder–like soil] so they had to transition from visual to instrument flight. They were on a slope and when they hit it the aircraft just kept rolling." The Rangers "clipped their [safety] lanyards into the nylon rigging." When the aircraft rolled over, "their lanyards were long enough that they [were] ejected from the aircraft and crushed."

General Richard B. Myers commented at a news conference that "Any claims (by the Taliban) that they shot this helicopter down are absolutely false. This is being classified as an aircraft mishap and it will be investigated as such. . . . This was a middle of the night landing. There was a significant amount of dust. . . . close to the ground, the rotor wash brings up the dust and makes landing very, very difficult. We think that had something to do with it, but it's going to be up to the mishap investigation board to tell us finally."

A Marine CH-53 Super Stallion aboard the USS *Peleliu* was tasked to lift out the Black Hawk. "We were awakened around 0320, and we imme-diately hashed out a plan in 15 to 20 minutes," Capt. Jay M. Holtermann, the mission commander, said. "An hour later pilots were on the flight deck getting the helicopters fired up while we had our confirmation brief. We were off the deck in less than two hours after waking up. If we had a week to plan the mission, we'd probably have spent 14 hours a day on it." After launching, the helicopters picked up several army aircraft mechanics and continued to the crash site.

"I was pretty nervous as we flew toward the border," said Sgt. Anthony D. Ritacco, a CH-53E crew chief. "Everything was going so fast, and I had a million things running through my mind. I went over everything a thousand times to make sure we were ready. We were of course."

After arriving at the crash site, "the army mechanics quickly stripped the Black Hawk almost all the way down to the frame," Cpl. Jose M. Pazos, a landing support specialist, said. "The Black Hawk is a very heavy bird, and we needed to get it as light as possible for the long haul back. We gathered up all the debris from the accident and packed it into one of the other birds with the panels and things being pulled off. Everyone was moving fast. There wasn't any sense of fear, just a strong sense of purpose." Pazos, other Marines, and the mechanics, rigged slings onto the now bare Black Hawk.

The CH-53E hovered a few feet above the landing support Marines and Black Hawk, creating a fierce 220-mile-per-hour downwash. "The loose, dusty ground made for terrible conditions for all of us involved," Pazos recalled. "It created a brownout that nearly blinded us. It pelted us with rocks, stones, dirt, and everything else. I don't know how much Pakistani dirt I swallowed." They fastened slings to a hook lowered through a hole in the Super Stallion's underbelly, lifted it off the ground, and made their way to a Pakistani air base near the coast to refuel.

The Marine helicopter set the Black Hawk down next to the runway, and the crew readied it to take on fuel. "We were sitting in the back of the helicopter eating and waiting when we a heard a whistling and crackling sound," Ritacco said. "We just stopped and listened. I think we all figured it out at the same time. We looked at each other in amazement and then we all hit the deck." The crews were under fire. "We were scrounging for our weapons when I saw the [downed Black Hawk's fuel] tank in the helo with us. I immediately thought about its Kevlar armor lining. With the help of one of the soldiers I removed the chains holding it down and pushed it into position to protect us from the incoming fire."

The Marines and soldiers began pulling out the CH-53's windows and returning fire with their M-16A2 service rifles. Gunnery Sergeant Brian A. Bonney, an aircraft technician, manned the powerful .50-caliber machine gun mounted in the door. "All the training the Marine Corps has provided us paid off at that moment," Ritacco recalled. "There was no time to get scared. Things just kicked in automatically. We did what we've been taught."

Captain Holtermann had just returned from a meeting with Pakistanis in the control tower when the rounds started flying. "We were sitting outside next to one of the helicopters when the dirt stared jumping up around us," he said. "One of the soldiers yelled 'Sniper fire,' and everyone crowded into the helicopter. I wasn't at my bird. We were screaming asking if anyone could see where the shots were coming from when Gunny Bonnie jumped on the .50-cal. I ran across the tarmac to my bird and jumped in."

Pazos was checking on the slings, "when we heard three pops and then two more. "We looked up just in time to see impacts about 20 feet away. It didn't really register for a moment. Once it did we jumped into a nearby ditch. We were in the prone scanning the area when we heard the M-16s and .50-cal open up. A few seconds later the rotors started turning, and a soldier sprinted the 200 meters between us. He covered us as we ran to the helos using smoke as concealment. I had so much adrenaline pumping that my head almost exploded."

In less than two minutes, both helicopters were ready to liftoff. "It takes 10 to 15 minutes normally," Holtermann said. Getting the Marines who were at the Black Hawk was all that was holding them up. "God bless the soldier who ran all the way across the field to gather them up and get them back," he exclaimed. "We counted heads and had accounted for everyone." The helicopters swiftly rose into the air, leaving the Black Hawk behind— temporarily at least.

"We lifted off with absolute minimum fuel," Holtermann said, "Plus, there were two more of our helicopters enroute to the same airfield we had just been attacked in, and we couldn't get communication with them to warn them not to land there. It was a total freak of luck we happened to fly right over the incoming birds," Holtermann continued. "We were able to get direct communication with them. They turned around and joined us." They made it safely back to the *Peleliu* after a very long day. The following night they returned to the ambush site, but with a large security detail and Cobra gunships for support. The platoon sergeant with the security detail said, "We could see them with our NVGs outside the fence around the base. I think they were scared off by the size of our force this time. They walked around looking at us, but never got within range to be any danger to us. They were as dead as dead can be if they tried anything. I think they realized that." This time the Black Hawk was successfully recovered without incident.

CHAPTER 25

The Marines Have Landed

"The zone is winter."
—Coded phrase, meaning no enemy in the landing zone

IN MID-OCTOBER, SEAL TEAM THREE established a headquarters on the island of Masirah, off the coast of Oman, in support of operations in southern Afghanistan. One platoon was assigned to conduct surveillance and reconnaissance of a desert airfield for a U.S. Marine helicopter assault scheduled for the evening of 21 November. The platoon's assignment came as a result of a chance meeting between Brig. Gen. James N. Mattis, commanding general of Task Force 58, and navy Capt. Robert Harward, commander of Joint Special Operations Task Force South (JSOTF-S) or Task Force K-Bar, the counterpart to Mulholland's JSOTF-N. Colonel Nathan S. Lowrey wrote in *Marine Expeditionary Operations in Afghanistan, Task Force 58 during Operation Enduring Freedom, September 2001–March 2002* that "their paths crossed under a lamppost in Bahrain."

"What the hell are you doing here?" Mattis had asked lightheartedly.

Harward said, "I'm trying to get into the fight, but I don't have any helicopters."

At that point "Mattis quickly extended an invitation and, based on a handshake, they decided that the SEALS would provide a liaison officer and conduct strategic reconnaissance near what would become Forward Operating Base Rhino."

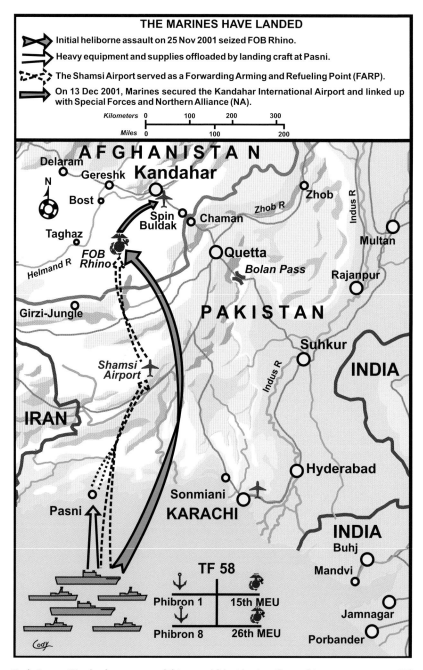

THE MARINES HAVE LANDED

Initial heliborne assault on 25 Nov 2001 seized FOB Rhino.

Heavy equipment and supplies offloaded by landing craft at Pasni.

The Shamsi Airport served as a Forwarding Arming and Refueling Point (FARP).

On 13 Dec 2001, Marines secured the Kandahar International Airport and linked up with Special Forces and Northern Alliance (NA).

Task Force 58, the longest amphibious raid in Marine Corps history . . . some 450 miles inland. *Bill Cody*

The SEAL platoon, reinforced with two combat controllers, was to be inserted by two MC-130s on one of the darkest nights of the year. "Our plan called for four Humvees to be put down about ten miles from the target site on the dry lake bed," one of the SEALs recalled. "We had to fly in, land, make our way to the target, and go to ground, and we had to do this in about eleven hours of darkness." The operation was risky because if the SEALs were discovered it might compromise the entire operation. After several delays—"We'd grown accustomed to saddling up and standing down," he said—the platoon boarded the aircraft for the three-hour flight to the objective. After crossing into Afghan air space, the aircraft flew low level. "At that height, the MC-130s fly themselves with their terrain-following radar." The pilots put the big aircraft right on the money. "They made a straight pass in and dropped us right on the insertion point." Within minutes the SEALs unchained the vehicles, exited the aircraft, and had taken up security positions. In the meantime, the aircraft pivoted, rolled down the runway, and quickly gained enough speed to take off. The roar of their engines gradually subsided as the aircraft disappeared into the night sky.

The SEALs stayed in position, listening for indications that their insertion had been discovered. They probed the darkness with their night vision goggles. Seeing and hearing nothing, the leader gave the signal to get ready. "When the word came to move out," a team member reported, "we came off the perimeter and found our assigned vehicle and assigned place in the vehicle—four Humvees, five guys in each Hummer." They had been inserted ten kilometers from the objective, a dry lake bed cum dirt landing strip and compound that had once been used by wealthy Arabs for hunting. The objective, code named Rhino, had been the site of the Ranger assault in October and was now to be Task Force 58's (TF 58) FOB from which to mount ground operations in southern Afghanistan. Task Force 58 was composed of a small headquarters, elements of the 15th and 26th Marine Expeditionary Units, Seabees from Naval Mobile Construction Battalion 133 and several countries in the Coalition.

When the vehicles were loaded, "the drivers started their engines and took station behind the lead vehicle," a SEAL recalled. "Using GPS navigation, we finally found the dirt road that led from the insertion point to the target area and headed out . . . it was eerie rolling across that flat, desolate land and watching it slip by in the green glow of my night-vision goggles." The platoon averaged fifteen to twenty miles an hour, despite the drifting sand and the need to maintain security in the desolate wasteland. By 0230, they reached their layup position (LUP), a knoll about a half mile from the objective. They quickly concealed the vehicles, dug an OP on the high ground, established security, and settled down to observe and report. "When the sun came up, we were in place and had good commo [communications] with the task unit back at the base. We rotated four guys at a time through the OP while the rest of us hunkered down in the LUP." The objective appeared to be deserted, but the team continued to remain hidden, waiting for confirmation that the Marines were on schedule.

* * *

The plan called for a two day mission. On the second day, the team received word that the operation had been postponed for twenty-four hours . . . and then a second twenty-four hour delay. "The days got up into the mid-sixties,

Combined Joint Special Operations Task Force-South Task Force K-Bar

Combined Joint Special Operations Task Force-South or Task Force K-Bar was under the command of U.S. Navy Capt. Robert Harward. Its mission was special reconnaissance (SR) and direct action (DA) against the al-Qaeda and Taliban networks. The 2,800-man task force was a multi-nation force composed of Special Forces from eight countries including:

- U.S. Special Forces (3rd Battalion, 3rd Special Forces Group)
- U.S. Navy Seal platoons from Teams 2,3,8 and SDV 1
- U.S. Army personnel from 4th Psychological Operations Group
- U.S. Air Force Special Operations personnel (Combat Controllers)
- Marine and army helicopter support
- Coalition special forces elements from:
- Denmark (Frømandskorpset and Jægerkorpset), 100+ personnel
- Germany (Kommando Spezialkräfte (KSK), 100+ personnel
- Australia (SASR or Task Force-64), 150+ personnel
- Norway (Jegerkommando and Marinejegerkommandoen}, 70+ personnel
- Canada (JTF-2), 40 personnel
- New Zealand (NZSAS), 120 + personnel
- Turkish Special Forces (Ozel Kuvvetler Komutanligi)

Combined Joint Task Force South/Task Force K-Bar received the Presidential Unit Citation: "For extraordinary heroism and outstanding performance of duty in action against the enemy in Afghanistan from 17 October 2001 to 30 March 2002. Throughout this period, Combined Joint Special Operations Task Force South/Task Force K-Bar, operating from first Oman and then from forward locations throughout the southern and eastern regions of Afghanistan, successfully executed its primary mission to conduct but the nights were in the low twenties, so we got a little cold," a SEAL recalled. "We had to ration our water and MREs to make them go the distance." On the fourth day, the team received word the Marines would land that night. "After dark, half of us with the Air Force CCTs [Combat Control Teams] made a foot patrol down the airstrip. We quickly searched the buildings in the compound . . . to make sure there were no bad guys hiding out." The team also sent real-time photos of the objective back to the intelligence section on the USS *Peleliu* (LHA 5). While the SEALs searched the compound, the two combat controllers set up beacons around the landing zone to guide the helicopters. When the two groups were finished, they made their way back to the LUP and waited.

special operations in support of the United States' efforts as delegated to Commander, U.S. Central Command through the Joint Forces Special Operations Component Command, to destroy, degrade, and neutralize the Taliban and al-Qaeda leadership and military. During its six-month existence, Task Force K-Bar was the driving force behind myriad combat missions conducted in Combined Joint Operations Area Afghanistan. These precedent setting and extremely high-risk missions included search and rescue, recovery dive operations, noncompliant bordings of high interest vessels, special reconnaissance, hydrographic reconnaissance, sensitive site exploration, direct action missions, apprehension of military and political detainees, destruction of multiple cave and tunnel complexes, identification and destruction of several known al-Qaeda training camps, explosion of thousands of pounds of enemy ordnance, and successful coordination of unconventional warfare operation for Afghanistan. The Sailors, Soldiers, Airmen, Marines and coalitions partners of Combined Joint Special Operations Task Force-South/Task Force K-Bar set an unprecedented 100 percent mission success rate across a broad spectrum of special operations missions while operating under extremely difficult and constantly dangerous conditions. They established benchmark standards of professionalism, tenacity, courage, tactical brilliance, and professional excellence while demonstrating superb esprit de corps and maintain the highest measure of combat readiness . . ."

U.S. Navy Vice-Admiral Robert Harward speaking at a homecoming reception for U.S. service members from Task Force Ramadi. As a captain he commanded Task Force K-Bar, the 2,800-man multi-national Special Forces teams that operated in southern Afghanistan. *U.S. Air Force photo by Staff Sgt. Joe Laws*

Suddenly the roar of engines filled the night air . . . and out of the darkness, three huge CH-53E Super Stallions from HMM-163 (nicknamed "Evil Eyes") swept onto the dirt runway, within 30 seconds of the planned L-Hour. Huge clouds of dust rose in the air. "The brownout conditions were very severe . . . aircraft within both divisions were forced to wave off," Capt. Jay M. Holtermann wrote in the June 2002 *Marine Corps Gazette.*

"The dirt was like silt," Maj. Lou Albano recalled. "Every time you'd land you'd kick up so much dust that you couldn't see anything . . . you'd just brown out." Sixty heavily armed Marines from Company C, Battalion Landing Team 1/1, the battalion commander, Lt. Col. Christopher Bourne,

Task Force 58 Organization

Task Force 58's primary ground components were the 15th and 26th Marine Expeditionary Units, consisting of two infantry battalions (1st Battalion, 1st Marine Regiment and 3rd Battalion, 6th Marine Regiment), two helicopter squadrons (HMM-163 and HMM-365), and two logistic support groups (MSSG 15 and MSSG 26), approximately 2,500 Marines and sailors. In addition, an Australian Special Air Service squadron and a Naval Construction Battalion (NMCB 133) were assigned.

The naval component was built around two Amphibious Ready Groups, Phibron 1 (USS *Peleliu* LHA-5, USS *Dubuque* LPD-8, and USS *Comstock* LSD-45); and Phibron 8 (USS *Bataan* LHD-5, USS *Shreveport* LPD-12, USS *Whidbey Island* LSD-41). Navy Captain William E. Jezierski, commander of Phibron 1, was designated deputy commander of the task force.

The task force headquarters consisted of approximately thirty-two personnel, a particularly lean organization, but one that suited its commander . . . " a light, lean staff ('everyone had to fill sandbags') that can take existing forces and mold them into a smooth functioning team." The task force headquarters was located aboard the USS *Peleliu*, with a forward Observation Post (OP) and a jump command post (CP) deployed ashore.

Brigadier General James N. Mattis, commanding general of Task Force 58, talking with a group of U.S. Navy Seabees at the airport in Kandahar. *USMC*

and his jump command post (CP) quickly disembarked and set up security around the airfield. Minutes later, the second flight of three CH-53s with an additional ninety-five Marines landed. Four AH-1W Super Cobras and three UH-1H Twin Huey gunships circled overhead, ready, willing, and able to fend off any Taliban that tried to interfere with the landing.

After establishing security, the Marines made contact with the SEAL platoon. "They came out to get us," a team member recalled. "We exchanged recognition signals, and they brought us back in through their perimeter." The linkup was made without incident, but it still was a touchy situation. "We're always worried about friendly fire," he said, "so they sent a patrol out for us." With their mission accomplished, the SEALs caught a bird out and returned to their base. "The ground force commander thanked us for freezing our butts off for them, and that was it."

The SEALs weren't the only ones that were cold and miserable. Combat Correspondent Joseph R. Chenelly noted that "Marines overcame temperatures that dipped below freezing and howling winds kicking up cyclones of sand that engulfed aircraft and blasted marching troops." Sgt. Anthony Anguiano, a squad leader, said, "There is ice in our canteens in the morning and the parkas we have practically save our lives."

The Marines from Task Force 58 had launched from the USS *Peleliu* in the North Arabian Sea, flew through Pakistani airspace to Rhino, a distance of over 450 miles, in the longest amphibious raid in history. It was absolutely essential to gain Pakistan's assistance in order to conduct operations that

U.S. Navy SEALs conduct special reconnaissance mission on a suspected location of a-Qaeda and Taliban forces. *U.S. Navy*

U.S. Navy SEALs on a search and destroy mission discover a large cache of munitions in one of more than fifty caves explored in the Zhawar Kili area. Used by al-Qaeda and Taliban forces, the caves and above-ground complexes were subsequently destroyed through air strikes called in by the SEALs. *U.S. Navy*

far from the sea. Before asking for Pakistani support, Gen. James N. Mattis paid a surprise courtesy call on Wendy Chamberlain, the U.S. ambassador to Pakistan, to ask for her assistance. Upon entering her office, Mattis was confronted by Chamberlain, who sternly demanded to know what a Marine was doing in her embassy. Mattis replied, without missing a beat, that he had come with a thousand of his best friends to "go to Afghanistan to kill some people." Chamberlain invited him to sit down, so they could talk about it. Mattis told a friend that she was a Marine "brat," born at the Camp Pendleton, California, base hospital and had "yanked his chain" to get his reaction. Mattis indicated that she was "magnificent," opening doors to the Pakistani military and helping to coordinate military details.

With Chamberlain's assistance, Mattis met with Major General Farooq, Chief of Plans for the Pakistani Joint Headquarters Staff, to brief him on his concept of operations and to gain Pakistan's support. Mattis told a friend that it was a difficult meeting because he had to sit patiently while the Pakistani lectured him for an hour and a half on all the incidents where the United States had let them down. "It started with the shoot-down of Francis Gary Powers, who flew out of Peshawar, and goes on about how many times our country has screwed theirs," Mattis said.

Finally Farooq turned to Mattis and asked, "What are you going to do about it?"

Mattis replied thoughtfully, "There is nothing I can do about the past, but I pledge my personal commitment to open and honest communication with you in the future." The Pakistanis accepted his word and asked how they could support the operation. Mattis had a laundry list ready. "I want to bring the ships in next to the beach where I can off-load supplies and have an airstrip nearby where I can fly stuff in and out. In addition, I want an intermediate support base where I can put some fuel."

15th MEU Press Release

"Marines Land, Seize Desert Strip"
By Sgt. Joseph R. Chenelly

Marine Forward Operating Base, Southern Afghanistan

The thunderous thumping of Marine CH-53E Super Stallion helicopters ripped through the cold, black desert night signaling the start of Operation Swift Freedom [renamed Operation Enduring Freedom] as the 15th Marine Expeditionary Unit (Special Operations Capable) seized a forward operating base in southern Afghanistan, November 25, 2001. Marines with Charlie Company, Battalion Landing Team 1/1, 15th MEU (SOC) charged down the helicopter ramps through clouds of dust and into the darkness sweeping across vast areas of deep sand, clearing buildings and establishing a secure airstrip for hundreds of follow-on forces who arrived before dawn.

The airstrip was setup less than an hour after the first helicopter stirred up the Afghan sand. Lights were added to the runway allowing KC-130 aircraft filled with Alpha Company Marines and tactical vehicles to land here. Planes and helicopters continued the inflow of troops and gear non-stop through the night and early morning. "It was exciting seeing the Marines go into action," First Sergeant Phil Fascetti said. "You know there is a possibility that there could be enemy forces out there." The raid force flew several hundred miles directly from the USS Peleliu to the desert strip aboard six Super Stallions. The long flight required tricky nighttime aerial refueling with the KC-130 Hercules aerial refueling and transport aircraft.

Hundreds of hours of planning, rehearsals and briefs preceded the mission back aboard the Peleliu in the North Arabian Sea. Terrain models were built. The raid force kept a special sleep schedule to prepare for the all-night mission. Fast attack vehicles, weapons and other gear were painted with desert camouflage patterns. Packs were put on pallets and flown in later to keep the force light on their feet. The new chapter of the international war on terrorism began without contacting enemy forces. Not a single shot was fired during the raid.

The Pakistanis had problems with the initial locations. "They said, 'No, you don't get that place, but we will give you this one,'" Mattis recalled. "If you can get ten miles over the sand dunes, you can use this civilian airstrip [and] hide your gear in the daytime. We will put troops around it and guard it." In fact, three hundred Pakistani Marines maintained security at the airfield and the beach during operations. Mattis was sensitive to the Pakistani internal politics. "They could not admit publicly that they were doing this . . . so we brought the ships in after dark and landed across the beaches. When the sun came up, there were just the waves washing some tire tracks away. The Pakistani government brought newsmen down who claimed the government was helping us. They said, 'Look, there are no Americans on the beach.' At night I brought the ships back in, and night after night we hid the stuff in the sand dunes. Marine KC-130s and air force C-17s would fly in, pick it up and take it into Afghanistan. It worked like a champ. The Chinese have a saying that if you drink the water, you ought to thank the guy who dug the well."

Colonel Nathan Lowery wrote that "without the unwavering support of the Pakistani government and Major General Farooq, TF-58 would not have been able to orchestrate the complex operation in southern Afghanistan." In a show of trust, Mattis told the Pakistanis the H-hour, D-day and the objective "three weeks in advance and [they] never revealed one word."

Pakistan granted access to a seaport and airfield along their southern coast at Pasni, a remote coastal fishing village located approximately three hundred kilometers west of Karachi. The village possessed suitable beaches for landing craft to off-load supplies, and it was located ten miles from a secluded commercial airport that could be used by U.S. aircraft to use as a logistics and refueling base. Internal political considerations forced the Pakistanis to restrict operations to the hours of darkness and to limit the number of U.S. forces ashore at any given time. The Amphibious Ready Group, operating 12–20 miles offshore, used thirteen Landing Craft Air Cushioned (LCAC) and four Landing Craft Utility (LCU) to transport troops and supplies ashore. After arriving at the beach, trucks were used for the one-hour trip over an improvised dirt road to the airfield. The convoys were limited to two per night. The airport at Shamsi was situated in a desolate area, forty nautical miles south of the Afghan border, one hundred eighty four nautical miles northeast of Pasni, and one hundred and seventy nautical miles southeast of Rhino. The airfield facilities were initially used to support Special Forces operations. They were taken over by TF-58 when the Special Forces moved out. Task Force 58 designated

Shamsi as a Forward Arming and Refueling Point (FARP), which became a critical refueling for helicopters transiting from ship to Camp Rhino.

The task force initial mission was to conduct "three to five raids for the purpose of destabilizing Taliban control in southern Afghanistan." The mission was soon changed to "seize a desert airfield and establish a forward operating base at Objective Rhino, the former United Arab Emirates hunting camp."

Vice Admiral Charles W. Moore, commander Naval Forces, Central Command (NavCent), and Combined Forces Maritime Component Commander (CFMCC), stressed that the task force was "not to conduct a show of force, they were to conduct raids that would quickly and decisively defeat Taliban and al-Qaeda forces. I want you to go in there and raise hell!" He added, "A squad of Marines running through Kandahar would turn the tide."

Admiral Moore, in a totally unexpected move, designated General Mattis as the sole commander of Task Force 58 and all amphibious operations in the theater. The designation went against tradition. "In conventional amphibious operations," Lowery wrote, "the principal authority had been the Navy commander of the amphibious task force (CATF), who relinquished operational control to the Marine commander of the landing force (CLF) once his forces were ashore." Moore told Mattis that "we are going to break a lot of rice bowls when we do this," according to Col. Clarke Lethin, TF 58's operations officer.

A U.S. Navy SEAL on a reconnaissance mission in southern Afghanistan. U.S. Navy Capt. Robert S. Harward's Joint Special Operations Task Force South (JSOTF), known as Task Force K-Bar, supported Marine Task Force 58. *U.S. Navy*

Within an hour and a half of the initial landing, the first of several KC-130 flights from VMGR-352 brought in reinforcements. Major Mitchell Hoines flew two sorties on the first night. "I flew from Jacobabad [Pakistan] direct to Camp Rhino in the number three aircraft, call sign Raider. We thought there might be anti-aircraft artillery around, especially the Stinger . . . so we did high approaches, with lights off, and then did a corkscrew to land." Once on the ground, the pilots had to worry about offloading in the dark. "We did not have any ground support so we left our motors running, which is a safety hazard. We blew a lot of sand on the Marines unloading cargo." The first KC-130s brought in Alpha Company and a section of the 81mm Mortar Platoon to provide close-in fire support. The two infantry companies split the airfield defense, Charlie Company secured the western half, while Alpha Company took the eastern sector. An engineer platoon cleared the buildings in the compound, while the reconnaissance platoon and the battalion's scout snipers pushed out from the perimeter to establish observation posts. Marines hunkered down in mortar pits carved into the hard and rocky earth, where they fought bitterly cold nights, warm days, and thick dust storms that made it necessary to shovel out the pits every morning. A total of 403 Marines and four Interim Fast Attack Vehicles (IFAVs) were brought in on the first night.

View through night vision goggles of U.S. Navy beachmasters and a Landing Craft Air Cushion (LCAC) hovercraft on the beach at Pasni, Pakistan. The beach could only be used at night because of Pakistani political concerns. *USMC*

The KC-130s were the work-horses of the first night. "We were in the emergency war weight category," Hoines explained. "You had to utilize all the fuel on the plane to do as many runs as possible, which required your first takeoff and landing to be overweight . . . It decreases the life of the plane . . . and it's also a safety factor; you're so heavy that if you lose a motor on takeoff, those three remaining propellers might not have enough lift to keep you flying on a hot night."

Sometimes peacetime rules went by the boards. Passenger seats were abandoned for the initial wave of Marines. "They showed up with these big tortoise shell packs, huge, 100 pounds," Hoines recalled, "and they won't fit in regular seats." The men were told to sit on the deck five across and lash a cargo strap across their laps. "You told the guy on the far right, 'Here's how you unlatch it' . . . So when you land, they march out just like the Roman Legion."

Marine humor in the midst of a barren landscape, where the temperatures dropped like a stone at night and barely warmed them during the day. Note the location of suspected Taliban. *USMC*

Camp Rhino was far from a Club Med. "It was desert," Major Albano explained. "They called it a hunting lodge . . . there were a couple of buildings off to one side and a very austere dirt runway that we weren't even using to land on, since the dirt was like silt. On the other side of the runway, opposite from where the small set of buildings [was,] [was] where we created landing pads [for helicopters]. They were just sandbags that were spray painted and had been set out in a crow's foot configuration. We'd just land on the sand pads. That's what it was; it was very austere."

On D-day +1, Brigadier General Mattis and his forward command group flew into Rhino, and assumed command ashore. Joseph R. Chenelly wrote, "In the first hour of dawn the morning Camp Rhino was secured, a platoon of Marines raised an American flag in a fashion reminiscent of the famous World War II flag raising at Iwo Jima." The event was captured on film and sent to media outlets around the world.

Mattis told reporters that the Marines now "own a piece of Afghanistan." His statement was immediately repudiated by the State Department. "The United States has no intention of owing any part of Afghanistan," the press release stated. The Pentagon immediately sent a directive to all troops in Afghanistan, ordering the Marines to no longer raise American flags in Afghanistan. Mattis later told a friend that Karzai thought it was a positive statement, and was amazed that the incident caused such a furor. That same day, a Joint Surveillance and Reconnaissance Attack Aircraft (JSTARS) detected several Taliban BMPs to the northwest of FOB Rhino. An airborne FAC confirmed the identification and ran several air strikes against the vehicles, with unknown results.

On 28 November, air force C-17s brought in a detachment of Naval Mobile Construction Battalion (NMCB) 133 to maintain and repair Rhino's runway which, after three nights of continuous use, was in desperate need of repair. NMCB 133 was, according to historian James P. Rife, "one of the most storied CB ("Seabee") units within the U.S. Navy. NMCB 133 is perhaps most famous for its bloody landing on Iwo Jima during WWII, where it sustained a twenty-five percent casualty rate." The Seabee advance party—27 men and nine pieces of equipment, including a small bulldozer named "Natasah II"—found the runway already badly deteriorated. The top six inches had been pulverized under the weight of the incoming C-17 and KC-130 transports, and there were numerous ruts, some in excess of ten inches deep, which threatened aircraft safety. The Seabees devised a way to use the more clay-like soil found deeper underground as a stabilizer. Each day they cleared the spoiled surface dirt generated by the previous night's air operations, and then replaced it with the dug-up clay-like material, wetting it down with what little water was available and then rolling it to create a temporary hard surface. This "just-in-time" method allowed the runway to stay operational for nearly two months. To facilitate helicopter operations, the Seabees imported a spray-applied soil stabilizer that came to be known as "Rhino snot," effectively reducing the dust levels.

The next day, TF 58 was notified that General Franks had established a ceiling (force cap) on the number of Marines and sailors that could be deployed at Camp Rhino. Initially the number was set at 1,000, later increased to 1,100, and finally set at 1,400. This arbitrary ceiling caused a temporary pause in operations and stopped the buildup of combat power in southern Afghanistan. Lowery wrote that "CentCom denied the existence of a force cap but other sources said that the cap was a strictly enforced reality." The issue was raised to the Secretary of Defense level but was

U.S. Marine Corps Gen. James Mattis, Task Force 58 Commander, greets Gul Agha Shirzai, governor of Kandahar, in a flag ceremony held at Kandahar airport, 1 January 2002. *USMC photo by Lance Cpl. Marcus L. Miller*

Senior Chief Equipment Operator John Lemmond piles rocks into a dump truck with a front-end loader at the U.S. Marine Corps Base in Kandahar, Afghanistan, December 2001. U.S. Navy Seabees of Naval Mobile Construction Battalion One Thirty Three have provided support to all coalition forces including airstrip and airport runway repairs and building construction. *U.S. Navy photo by Chief Photographer's Mate Johnny Bivera*

only resolved when the task force was assigned additional missions. On 3 December, a squadron of the Australian Special Air Service Regiment (SASR) under the command of Lt. Col. Peter "Gus" Gilmore flew into Rhino. The veteran Aussie soldiers were a welcome addition to the task force and quickly earned the respect of the Marines. Mattis commended the Australians in a letter to Maj. Gen. Duncan Lewis, the commander of the Australian Defense Force.

The task force received an order to interdict Route 1, a beltway-type road that circles Afghanistan to the west and south of Kandahar, to "prevent/deny the escape of Taliban and al-Qaeda forces from Afghanistan." Elements of the Light Armored Reconnaissance Company (LAR), Combined Anti-Armor Team (CAAT), and Force Reconnaissance platoon left Rhino for "the 120-kilometer, 19-hour motor march across the unchartered desert," to interdict the road. In the early morning hours of 6 December, a Lockheed

Mattis Letter

"Dear Duncan, As the Commander Task Force 58 it was my pleasure to serve alongside the Australian Special Air Service contingent during active operations in southern Afghanistan from November 2001 through February 2002. At this time I desire to acknowledge the high qualities of

Australian Special Boat Service operatives (Task Force 64), led by Lt. Col. Gus Gilmore, performed reconnaissance and surveillance missions as well as sensitive site exploitation. USMC

P-3 Orion Maritime Patrol Aircraft spotted a column of six vehicles approaching the Marine roadblock/ambush site. The column stopped, while one truck carrying nine men sped toward the concertina wire the Marines had strung across the road. The truck stopped when it became tangled in the wire and the Marines took it under fire, killing all the occupants and setting it ablaze. As the firing died down, the other vehicles quickly moved into a position north of the ambush site. Major Tim Oliver, the task force observer in the P-3, saw up to thirty individuals dismount from the vehicles and form a skirmish line. The P-3 and a FAC called in an airstrike that destroyed the vehicles and eliminated the threat. Villagers reported the next day that an estimated 120 Taliban had been killed or wounded. The ambush served its purpose. No other attempts were made to use the road.

Just after dark on 6 December, Marines on the front lines observed light

leadership, devotion to duty and aggressiveness displayed by the men of the SAS. Uncritical is their acceptance of missions, the sun has seldom shone on soldiers as competent and confident. I am familiar with the standards set by the fighting men of Australia. No Marine can fail to be impressed by your force's combat achievements from Gallipoli to North Africa and beyond. The performance of Lieutenant Colonel Gus Gilmore and these super fighters continues that tradition. The conduct of your officers and men has earned them the full admiration of the Sailors and Marines of Task Force 58. Please pass to them my personal respect and appreciation for a job well done. We Marines would happily storm hell itself with your troops on our right flank."

Mattis's tribute to the Australians was in keeping with his character and fighting spirit. One of his officers was checking the lines one night and related the following story. "In the middle of a gravelly flat near the runway's end, I approached another fighting hole…It was an assault rocket team, and there should have been two Marines awake. In the moonlight, I saw three heads silhouetted against the sky…General Mattis leaned against a wall of sandbags, talking with a sergeant and a lance corporal. This was real leadership. No one would have questioned Mattis if he'd slept eight hours each night in a private room, to be woken each morning by an aide who ironed his uniforms and heated his MREs. But there he was, in the middle of a freezing night, out on the lines with his Marines.

"General Mattis asked the assault men if they had any complaints. 'Just one, sir. We haven't been north to kill anything yet.' Mattis patted him on the shoulder… 'You will, young man. You will. The first time these bastards run into United States Marines, I want it to be the most traumatic experience of their miserable lives.'"

flashes to the north and northwest of the base. "All of a sudden flares go off, big trip flares, looks like *Apocalypse Now* out there," Maj. Mitchell Hoines exclaimed. "Everything lights up and it's surreal." A P-3 aircraft orbiting Rhino confirmed several individuals loading vehicles. The group was taken under fire by the 81mm Mortar Platoon. "Explosions and machine gun fire . . . the helicopter guys run for their aircraft," Hoines exclaimed. "A Huey takes off, gets to 10 or 15 feet, crashes, and bursts into flames!"

Albano was nearby. "You heard the crash and you heard the ammunition pop off." The pilot got disoriented in the dense cloud of dust.

"I told my guys in the back to grab fire extinguishers and see what you can do to help," Hoines yelled, "Let's take care of those Marines." He saw the crew climb out of the wreckage, as rescuers came from all points of the compass to help them and put out the fire. The task force narrative summary noted, "All crewmembers survived, due to the quick thinking and rescue efforts of fellow Marines. As flames engulfed the aircraft and ammunition began to cook off, ordnance personnel . . . succeeded in moving a fuel truck parked only fifteen feet away."

The task force received a warning order to be prepared to receive detainees and provide temporary holding facilities until they could be transported elsewhere. John Walker Lindh was the first to arrive. Capt. Stewart Upton explained his status. "Walker is a battlefield detainee and is being held here pending disposition instructions from higher headquarters." The Task Force narrative summary stated that "upon arriving at Rhino, Walker immediately received medical attention. Under a 24-hour guard, his sanitation needs were met and medical personnel evaluated his condition twice a day. He was given two MREs per day [the same as the Marines], later raised to three, and all the water he wanted." While at Camp Rhino, Walker was photographed by the FBI and then interviewed and fingerprinted by the Naval Criminal Investigative Service (NCIS). On the fourteenth, he was transferred to the USS *Peleliu.*

On 1 January, Camp Rhino was closed and the 15th MEU re-embarked aboard the *Peleliu* 's Amphibious Ready Group. The task force summary noted, "15th MEU made every attempt to leave Rhino in "pre-war" condition upon their departure. Fighting holes were filled in, concertina wire was collected and buildings were policed and markings painted over." Elements of TF 58 had occupied Rhino for fourty days, and, with its departure, the task force focus shifted to operations in the vicinity of Kandahar, the spiritual home of the Taliban.

CHAPTER 26

Spiritual Home

A S THE TALIBAN'S HOLD IN the south deteriorated, Task Force 58 was tasked to occupy the airfield at Kandahar in conjunction with the Special Forces in the area. A combined Light Armored Vehicle force and Combined Anti-Armor team from both the 15th MEU and the 26th MEU, named Task Force Sledgehammer, proceeded overland to the airfield, arriving without incident in the early morning hours of 13 December. Combat correspondent Joseph Chenelly wrote that "the Marines entered the airport grounds at the outskirts of the war torn town. No time was wasted securing the abandoned International Airport. Vehicles and their scouts established a perimeter as the sky's first sunbeams raced down the lengthy runway." After they secured the runway, helicopters flew in with India Company, 3rd Battalion, 6th Marines.

"An infantry company was inserted by CH-53E Super Stallions and immediately scoured the runway and its taxiways for countless pieces of shrapnel—some as minute as a pennies and others as large as station wagon bumpers," Chenelly said. "Shattered glass littered the ground and the floors around and inside the airport terminal. Old luggage tags, passports and advertisements were strewn throughout the baggage check counters and lobbies. Calendars, photos and bulletin boards were still hung on walls in apparent office spaces."

As additional forces arrived, it became absolutely essential to clear the runway and the adjacent area of landmines and unexploded ordnance. Lieutenant Commander Michael Runkle, a U.S. Navy Explosive Ordnance Disposal (EOD) officer, and an EOD detachment from Mobile Unit Two

275

flew into the airfield. "The minute we landed and went to ground there was an RPG sitting behind me and a 2.75" rocket just a few feet away. It was an EOD technician's dream job!"

Runkle recalled a tragic incident. "One of the Marines stepped on a mine and it blew his leg off below the knee . . . another Marine had his arm torn up by shrapnel and my EOD tech was down with shrapnel in his head." Several men who came to their assistance, ran into a minefield. "I grabbed three Marines, got down on our hands and knees, crawled in, and probed a clear path." The badly wounded Marine survived because the blast cauterized his leg, keeping him from bleeding to death. The men were checking out a building in an area that had already been swept for mines, but either a mine had gone undetected or a ceramic or plastic mine was in the ground. The American EOD team was augmented by a Norwegian army contingent, equipped with a mine flail, which was used to "mine proof" the airfield perimeter. A Jordanian mine clearing detachment also assisted in the effort. Their expertise in area clearing was a Godsend. "Soil you could walk and live on was at a premium," one officer recalled.

Once the area was cleared of unexploded ordnance, the Marines moved into the airport building. "Crews cleared large chunks of concrete, furniture and flowerpots obstructing covered sidewalks that wrapped around the terminal," Chenelly wrote. "Dangerous shards of glass were pulled from hundreds of

U.S. Navy explosive ordnance disposal expert briefing his Norwegian counterparts, who had arrived to assist with mine clearing. *USMC*

Kandahar's air field control tower. Very few of its occupants knew that Texas 17 had pulled a "Kilroy was here" moment to announce that they had been the first to arrive. *USMC*

15th MEU Press Release

"U.S. Marines Reach Kandahar, Take Airport,"
by Sgt. Joseph R. Chenelly

Nearly fifty set of headlights illuminated the cratered streets here as the heavily armed, lightly armored vehicles of Marine Task Force 58 rolled into the former Taliban stronghold securing the city's airport on December 13, 2001. Scattered fires and the city's few streetlights revealed armed men and packs of dogs roaming the streets. Virtually every man and even children toted deadly, assault weapons as the long convoy rumbled through the late hours of the evening. "It was crazy seeing people standing around with AK-47s and RPGs," said L/Cpl Randy S. Starks, 19, a scout with 15th MEU (SOC) and Sacramento, California. "We were briefed that these were the good guys, but we were ready for anything. No one was going to relax that night."

The convoy maneuvered around bomb craters, over rubble from recently shelled buildings and in between decimated vehicles. Evidence of the recent battles for the city were visible everywhere. "It looked like Tijuana (Mexico) on a real bad night. The craters were big enough to swallow a LAV (Light Armored Vehicle), and there were a lot of burnt cars in the street," L/Cpl Jason A. Haislar, and LAV driver with the 15th MEU (SOC) and an Edwardsville, Ill. native. "Obstacles like that create a high-risk because you never know who or what is waiting for you in a hole or around a car. I had to keep the LAV moving fast—speed is our best security in situations like that." Those Kandaharis who bothered to look up from the fires in their yards and alongside the roads waved their guns in the most cordial way possible. Shouts of "welcome Americans" were heard from crowds gathering on corners.

broken windows—some were more than three stories high. Office spaces were converted into command posts and lobbies into berthing spaces. Tents began popping up around the complex, and the lone control tower into an observation post for Marine scout snipers. The one road in and out of the area was barricaded and a controlled entry point was established." Cardboard signs were posted proclaiming the base "Camp Justice." Major Mark Quander, 326th Engineer Battalion, arrived in January with his company. "It was extremely cold and windy. The highs were in the mid-40s or mid-50s but the temperature really dipped at night. We didn't have a building to sleep in. The Marines from TF 58 had some tents that we were housed in initially."

The Seabees started repairing the runway, taxiways, and aprons, which were heavily cratered. Lieutenant Commander Leonard W. W. Cooke, officer in charge of NMCB 133 Air Detachment said that "the crater damage caused by Coalition bombing was severe but not devastating. With expeditious field repairs, it was determined the Seabees could open the runway for KC-130 and C-17 flights within 48 hours." Cooke's men were also tasked to build a short-term holding facility to house Taliban and al-Qaeda detainees. They converted a rubbish- and ordnance-strewn compound into an austere detainee camp. The facility was large enough to hold five hundred detainees, but small enclosures were constructed inside to hold no more than twenty to reduce the possibility of a mass breakout.

Lieutenant Colonel Mark Faulkner, commander of the facility, said that "all detainees are thoroughly searched, fingerprinted, and medically screened. They were given new clothes and blankets. We check everything to ensure they're hiding nothing, because of lessons learned, that we've gained, from this conflict."

Brigadier General Mattis was very concerned about the detainees' legal status, and dictated they would be treated in accordance with Geneva Convention rules for the treatment of POWs. At the same time, he ordered that "any prisoner who tried to escape was to be shot." There had been two jailbreaks that had influenced his decision; one in Pakistan, where detainees had overpowered their guards, and the other at Qala-i-Jangi. As soon as the facility opened, the International Committee of the Red Cross was welcomed to ensure complete compliance with the Geneva Convention. A U.S. Army military police unit from the 16th Military Police Brigade was brought in to assist with detention security and running the facility.

"One of my platoons led by Lt. Allison Kilborn went to Mazar-e Sharif, picked up a number of detainees and transferred them down to the Marines

Short-term prisoner of war holding facility. The facility was designed to separate detainees into small groups for ease of control. The guards had orders that "any prisoner who tries to escape was to be shot." USMC

in Kandahar," Maj. Sara Albrycht recalled. "She wound up being all alone down there for about three or four months."

The prisoners were interrogated by Marine Interrogator Translators, the 202nd Military Intelligence Battalion, the CIA, DEA (Drug Enforcement Agency, CID (Criminal Investigative Division), and MI-5 (British Intelligence). "We have experts in here that want to know anything they can about the affiliations of these individuals, who they're tied in with, what other information they may know about training facilities—anything," Faulkner said. Mattis granted full access to the detainees with the proviso that the results of the interrogation would be shared with each other and, "alarm" type information (pending attack, actionable intelligence, etc.) was to be reported immediately. He made it clear that anyone who violated the rules was to be put on the next available plane out of Kandahar.

Lieutenant Commander Runkle and his EOD specialists were tasked to support a team from the Defense Threat Reduction Agency (DTRA) in clearing the "Karnak Farm," an al-Qaeda training camp. The farm was one of many Sensitive Site Exploitation (SSE) missions that Task Force 58 conducted in coordination with Task Force K-Bar. Runkle said the farm "was a fascinating thing to see. We had bombed the heck out of it so it was smashed but you could clearly see that it was a demo training area . . . with blasting caps . . . demolition equipment all over the place [and] labs where they were manufacturing chemicals. There were shooting houses where they had pictures of President Bush and the Israeli prime minister hung up on targets." The team found "reams and reams" of files that contained reference and training manuals, as well as "gobs of paperwork that the intel guys went nuts over." At one point they discovered several military-style boxes. "We opened them up and it's a missile and right in the middle of the missile is a nuclear radiation symbol," Runkle said. "The DTRA guy flipped out, 'Oh my God,' he exclaimed, 'we've got nuclear missiles!'" Runkle was able to calm the man down after he explained that the radiation symbol referred to the depleted uranium in the Russian Aphid air-to-air missile, designed for use by Soviet fighter aircraft.

The task force conducted several SSE missions in an area believed to be linked to chemical and biological warfare research. A special Chemical Biological Inspection Site Team (CBIST) was flown in to assist the Australians of Task Force 64. The combined unit, along with a Marine Corps security force, was inserted into the Dewaluk area to check out eight villages. Nothing unusual was discovered during the searches, and the mission was completed without incident. One of the most productive missions occurred in early January 2002, when a combined force from TF 58 and TF K-Bar was tasked to search a series of caves in the vicinity of Zhawar Kili, Afghanistan. The mission was expected to last a few hours but instead went on for twelve days. The caves yielded a tremendous amount of intelligence . . . as well as the destruction of tons of ammunition and explosives. Captain Lloyd Freeman, commanding officer of Lima Company, 3rd Battalion, 6th Marines, recalled, "Things are going great out here. We have been doing everything from digging graves to clearing rooms of deserted villages. The air guys have been very busy with JDAMS and bunker busters daily and nightly . . . the area is target rich." Another SSE mission west of Kandahar, near the town of Garmabak-Ghar, did not go as well. During the insertion, a helicopter experienced a hard landing that damaged its nose wheel and required a security force to guard the site until the aircraft was repaired.

The mountainous terrain and bad weather continued to plague the aircrews. Major Albano remembered a flight from Kandahar to Bagram. "It snowed the entire flight. There was just snow; snow covered mountains that were pristine for hundreds of miles." On 9 January, a Marine KC-130 from VMGR-352, with seven passengers and crew, crashed and exploded while on final approach three miles from Shamsi, Pakistan. The towering flames could be seen twenty miles away. Residents claimed the noise from the crash was "deafening." The crash site was located in steep, difficult terrain, complicating search and recovery efforts.

A joint team of U.S. Marines and Pakistani troops finally reached the site. "They made it to the crash site on foot," an American spokesman said. "But they were unable to remain there. It is a very steep grade and they were unable to get footing." The remains were finally recovered over several days. The deceased Marines were: Capts. Matthew Bancroft and Daniel McCollum, Gunnery Sgt. Stephen Bryson, Staff Sgt. Scott Germosen; Sgts. Nathan Hays and Jeanette Winters; and Lance Cpl. Bryan Bertrand.

Two weeks later, a Marine CH-53E from Heavy Helicopter Squadron HMH-361, with seven passengers and crew, crashed while transiting a rugged area in the vicinity of Khowst. "They were just coming over a ridgeline, very high up [in the mountains] when they had a compression stall," Albano related. "One engine flamed out; the aircraft lost power and crashed into a 9,500-foot mountain." Captain Douglas V. Glasgow, the pilot, was knocked unconscious and awoke to find the aircraft on fire. Despite a broken wrist, he assisted the injured crew. "He actually dragged a couple of guys out of the plane because they were unconscious," Albano said. Glasgow then stomped out an SOS in the snow and rendered aid to the injured until a rescue team arrived. Albano flew over the crash site the next day. "All that was left was a main gear box, a probe, and a tail. Everything else had burned, there were just black cinders." Two Marines died in the crash, Staff Sgt. Walter Cohee III and Sgt. Dwight Morgan. Albano commented, "It was just such a treacherous place to fly around and there were a lot of accidents."

On 19 January, 26th MEU turned over control of the airport to elements of the 101st Airborne Division, Task Force Rakkasan, while Task Force 58 continued to support Special Forces operations throughout the remainder of the month. On 5 February, General Mattis and his staff repositioned to Bahrain, ending Task Force 58's initial participation ashore in Afghanistan. During the three months ashore, the TF conducted a wide variety of missions in support of the war effort. The sailors and Marines blocked western escape routes along Highway 1, provided security for the U.S. embassy in Kabul and a special operations facility in Khowst, occupied Kandahar International Airport and established a short-term holding facility for detaining enemy prisoners, and conducted numerous sensitive site exploitation missions.

Epilogue:
Takur Ghar

O N 6 JANUARY 2002, COLONEL Mulholland's JSOTF-N was ordered to conduct a sensitive site exploitation (SSE) mission in the Gardez-Khost region, where it was estimated that up to a thousand foreign fighters were located. The mission was originally planned as an unconventional warfare (UW) operation, using Afghan militia assisted by ODAs from the 5th Special Forces Group. Over the next three weeks, several teams of ODAs, Australia's Task Force 64, and Afghan militia attempted to infiltrate the Shahi Kowt Valley, where the enemy was suspected of holding out. The teams were unable to penetrate the valley. In late January, ODA 594 (Texas 14) attempted to conduct a ground reconnaissance of the valley, only to turn back after their Afghan security forces warned them of a major enemy concentration there.

Based on the intelligence he had gained, Mulholland decided that he did not have a large enough force to accomplish the mission. "It was beyond my ability with my small force to do something about it because we were confident there was a sizable concentration of bad guys in there," he explained. Mulholland recommended that conventional U.S. forces assume the mission, supported by both his own Task Force Dagger and Harward's Task Force K-Bar.

Mulholland's recommendation was accepted, and dubbed Operation Anaconda. Troops from the 10th Mountain Division (Light Infantry), 101st Airborne Division (Air Assault), and nearly a thousand Afghan military forces, under the command of Maj. Gen. Franklin L. Hagenbeck, commander of the 10th Mountain Division, were assigned. The first phase of the operation kicked off on 2 March, when an Afghan militia force under

Final troop disposition at the battle of Tora Bora. *U.S. Army*

the direction Chief Warrant Officer Stanley L. Harriman attempted to reach the northern entrance of the valley. The joint force convoy seemed to be snakebit. Many of the vehicles had difficulty negotiating the dirt roads that had turned into mushy, slippery quagmires from the recent snow and rain. At one point a truck tipped over, injuring several Afghanis. Further on, Harriman's vehicle was mistakenly hit by an AC-130, and he was killed, along with two Afghans. Two other Special Forces soldiers were wounded, as well as twenty Afghans. The leader of the Afghans decided to withdraw his force after receiving enemy mortar and small arms fire and the promised air support did not materialize. Meanwhile, conventional American forces were inserted into various landing zones and immediately ran into heavy enemy resistance that continued throughout the nineteen-day operation. "The most dangerous course of action, which was that the enemy would try to stay and fight American soldiers toe-to-toe," Lt. Col. David Gray explained. "In this particular case, he decided to stay and fight."

On the second day of Operation Anaconda, two SEAL teams commanded by Lt. Cmdr. Vic Hyder were to be inserted into the Shah-e Kot Valley. The two SEAL teams, Mako 30 and Mako 31, planned to establish an observation point on either end of the valley. Mako 30 drew the southern approach,

An MH-47E Chinook from Echo Company, 160th Special Operations Aviation Regiment. This is the same model helicopter as "Razor 03," which landed SEAL team Mako 30 on Takur Ghar. During Operation Anaconda, several Chinooks were shot down or badly damaged by al-Qaeda, who were waiting in ambush.
U.S. Navy photo by Photographer's Mate 2nd Class Andrew Meyer

a peak known as Takur Ghar, dubbed "Ginger" by the military. Prior to the mission, surveillance aircraft overflew the objective and did not detect any signs of life. "With a recon mission like this, you don't want to land where the enemy is," a pilot said. As the MH-47E, call sign "Razor 03," touched down, an RPG round exploded in the left side electrical compartment, knocking out its electrical power, hydraulics, miniguns, and the pilot's multifunctional displays, radios, and other flight equipment.

The pilot, Chief Warrant Officer Alan Mack, said it was launched about fifty feet from the helicopter. "It was very close," Mack said. "I saw him just outta the corner of my eye, hit the aircraft. You hear a big, y'know, big boom, and—all the generators go out. It set the inside of the aircraft on fire. The team was in the back trying to put it out." Within seconds, the right rear gunner shouted, "We're taking fire! Go, go, go, go."

Mack managed to get the damaged helicopter in the air. "The aircraft was shaking like a washing machine out of balance," he said. "There were holes in the rotor blades, and the hydraulics were doing some funny things. You know it was obvious we were gonna have to put it down somewhere. And then I started thinking, 'Well, where are we gonna put this?' I mean there's a big battle going on right—just out my right door." He managed to find a clear space in the valley below, approximately four miles away, and landed hard.

A crewman shouted, "Hey, we lost a man. We lost a man in the LZ."

Mack was stunned. "You can't be serious," he replied skeptically, "do another head count."

The crewman replied firmly, "No, we saw him go out. He's on the LZ right now!" Mack found out that as he took off Petty Officer 1st Class (ABH1) Neil Roberts and the rear gunner had slipped on the oil-slickened ramp and fallen out. The gunner was still tethered to the helicopter and was able to be pulled back in, but Roberts fell eight to ten feet to the ground. With the intercom system out, Mack unknowingly continued flying north, trying to assess the damage, until he was finally forced to crash-land the aircraft.

Forty-five minutes after the forced landing, a second helicopter, Razor 04, picked up Razor 03's crew and the remainder of Mako-30. After taking the aircrew to safety, the helicopter returned to the LZ where Roberts had fallen and inserted the remainder of his team. Immediately upon landing, the helicopter took heavy fire—the pilot saw the flash of a machine gun and thought, "Oh, this is going to hurt!"—but was able to safely insert the SEALs before leaving the zone.

Once on the ground, the team moved toward the most prominent features on the hilltop, a tree shading a large boulder. Unknown at the time, the hilltop boulder concealed an enemy position, while a network of slit trenches covered the hilltop. As they approached the boulder, two enemy soldiers popped up. Before they could shoot, Air Force Tech. Sgt. John A. Chapman and one of the SEALs killed them. The Americans were then taken under fire from a bunker only twenty meters away. Chapman continued to advance through the fire in an effort to find Roberts until struck by a burst of gunfire and killed. As the team moved to a covered position, two more SEALs were wounded, forcing the team to withdraw in the face of overwhelming enemy fire. An AC-130, call sign "Grim 32," provided covering fire.

Meanwhile, a twenty-three-man Ranger QRF was alerted for the rescue mission. "I was in the operation center planning for some kind of contingency," Capt. Nathan Self, the Ranger platoon leader, recalled. "And I hear a little bit of traffic come over the radio about one of our helicopters being forced to land, or that it went down." The Ranger platoon headed to the tarmac, where two choppers were "spinning up." Self split his men into two squads ("Chalk 1" and "Chalk 2"), and boarded the aircraft, which immediately launched.

Chief Warrant Officer Don Tabron, the air mission commander, recalled, "We proceeded inbound. Now the sun is up at this point. So we're out there in broad daylight. We're really feeling exposed, you know. You're a black helicopter with snow covered everything. So you really stood out." The pilots circled the landing zone three times in an attempt to see what was going on.

"Everyone moved from a seated position to a kneeling position looking out of every window they could find searching, searching for RPG launches,

Technical Sergeant John A. Chapman
Air Force Cross Citation

"The President of the United States awards the Air Force Cross to Tech. Sgt. John A. Chapman for extraordinary heroism in military operations against an armed enemy of the United States as a 24th Special Tactics Squadron combat controller in the vicinity of Gardez, in the eastern highlands of Afghanistan, on 4 March 2002. On this date, during his helicopter insertion for a reconnaissance and time sensitive targeting close-air support mission, Sgt. Chapman's aircraft came under heavy machine gun fire and received a direct hit from a rocket-propelled grenade which caused a United States Navy SEAL member to fall from the aircraft. Though heavily damaged, the aircraft egressed the area and made an emergency landing seven kilometers away. Once on the ground Sgt. Chapman established communication with an AC-130 gunship to insure the area was secure while providing close-air support coverage for the entire team. He then directed the gunship to begin the search for the missing team member. He requested, coordinated and controlled the helicopter that extracted the stranded team and aircrew members. These actions limited the exposure of the aircrew and team to hostile fire.

Without regard for his own life, Sgt. Chapman volunteered to rescue his missing team member from an enemy stronghold. Shortly after insertion, the team made contact with the enemy. Sgt. Chapman engaged and killed two enemy personnel. He continued to advance, reaching the enemy position, then engaged a second enemy position, a dug-in machine gun nest. At this time the rescue came under effective enemy fire from three directions. From close range, Sgt. Chapman exchanged fire with the enemy from minimum personal cover until he succumbed to multiple wounds. His engagement and destruction of the first enemy position and advancement on the second enemy position enabled the team to move to cover and break enemy contact. In his own words, his Navy SEAL team leader credits Sgt. Chapman unequivocally with saving the lives of the entire rescue team. Through his extraordinary heroism, superb airmanship, aggressiveness in the face of the enemy, and the dedication to the service of his country, Sgt. Chapman reflects the highest credit upon himself and the United States Air Force."

trying to protect the helicopter," Self explained. "The flight became very, very rough."

Razor 01, piloted by Chief Warrant Officer Gregory Calvert, began its approach. "I pop over the hilltop. I've picked my landing point out. And I set up for my approach. And then everything just, all hell breaks loose." The helicopter was riddled by small arms fire.

"We had rounds entering from both sides of the helicopter just really tearing up the inside of the aircraft," Self described. "It sounded like several people hitting the side of the helicopter with sledge hammers."

Calvert distinctly remembered "bullets coming through the windshield." The pilot flew backwards in his seat as a heavy-caliber round struck his flight helmet and shattered his left leg, taking out two inches of bone. An RPG exploded, destroying the right engine. The left engine howled in protest as it took the strain. "Crew members are calling targets," Calvert said. "Phil Svitak [flight engineer and crew chief], I remember him calling, 'One-o'clock, three-o'clock, engaging.' That was the last words I heard him speak. He was calling out targets and he engaged them all the way down." Svitak was mortally wounded while manning one of the mini-guns, and the other gunner, Staff Sgt. David Dube, was severely wounded.

The helicopter landed hard, bouncing men and equipment around the interior. "Almost everyone inside the aircraft had been thrown to the floor on the impact," Self exclaimed, "and we're trying to get out. Crawling and scratching, whatever we had to do get out of the aircraft." Razor 01 immediately became the focal point of enemy fire, which tore through the aluminum skin, striking three of the Rangers. Private First Class Matt Commons (posthumously promoted to corporal), Sgt. Brad Crose, and Spc. Marc Anderson were killed. The rest of the men piled off the helicopter and set up a defensive position.

"The pilot on the left side of the helicopter popped his door out, grabbed his rifle, fell out into the snow and began fighting from the front of the aircraft [the pilot was severely wounded in the hand]," Self recalled. "I knew that we had several people that did not make it out of the helicopter. But I had no idea what the extent of it was. I could hear some people inside the helicopter in pain, so I mean, we always train that if we take a casualty the best thing you can do for that casualty is to kill the enemy." Senior Airman Jason D. Cunningham, a pararescueman, and Sgt. 1st Class Cory Lamoreaux tended to the wounded inside the fuselage.

Small arms fire continued to pour into the surviving Americans. "We took fire from above, above us to our right," Self explained. "And an RPG was fired at us as well." The round exploded on the right side of the helicopter and wounded Self in the thigh. "You feel it to the bone," he recalled, "like maybe a ball-peen hammer with the tip of a nail at the end of it." The Rangers suppressed some of the enemy's fire long enough for one of the combat controllers to bring in air support. Unfortunately it was not enough to stop an enemy mortar crew from lobbing 82mm rounds toward their position. "The first round that came in from the mortar landed off the nose of the helicopter," Self recalled. Staff Sergeant Kevin Vance said, "At one point they had bracketed us with mortars but then they started shooting down the hill to try and hit the second team as they were coming up the hill to reinforce us." At this point, Self directed his men to drag the wounded to a depression some meters from them, out of the line of fire, where the medics could treat them. Cunningham and Lamoreaux went from man to man, tending to their wounds.

As Self's Chalk 1 fought for its life, Chalk 2, under Staff Sgt. Arin K. Canon, landed 300 meters from the remnants of the SEAL team but 800 meters east of the Rangers—a 2,000 foot climb at altitudes of over 8,000 feet. While Canon's men slogged their way up the mountain, airstrikes continued to pound the al-Qaeda positions. Australian SAS soldiers had infiltrated the area prior to the first helicopter crash as part of a long range reconnaissance mission and had remained undetected in an observation post through the firefight, proving critical in coordinating multiple Coalition air strikes to prevent the Taliban fighters from overrunning the downed aircraft. After two F-16s failed to knock out a critical bunker, a CIA Predator UAV fired two Hellfire missiles, one of which scored a direct hit and killed the occupants. "It came over all of us, landed off the nose, I don't know 40 meters off the front of the helicopter," Self recalled. "The second one had to have been right into the bunker. When it hit, there were pieces of the tree flying everywhere."

By 1030, Chalk 2 linked up after a four hour climb. "Just the grade of the ridge made it an unbearable walk, not including the altitude," Cannon recalled. "It was enough to where my guys' chests felt heavy and my joints were swollen." The men were completely exhausted, but still had to defeat the enemy controlling the top of the hill—a mere fifty meters from their position. With the arrival of the ten men of Razor 02, the Rangers prepared to assault the enemy bunkers. As the combat controller called in a last airstrike

Senior Airman Jason D. Cunningham
Air Force Cross Citation

"The President of the United States awards the Air Force Cross to Senior Airman Jason D. Cunningham for extraordinary heroism in military operations against an opposing armed force while serving as a pararescueman near the village of Marzak in the Paktia Province of Afghanistan on 4 March 2002. On that proud day, Airman Cunningham was the primary Air Force Combat Search and Rescue medic assigned to a Quick Reaction Force tasked to recover two American servicemen evading capture in austere terrain occupied by massed Al Qaida and Taliban forces. Shortly before landing, his MH-47E helicopter received accurate rocket-propelled grenade and small arms fire, severely disabling the aircraft and causing it to crash land. The assault force formed a hasty defense and immediately suffered three fatalities and five critical casualties. Despite effective enemy fire, and at great risk to his own life, Airman Cunningham remained in the burning fuselage of the aircraft in order to treat the wounded. As he moved his patients to a more secure location, mortar rounds began to impact within fifty feet of his position. Disregarding this extreme danger, he continued the movement and exposed himself to enemy fire on seven separate occasions. When the second casualty collection point was also compromised, in a display of uncommon valor and gallantry, Airman Cunningham braved an intense small arms and rocket-propelled grenade attack while repositioning the critically wounded to a third collection point. Even after he was mortally

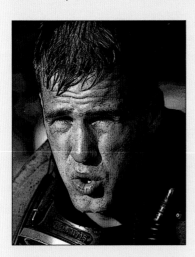

wounded and quickly deteriorating, he continued to direct patient movement and transferred care to another medic. In the end, his distinct efforts led to the successful delivery of ten gravely wounded Americans to life-saving medical treatment. Through his extraordinary heroism, superb airmanship, aggressiveness in the face of the enemy, and in the dedication of his service to his country, Senior Airman Cunningham reflected the highest credit upon himself and the United States Air Force."

Senior Airman Jason D. Cunningham, a pararescue jumper (PJ), was posthumously awarded the Air Force Cross for extraordinary heroism during the fight on Takur Ghar. Despite being severely wounded himself, he continued to treat the other wounded. Here he sweats it out between tasks at the U.S. Army Special Operations Underwater School at Key West, Florida. *U.S. Air Force* on the enemy bunkers, and with two machineguns providing suppressive fire, seven Rangers stormed the hill as quickly as they could in the knee-deep snow—shooting and throwing grenades. "With the supporting fire opened up, everybody just went for it," Staff Sgt. Harper Wilmoth said. Within minutes, the Rangers attacked, killing multiple al-Qaeda fighters.

"Once we took the top of the hill we found two friendly bodies," Vance recalled. "Both had been shot and killed."

Despite Self's pleas for extraction, Major General Hagenback decided to wait until dark before allowing the helicopters to pick them up. For the remainder of the day, the Americans traded long-range fire with the enemy. A little after 2000, two MH-47Es landed to extract the wounded and a portion of the QRF. Two others followed to pick up the remainder and the bodies of the dead, including Roberts. "I was on the last helicopter to leave with our force on it," Self explained. "It also contained all of our bodies. And I think it took us over two hours to get back to Bagram. And to sit there with . . . our dead brothers was not easy to do." The entire operation had lasted seventeen hours and cost six men killed in action and numerous wounded. The military awarded two Air Force Crosses, nine Silver Stars, and eight Bronze Stars for Valor to the men who fought on Takur Ghar.

On 6 March, ODAs 394, 594, and 372 assisted a large force of Pashtun militiamen in attacking the northern entranceway to the valley. They were to coordinate their attack with a mechanized force of ethnic Tajiks, their traditional adversaries. Despite several days of negotiations and planning between the two groups, the operation failed to achieve anything more important than confirming that the enemy had made its escape. On 15 March 2002, Colonel Mulholland sent a message to the U.S. Army Special Forces Command stating that the last 5th Special Forces Group A-Team had left Afghanistan. Four days later, General Tommy Franks announced that Operation Anaconda was officially over. Mulholland assessed the performance of his men. "We put these small groups of highly trained, very dedicated professional unconventional warriors . . . into an alien country . . . and destroyed al-Qaeda and the Taliban in his backyard, in his stronghold."

Operation Anaconda was the last major Coalition operation in Afghanistan before the United States turned its attention to Iraq. Gary Schroen witnessed the shift. "You could see changes being made in the staffing—U.S. military staffing—in Afghanistan, the Green Beret units, the Special Forces Group were being pulled out to refit and get ready for

Iraq. So we began to have some difficulty staffing Afghanistan on our side, and it was clear that the kind of guys that I think a lot of us believed was essential—U.S. military personnel with special operations capabilities—was being pulled away." With the focus on Iraq, the Taliban regrouped in Pakistan, and prepared to start round two in the fight for Afghanistan.

Chronology

February 1979

2/14: U.S. Ambassador Debs assassinated by Afghan government security forces under instructions of the Soviet KGB, secret police.

December 1979

12/25: The Soviet 40th Army, 80,000 soldiers, 1,800 tanks and 2,000 armored fighting vehicles launch a surprise attack.

February 1989

2/15: The total withdrawal of all Soviet troops from Afghanistan was completed on 15 February 1989, in compliance with the terms of the Geneva Accords signed ten months earlier. Lieutenant General Boris Gromov, commanding general of the 40th Army is the last Soviet soldier to leave Afghanistan.

December 1991

12/26: On December 26, 1991, the Council of Republics of the Supreme Soviet of the Soviet Union formally recognized the dissolution of the Soviet Union and dissolved itself. By December 31, 1991, all official Soviet institutions had ceased operations, as individual republics assumed the central government's role.

1989–1992

The Soviet withdrawal from Afghanistan was accompanied by a battle for power among various warlords after the fall of the Najibullah regime in the so-called Afghan Civil War.

1994–1996

The rise of the Taliban under the reclusive Mullah Omar, Commander of the Faithful, culminates in the capture of Kabul in 1996 and the establishment of the Islamic Emirate of Afghanistan.

September 2001

9/11: Attack on the World Trade Center in New York City, the Pentagon in Arlington, Virginia, and Flight 93 in Shanksville, Pennsylvania.

9/12: President Bush announces to his cabinet that "the deliberate and deadly attacks which were carried out yesterday against our country were more than acts of terror, they were acts of war."

9/14: Congress authorizes military response—"Use all necessary and appropriate force against the perpetrators of the September 11 attacks, their sponsors, and those who protected them."

9/16: National Security Team Plans for War—Bush assembles a meeting of the national security principals at Camp David. Bush agrees to adopt a plan proposed by CIA Director George Tenet to prosecute a covert war using CIA paramilitary officers to link up with anti-Taliban warlords inside Afghanistan.

9/20: President Bush addresses Congress—just before his speech he instructs the military to begin planning for war.

9/25: Defense Secretary Donald Rumsfeld announces that the military action against terrorism would be called "Operation Enduring Freedom."

9/26: The first of seven CIA Special Activities Division teams is inserted into the Panjshir Valley. Designated the Northern Afghanistan Liaison Team (NALT) it was known by its code name "Jawbreaker."

October 2001

10/6–7: U.S. troops fly to Uzbekistan, which agrees to allow U.S. troops to base humanitarian and search-and-rescue operations there.

10/7: The bombing campaign begins with U.S. and British airstrikes against Taliban government installations and al-Qaeda training camps.

Mid-October: Hamid Karzai crosses into Afghanistan from Pakistan in secret, in the hopes of leading an anti-Taliban uprising. He arrives at a small Pashtun village on the outskirts of Kandahar. Within days of his arrive, he finds himself surrounded by Taliban forces, and calls for help. He is airlifted out of Afghanistan by a U.S. helicopter along with some of his senior supporters.

10/19: U.S. Army Rangers and Delta Force operators stage a nighttime raid on an airfield in southern Afghanistan and on a Taliban compound in Kandahar.

10/19–20: U.S. Special Forces arrive in Afghanistan. Operational Detachment Alpha 555 (ODA 555) is inserted into the Panjshir Valley to support Mohammad Faim Khan. ODA 595 (Tiger 02) is inserted into the Dari-a-Souf Valley to support General Abdul Rashid Dostum.

10/25: ODA 585 (Tiger 03) is inserted near the village of Dasht-e-Qaleh in the upper northeast corner of Pakistan to support General Bariullah Khan.

10/30: Rumsfeld acknowledges ground troops by publically admitting that there are "a very modest number of ground troops in Afghanistan."

10/31: ODA 553 (Tiger 07) is inserted into the southern Hindu Kush to support General Kareem Khalili.

November 2001

11/2: ODA 534 (Tiger 04) is inserted into the Dari-a-Balkh Valley to support General Ustad Atta Mohammed. Tiger 04 joins Tiger 01 and General Dostum's forces to capture the northern city of Mazar-e Sharif.

11/8: ODA 586 (Texas 11) is inserted near the village of Farkhar to support General Daoud Khan.

11/9: Fall of Mazar-e Sharif triggers the collapse of Taliban positions throughout the north. Thousands of Taliban and al-Qaeda flee east to Kunduz.

11/12-13: Northern Alliance forces capture Kabul and Herat after weeks of American airstrikes.

11/14: ODA 574 (Texas 12) is inserted into the southern Afghanistan Province of Oruzgan to support Pashtun leader Hamid Karzai.

11/18: Battle of Tarin Kowt a key city in southern Afghanistan. Texas 12 and Karzai's forces successfully rout the Taliban, opening the way for the capture of Kandahar, Omar's spiritual capital.

11/24–26: Kunduz falls, after a two-week siege by Northern Alliance forces and U.S. airstrikes. It is the last major Taliban stronghold in Northern Afghanistan. Thousands of Taliban are taken prisoner. Those suspected of being al-Qaeda are transferred to American custody, and the remaining are turned over to Dostum and his troops.

11/25–12/1: Taliban and al-Qaeda prisoners revolt at the Qala-I-Jangi prison west of Mazar-e Sharif. The prisoners gain access to Northern Alliance weapons, and a bloody battle ensues. Johnny "Mike" Spann, a CIA agent sent to question the prisoners, becomes the first American to die in combat in the war in Afghanistan.

11/26: Marine Task Force 58 seizes Camp Rhino, an airstrip southwest of Kandahar in the longest amphibious raid in history, 450 miles from the sea.

December 2001

12/1: Karzai and his Special Forces A-Team begin to advance south toward Kandahar, the Taliban's last holdout. Simultaneously, forces led by commander Gul Agha Sherzai move toward the city from the south.

12/5: In the worst friendly fire incident of the war, a misdirected U.S. bomb explodes, killing three U.S. soldiers and at least twenty-three Afghani fighters. Dozens more, including all the members of ODA 574 and Hamid Karzai were wounded.

12/6: ODA 572 (Cobra 25) inserted into the Tora Bora Mountains to destroy al-Qaeda forces trying to flee into Pakistan. Osama bin Laden is believed to be present.

12/7: Kandahar falls to Hamid Karzai. It is the last remaining Taliban stronghold in the country. Al-Qaeda and Taliban leadership, including Mullah Omar, have fled.

12/17: Afghan commanders proclaim victory in the Tora Bora offensive, as the last al-Qaeda troops retreat from their fortified mountain caves toward Pakistan.

Many, including bin Laden, have slipped across the border into Pakistan.

12/22: Hamid Karzai sworn in as the interim head of the Afghan government. During his confirmation speech, Karzai said, "Today we are happy that we can see the sun rising again on our land. I think a wave of peace and unity is coming to our country."

March 2002

3/2: Elements of the 10th Mountain Division and the 101st Airborne Division, supported by Special Forces Task Force Dagger and Task Force K-Bar commence Operation Anaconda.

3/15: The last element of 5th Special Forces Group leaves Afghanistan.

3/19: General Tommy Franks announces that Operation Anaconda is officially over.

Bibliography

BOOKS

Aid, Matthew M. *The Secret Sentry: The Untold History of the National Security Agency.* New York: Bloomsbury Press, 2009.

Anderson, Jon Lee. *The Lion's Grave, Dispatches from Afghanistan.* New York: Grove Press, 2002.

Bearden, Milton, and James Risen: *The Main Enemy, The Inside Story of the CIA's Final Showdown with the KGB.* New York: Random House, 2003.

Beattie, Doug. *An Ordinary Soldier.* London: Pocket Books, 2008.

Beattie, Doug. *Task Force Helmand: A Soldier's Story of Life, Death and Combat on the Afghan Front Line.* London: Simon & Schuster, 2009.

Bergen, Peter L. *The Enduring Conflict between America and al-Qaeda.* New York: Free Press, 2011.

Bergen, Peter L. *The Osama bin Laden I know, An Oral History of al Qaeda's Leader.* New York: Free Press, 2006.

Berntsen, Gary. J*awbreaker: The Attack on Bin Laden and Al-Qaeda: A Personal Account by the CIA's Key Field Commander.* New York: Crown Publisher, 2005.

Blehm, Eric. *The Only Thing Worth Dying For: How Eleven Green Berets Forged a New Afghanistan.* New York: Harper, 2010.

Boot, Max. *War Made New, Technology, Warfare, and the course of History 1500 to Today.* New York: Gotham, 2006.

Clarke, Richard A. *Against All Enemies: Inside America's War on Terror.* New York: Free Press, 2004.

Coll, Steve. *The Bin Ladens, An Arabian Family in the American Century.* New York: The Penguin Press, 2008.

Coll, Steve. *Danger Close, The Tactical Air Controllers in Afghanistan and Iraq.* Texas: Texas A & M University Press, 2007.

Coll, Steve. *Ghost Wars: The Secret History of the CIA, Afghanistan, and Bin Laden, from the Soviet Invasion to September 10, 2001.* New York: Penguin Books, 2001.

Combat Studies Institute. *Weapons of Choice, ARSOF in Afghanistan.* Kansas: Combat Studies Institute Press, 2003.

Corbin, Jane. *Al-Qaeda: In search of the Terror Network that Threatens the World.* New York: Thunder's Mouth Press/Nation Books, 2003.

Corovez, Diego, and Selig S. Harrison. *Out of Afghanistan: The Inside Story of the Soviet Withdrawal*. New York: Oxford University Press, 1995.

Couch, Dick. *Down Range, Navy SEALs in the War on Terrorism*. New York: Crown, 2005.

Crile, George. *Charlie Wilson's War, The Extraordinary Story of How the Wildest Man in Congress and a Rogue CIA Agent Changed the History of our Times*. New York: Grove Press, 2003.

Feifer, Gregory. *The Great Gamble, The Soviet War in Afghanistan*. New York: Harper Perennial, 2009.

Feith, Douglas J. *War and Decision: Inside the Pentagon at the Dawn of the War on Terrorism*. New York: Harper, 2008.

Filkins, Dexter. *The Forever War*. New York: Vintage Books, 2009.

Franks, Tommy. *American Soldier, Tommy Franks*. New York: Regan Books, 2004.

Fury, Dalton. *Kill Bin Laden, A Delta Force Commander's Account of the Hunt for the World's Most Wanted Man*. New York: St. Martin's Griffin, 2008.

Grau, Lester W. *Afghan Guerrilla Warfare: In the Words of the Mujahideen Fighters*. Minneapolis: Zenith Press, 2001.

Grau, Lester W. *The Bear Went over the Mountain" Soviet Combat Tactics in Afghanistan*. Wash: National Defense University Press, 1996.

Grau, Lester W., and Michael A. Gress. *The Soviet-Afghan War, How a Superpower Fought and Lost*. Kansas: University of Press of Kansas, 2002.

Gul, Imtiaz. *The Most Dangerous Place, Pakistan's Lawless Frontier*. New York: Viking, 2009.

Hafvenstein, Joel. *Opium Season: A Year on the Afghan Frontier*. Connecticut: The Lyons Press, 2007.

Hirsh, Michael. *None Braver, U.S. Air Force Pararescuemen in the War on Terrorism*. New York: New American Library, 2003.

Holmes, Tony. *F-14 Units of Operation Enduring Freedom*. New York: Osprey Publishing Limited, 2008.

Isby, Daniel C. *Liberation and Capture Missions*. London: Weidenfeld & Nicobsen, 2004.

Jones, Seth G. *In the Graveyard of Empires, America's War in Afghanistan*. New York: W.W. Norton & Company, 2009.

Kakar, Hassan. *Afghanistan: The Soviet Invasion and the Afghan Response, 1979–1982*. CA: University of California Press, 1995.

Lambeth, Benjamin S. *Air Power against Terror, America's Conduct of Operation Enduring Freedom*. California: Rand, 2005.

MacPherson, Malcolm. *Roberts Ridge: A Story of Courage and Sacrifice on Takur Ghar Mountain, Afghanistan*. New York: Bantam Dell, 2005.

Maley, William. *The Afghanistan Wars*. New York: Palgrave, 2002.

Marsden, Peter. *The Taliban: War and Religion in Afghanistan*. London: Zed Books Ltd, 2002.

Matinuddin, Kamal. *The Taliban Phenomenon, Afghanistan 1994–1997*. London: Oxford University Press, 1999.

Moore, Robin. *The Hunt for Bin Laden: Task Force Dagger, on the Ground with the Special Forces in Afghanistan*. New York: Ballantine Books, 2003.

Nojumi, Neamatollah. *The Rise of the Taliban in Afghanistan: Mass Mobilization, Civil War, and the Future of the Region.* New York: Palgrave, 2002.

North, Ollie. *American Heroes in Special Operations.* Nashville: Fidelis Books, 2010.

Peters, Gretchen. *Seeds of Terror: How Heroin Is Bankrolling the Taliban and Al Qaeda.* New York: St. Martin's Press, 2009.

Pushies, Fred. *Deadly Blue, Battle Stories of the U.S. Air Force Special Operations Command.* New York: AMACOM, 2009.

Rashid, Ahmed. *Descent into Chaos, the U.S. and the Disaster in Pakistan, Afghanistan, and Central Asia.* New York: Penguin Books, 2009.

Rashid, Ahmed. *Taliban, Militant Islam, Oil and Fundamentalism in Central Asia.* New Haven: Yale University Press, 2010.

Robinson, Linda. *Masters of Chaos, The Secret History of the Special Forces.* New York: PublicAffairs, 2004.

Rohan Gunaratna. *Inside Al Qaeda, Global Network of Terror.* New York: Columbia University Press, 2002.

Rubin, Barnett R. *The Fragmentation of Afghanistan: State Formation and Collapse in the International system.* New Haven: Yale University Press, 2002.

Rumsfeld, Donald. *Known and Unknown, A Memoir.* New York: Sentinel, 2011.

Scheuer, Michael. *Marching toward Hell: America and Islam after Iraq.* New York: Free Press, 2008.

Schroen, Gary C. *First In, An Insider's Account of how the CIA spearheaded the war on terror in Afghanistan.* New York: Ballantine Books, 2005.

Sebestyen, Victor. *Revolution 1989, The Fall of the Soviet Union.* New York: Pantheon, 2009.

Self, Nathan E. *Two Wars: One Hero's Fight on Two Fronts—Abroad and Within.* Colorado: Alive Communications, Inc., 2008.

Stanton, Doug. *Horse Soldiers, the Extraordinary Story of a Band of U.S. Soldiers Who Rode to Victory in Afghanistan.* New York: Scribner, 2009.

Tootal, Stuart. *Danger Close.* London: John Murray, 2009.

Volodarsky, Boris. *The KGB's Poison Factory, From Lenin to Litvinenko.* London: Frontline Books, 2009.

Wawro, Geoffrey. *Quicksand: America's Pursuit of Power in the Middle East.* New York: Penguin, 2010.

Weaver, Mary Anne. *Pakistan in the Shadow of Jihad and Afghanistan.* New York: Farrar, Straus and Giroux, 2002.

West, Bing. *The Wrong War: Grit, Strategy, and the Way Out of Afghanistan.* New York: Random House, 2011.

Woodward, Bob. *Bush at War.* New York: Simon & Schuster, 2002.

Wright, Donald P. *A Different Kind of War: The United States Army in Operation Enduring Freedom, October 2001–September 2005.* Kansas: Combat Studies Institute Press, 2010.

Wright, Lawrence. *The Looming Tower: al-Qaeda and the Road to 9/11.* New York: Alfred A. Knopf, 2006.

Zaeef, Abdul Salam. *My Life with the Taliban.* New York: Columbia University Press, 2010.

OTHER SOURCES

"Campaign Against Terror, Interview: Colonel John Mulholland." *PBS Frontline* (undated). www.pbs.org/wgbh/pages/frontline/shows/campaign/interviews/mulholland.html.

"Campaign Against Terror, Interview: Lt. Col. David Fox." *PBS Frontline* (undated). www.pbs.org/wgbh/pages/frontline/shows/campaign/interviews/fox.html.

"Campaign Against Terror, Interview: President Hamid Karzai." *PBS Frontline,* 7 May 2002. www.pbs.org/wgbh/pages/frontline/shows/campaign/interviews/karzai.html.

"Campaign Against Terror, Interview: U.S. Army Captain Jason Amerine." *PBS Frontline,* 12 July 2002. wwe.pbs.org/wgbh/pages/frontline/shows/campaign/interviews/amerine.html.

"Campaign Against Terror, Interview: U.S. Special Forces ODA 555, Frank [No last name available] (SFC)." *PBS Frontline* (undated). www.pbs.org/wgbh/pages/frontline/shows/campaign/interviews/555.html.

"Campaign Against Terror, Interview: U.S. Special Forces ODA 572, Bill [No last name available] SSSG)," *PBS Frontline* (undated) http://pbs.org/wgbh/pages/frontline/shows/campaign/interviews/572.html.

Dick, C. J. *Mujahideen Tactics in the Soviet-Afghan War.* Conflict Studies Research Centre.

Gvosdev, Nikolas K. "The Soviet Victory That Never Was." *Foreign Affairs,* December 10, 2009.

Priest, Dana. "Team 555 Shaped a New Way of War, Special Forces and Smart Bombs Turned Tide and Routed Taliban," *Washington Post,* April 3, 2002.

Hersh, Seymour M. Annals of National Security: "Escape and Evasion: What happened when the Special Forces landed in Afghanistan?" *The New Yorker.* November 12, 2001, p.50.

United States Special Operations Command History Office, United States Special Operations Command HISTORY, 1987–2007, 20th Anniversary Edition (MacDill AFB, FL: USSOCOM, 2007).

Combat Studies Institute

At the Combat Studies Institute project, the Operational Leadership Experiences interview collection archives firsthand multiservice accounts from military personnel who planned, participated in, and supported operations in the Global War on Terrorism.

Aaknes, Dale G., Master Sgt. 29 Sept. 2006

Albano, Lou, Maj. 29 Jan. 2009

Albryacht, Sara, Maj. 13 Mar. 2007

Bowers, Robert, Maj. 1 February 2006

Creasman, David, Maj. 20 August 2007

Crombie, Roger, Maj. 20 March 2006

Diehl, David, Maj. 6 Dec. 2005

Doyle, David, Maj. 14 Feb. 2005

Hoines, Mitchell, Maj. undated

Levin, Robert Maj. 4 Nov. 2005

Lovell, Kevin, Maj. 24 Aug. 2007

King, David, Maj. undated

Nawatney, Nick S. Master Sgt. undated

Ninkowich, Christopher, Master Sgt. undated

Noyes, Jack, Maj. 27 Aug. 2007

Quander, Mark, Maj. undated

Runkle, Michael, Lt. Cmdr. undated

Short, David, Maj. 4 Jan. 2006

Index